Ysabella

de Trastámara

First Lady of the Renaissance

By

Elizabeth Long

ALHAMAR PUBLISHING, INC.

Sherman Oaks, California

ILLUSTRATION ACKNOWLEDGEMENTS

The following illustrations are used with the permission of the owners
indicated below

Robert Frerck, Odyssey Productions, Chicago: Trastamara of Castile
Family Crest, Alcazar of Sergovia, Sergovia Thrones of Ysabella and
Ferdinand, Alcazar of La Moto, Ysabella, Ferdinand, Ysabella and
Ferdinand Entering Granada, Courtyard of Lions - Alhambra, Cristobol
Colon, Colon Meets Ysabella and Ferdinand; Arxiu Mas Barcelona, Spain:
Crown of Ysabella, Sepulchres of Juan II and Isabel of Portugal; Museum
of Granada, Spain: Queen Mother with Children in Court; SEF/Art
Resource, N.Y.: Frontispiece - Ysabella; Arxiu Mas, Barcelona, Spain:
Cover - Ysabella in Full Length Red Dress with Scepter.

FOREWARD

Most Americans, if they think of Queen Isabella of Spain at all, remember a bit player in the saga of the discovery of the New World by Christopher Columbus -- or Cristobol Colon, as he called himself when he came to Spain. There may be a dim remembrance that Isabella overruled the doubts of her husband, King Ferdinand, to authorize spending precious royal money on a madcap voyage to find a shorter, more direct (and non-Portuguese) route to the riches of India and the Far East. Whether this represented the whim of a flighty woman taken with the dreams of an impressive would-be adventurer, or the considered judgment of a shrewd ruler accustomed to taking calculated risks, few people would be prepared to venture an opinion.

Some people who know a little more history may remember that Isabella was responsible for the expulsion from Spain of Moors and Jews who declined to convert to Catholicism, and authorized the beginning stages of the infamous Spanish Inquisition. Whether inhabitants of a century that has seen untold millions slaughtered or made into refugees in the name of various secular utopias can view such actions from a position of moral superiority is open to question. Each age seems to nurture its own special infamies. The belief, so widespread in the 19th century and still stubbornly clung to in our own exquisitely bloody century, that the passage of time can be equated with progress and improved moral sensibilities may turn out to be nothing more than a modern superstition, no more defensible than a previously widely-held belief that the world was flat.

Who was Isabella, and how did she get to be who she was? In this book, written in the first person as if it were an autobiography, Dr. Elizabeth Long goes a long way toward making a relatively obscure historical personage a real person. We are approaching the 500th anniversary of the discovery of America. Christopher Columbus was not the first explorer who discovered this body of land nor was he the first European adventurer. His maiden voyage was the epic historic discovery propelling future events which ultimately led to the widespread exploration, colonization, and eventual establishment of an independent New World. A New World that was to make its own unique contributions to the on-going process of civilization. To understand how Isabella played such a crucial role in beginning that process can enrich and enhance our understanding of where we came from and where we might be going.

One of the more difficult tasks of any historian is to gain and communicate an understanding of the context and texture of a previous era, the way people thought and lived. However conscientious and knowledgeable, a historian is a creature of his or her own era, affected and influenced in ways one may not be fully aware of by the assumptions, customs, and standards of the current times. In trying to take us into Isabella's mind and heart, Dr. Long has undertaken a formidable and difficult task, whose rewards are a better understanding not just of the Queen, but of the time and place in which she lived.

Thus we learn that someone of royal birth can live a childhood bordering on deprivation because of Court intrigues, and we get a sense of how history can be affected -- even made -- because of strictly personal likes and dislikes. We have a glimpse of the forces behind her marriage to Ferdinand and its importance to the making of Spain as a unified country rather than a collection of provinces. We understand plots against her and how she handled them, experience her vision for a modern Spain, live through the conquest of Granada, and come to understand what an impressive individual Columbus must have been.

It is possible to have a vague impression that royalty live lives of privilege and leisure, but this was a Queen who worked and scrambled to accomplish her ends. She made good and bad decisions, but they were seldom bad through lack of consideration or forethought. She absorbed advice and took risks for what she believed in. Her patronage of Columbus, remembered as the most significant event of her reign, was far from the most risky or portentous decision she made during a life of action. All in all, she comes across as an impressive leader we are glad to know a little better.

The age of Ferdinand and Isabella was one of discovery and adventure when people were pushing the limits of what was then known about the world and seeking to understand what lay beyond apparent barriers. The Portuguese may have begun it with their sponsorship of trips that eventually led to opening a sea route around Africa to Asia. The Spanish began adventures in other directions. The voyages of discovery were impelled, in part, by a desire for gold and riches but there was also human curiosity, a compulsion to spread religion, and the yearning to know more.

Five hundred years later, we are far from exhausting the possibilities of further discovery. It has been fashionable to compare the voyages of Columbus and other discoverers to recent adventures in outer space, but a similar curiosity is leading people to plumb the depths of the sea in search of knowledge and surprise. Todays' world of the microcosm, represented by the incredible miniaturization of electronic equipment, offers opportunities for discovery of a different character. Medieval scholars used to debate how many angels could dance on the head of a pin (a less frivolous disputation in context than most modern minds understand). Modern technologists wonder how many computers they can get on a thin slice of silicon. And our world changes as they discover the answers.

As we ponder discoveries yet to come and the changes they will bring, we could do worse than to recapture some of the spirit of the Queen who made Columbus's voyages possible. She was a creature of her time to be sure but she had an indomitable religious faith combined with open-minded curiosity, the ability to make a decision and carry through on it, determination of heroic proportions, and the capability to improvise when things got tough. Our times and our challenges are different, but those qualities are unlikely to become obsolete.

Alan W. Bock
Senior Columnist
The Orange County Register

ACKNOWLEDGEMENTS

My sincere appreciation for the major contributions of friends and associates helping to make this an exceptional book. I wish to acknowledge the information and research contributed by Francisco Garcia, Madrid, Spain, providing the historical background of the artisans who carved and sculpted the Choir Chairs and Sepulchers placed before the altar of the Carthusa de Miraflores in Burgos.

My noteworthy editor/author Auriel Douglas' experienced eye and keen editorial instinct provided constructive suggestions adding measurably to the final manuscript.

Robert Buckley never failed to come to my rescue when my computer "went on strike" and also thoroughly, painstakingly line proofed the completed manuscript.

Gilbert Peters shared his knowledge of the publishing industry, unselfishly guiding me through the maze of "prepublishing jitters."

PHOTOGRAPH RESEARCHERS

Debra Lemonds Hanna, Burbank, California
Cezanne Solis de Winter, Madrid, Spain

• YSABELLA

AUTHOR'S NOTE

Imagine stepping back into the annals of history to experience the medieval reign of Queen Isabella of Castile and Leon, signing her name Ysabel de Trastamara. Ysabella and Ferdinand resided in Alcazars (Royal palaces - some opulent and others semi-modest), with their Infante (Prince) Juan III (John) and Infantas (Princesses) Ysabel (Isabel, Elizabeth), Juana (Joanna), Maria (Mary) and Catalina (Catherine). Queen Ysabella's world famous explorer, Cristobol Colon (Christopher Columbus) secured her place in history.

Glimpse the epic reconstruction of her nation as Ysabella raced against time throughout her kingdoms (provinces), visiting the Alcaydes (Mayors) of the cities of Sevilla (Seville), Cordoba (Cordova), and Zaragosa (Saragosa).

Share the triumphs and disappointments, joy and sorrow of the Queen who redefined her nation and the world leaving a legacy of accomplishments unmatched by others in the chronicles of modern history.

ELIZABETH LONG

ROYAL AND NOBLE PERSONAGES

Ysabel of Portugal - Second wife of King Juan II, and mother of Ysabella and Alfonso.

Enrique IV - Heir to the Crown of Castile and Leon, son of King Juan II and Maria of Aragon. Ysabella and Alfonso's half-brother.

Juana of Portugal - Second wife of Enrique IV and mother of 'La Beltraneja'.

Juan Pacheco, Marquis de Villena - Powerful, wealthy noble and member of Enrique IV's Royal Council.

Alonso Carrillo, Archbishop of Toledo - Uncle of Juan Pacheco, using his vast wealth and influence aiding Ysabella during Enrique's life.

Pedro Gonzales de Mendoza - Grand Cardinal of Spain, Chancellor and Primate of Castile and Leon during Ysabella's reign, and after the death of Alonso Carrillo, Archbishop of Toledo.

Pedro Giron, Master of the Order of Calatrava - Brother of Juan Pacheco, Marquis de Villena.

Beltran de la Cueva, Count de Ledesma, Duke de Albuquerque - Close friend of Enrique IV and Queen Juana, and probable father of 'La Beltraneja'.

Count de Haro - Constable of Castile during Enrique IV and Ysabella's reign.

Beatriz Bobadilla de Cabrera, Marchioness de Moya - Lifelong friend of Ysabella and wife of Andres Cabrera, Marquis de Moya.

Gutierre de Cardenas - Treasurer of Castile and Leon during reign of Queen Ysabella.

Frederick Enriques, Admiral of Castile - Ferdinand's grandfather.

Fadrique de Hernandes, Admiral of Castile - Ferdinand's uncle.

Enrique de Guzman, Duke de Medina Sidonia - Wealthy and powerful noble residing in Sevilla. Bitter enemy of Marquis de Cadiz.

Rodrigo Ponce de Leon, Marquis Duke de Cadiz, Marquis de Zahara - Military strategist serving Ysabella and Ferdinand during Granada conflict.

Louis de Santangel - Member of Ferdinand's Royal Council, friend and ardent supporter of Cristobol Colon's proposed expedition.

Tomas de Torquemada - Appointed Inquisitor General of the Spanish Inquisition by the Pope setting the stage for the reign of terror devastating the nation and colonies for more than three hundred years.

Ximenes Cisneros, Archbishop of Toledo - Undertook reformation of the Church, and upon the death of Cardinal Mendoza, appointed Archbishop. After death of Ysabella and Ferdinand, Regent of Spain until Juana and Philip's son, Carlos I, assumed the Thrones of Castile and Aragon.

Hernando del Pulgar - First Secretary to Ysabella.

Pietro Martire - First Secretary to Ysabella after del Pulgar's resignation.

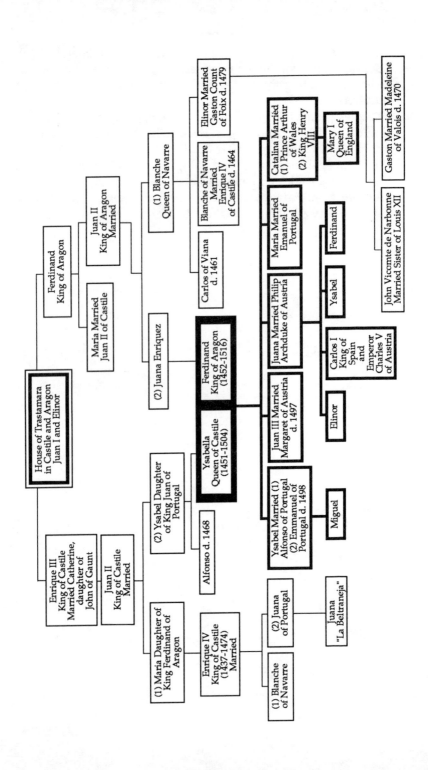

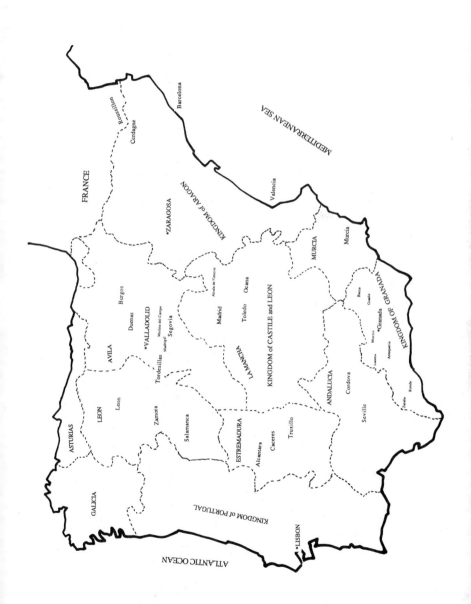

CONTENTS

PART III Granada Conflict

PART IV Cristobol Colon

PROLOGUE
July - 1454
Valladolid

The bright Spanish sun burst through the clouds that eventful day in July, 1454. It was high noon and the bells tolled across the entire land of Castile and Leon. The nation was plunged into grief. Juan II, their King, was dead.

The tolling of the bells in Valladolid were especially mournful. The heavy doors of the cathedral swung open, and the silent crowd watched, waiting for the emergence of the King's young widow, Ysabel. The choir was still singing softly as Ysabel and her two children, three year old Ysabella and eight month old Alfonso made their way out the door and down the steps toward the waiting horses. Following directly behind the Queen was seventeen year old Enrique IV, Juan's son from his first marriage to Maria of Aragon.

The Queen carefully made her way down the steps as the bells continued to echo throughout the city. Horsemen waiting at the foot of the steps helped Ysabel and her children to mount, ready for the slow procession through the quiet, tree lined streets of the city. Her entourage moved with a deliberate slow pace for she wanted the people to remember their King and his grieving Queen.

The procession was moving too slowly for Enrique. After the first mile he reined his horse to the side and with a signal to his aides to follow turned and cantered off taking a shorter route back to the Alcazar.

It took nearly an hour for the Queen to weave her way through the crowds gathered along the streets. Some of the people waved their hands in greeting, others seemed to stare blankly ahead. She looked into those faces and felt she recognized their grief, but beyond that there was an air of apprehension and tension evidently brought on by great uncertainty. What would the death of their King bring to them -- prosperity or continued hardship? The expressions on their faces seemed to cry out with the pain they had endured under the forty-eight year reign of a weak and vacillating King Juan II.

Arriving at the Alcazar, Ysabel immediately summoned her First Secretary and issued the command for the nation to remain in mourning for the next thirty days. Just as her secretary rose from his chair to carry out her command, the double doors burst open and in strode Enrique with four of his aides. The startled Queen looked up and before she could inquire about the abruptness of his actions, Enrique confidently swaggered across the room, the sounds of his polished high-top boots echoing with each measured step.

Enrique had a sheaf of papers in his hand, and waving them in front of Ysabel, he burst into high-pitched laughter, and then his swarthy face took on an ominous expression. Snarling, he continued to wave the papers yelling, "Your King, your King, the father of your children, he loved you all so much he has left you penniless. Penniless! Do you hear me? Your new home is to be the abandoned Alcazar of Arevalo in Avila. Quickly now, you must pack your things. You are leaving today!"

Enrique immediately demanded the chest and the keys to the Crown jewels. Ysabel seemed to be in total shock and hesitated as if she had been struck in the face by his harsh command. She looked into his face and sensed an evilness that she had not known before. She knew it was fruitless to argue. Reluctantly she went to a cupboard, unlocked the door, and as it opened, motioned for a servant to bring the chest of jewels forth. She went to a small table and unlocking a drawer took out a key. She handed it to the servant, who then handed it to Enrique. Enrique grabbed the key with a swift movement, motioned for his aide to unlock the chest for he wanted to examine his prize. The aide lifted the lid and Enrique began rifling through the gems. He lifted some out and exclaimed with sheer delight as the jewels gleamed in his hands. Suddenly he looked at Ysabel and demanded the emerald and diamond necklace, the diamond and ruby broach, and the ruby ring. They were missing.

The incredulous expression on Ysabel's face seemed not to move Enrique. She was so shocked she was unable to speak. Enrique again demanded those three missing pieces. Finally, Ysabel regained her composure and in her quiet voice reminded Enrique those three pieces of jewelry were bridal gifts from her Grandfather, the King of Portugal. They did not belong to the crowned head of Castile and Leon.

Enrique took another few steps toward Ysabel, and waving his clenched fist he again demanded her jewels. Ysabel's expression was firm and defiant. Her face seemed to say, "No, never will those jewels be yours!"

Enrique was impatient. He looked at her eight-month-old baby fussing in his bed, and with a quick motion to an aide holding a sword in his hand, he signaled for him to move towards the child. The aide flashed his sword and held it at Alfonso's throat.

Ysabel's face was filled with fright. Enrique again demanded the jewels..."or the blood of your son will be on your shoulders Death to Alfonso!" was his high-pitched cry. Ysabel took a key from a small drawer, and unlocking another drawer she removed the three pieces of jewelry. Without another word she handed them to Enrique.

Enrique's closest advisor, the Marquis de Villena, then issued orders to Ysabel's servants to pack her things quickly. They were only to pack the clothing, a few pieces of kitchenware, pottery plates and mugs, beds and bedding. She would be permitted to have only one old servant. There was also a command issued for a broken-down wagon and an ancient mule.

The servants flew into a frenzy of activity grabbing the clothes from the closet and piling them into the wagon. At last Ysabel was summoned. They were ready to depart.

They climbed up onto the wagon behind the old driver, and Ysabel turned for one last look at her home. Out of the corner of her eye, she was suddenly aware that her Throne Chair had not been packed. Hastily she gave orders to a waiting servant to bring it to her. The servant raced back into the Alcazar and emerged with the gold-leafed Throne. Ever so gently it was lifted up and secured to the top of the heap.

The old man lifted the reins and after several tugs the recalcitrant mule began its lumbering steps, pulling the heavy wagon along the cobblestone streets.

The city was quiet, its people had closeted themselves behind their doors. As they looked out their windows, they saw the cumbersome wagon slowly trundling along the quiet streets with the Queen Mother and her two small children. What did it all mean? They wondered.

PART I

**Ysabella's childhood,
death of young brother,
marriage and
death of Enrique IV**

CHAPTER I

1454 - The Alcazar Of Arevalo
Don Alvaro de Luna

 The plodding mule laboriously pulled the wagon along the dusty roads. I suddenly realized that no longer were there cheers of joy and shouts of glee as mother passed by. Everything was eerily quiet as we wound our way southward toward the mesa upon which Arevalo had been built.

The kingdom of Avila in which the Alcazar was built is contained by the Guadarrama mountains on the north, and to the south and east the green hills and valleys are covered with thick forests. Today the sun was not shining as bright as usual for dark clouds were forming in the skies. Mother looked up at the dark sky and urged our driver, Felipe, to strike the tired old mule pulling our heavy load until the plodding walk merged into a trot. Removing her rosary from her small satchel, she silently prayed for the clouds to go away. Suddenly Felipe began gesturing towards the Alcazar off in the distance situated on the flat mesa. This Alcazar was to be my childhood home. It was here in these high plains at Madrigal de las Alta Torres, that I, Ysabella de Trastamara, daughter of King Juan II of Castile and Leon and Queen Ysabel of Portugal, was born on a Thursday afternoon, April 22, 1451.

Our driver suddenly pulled the wagon up short by an old river bed scattered with piles of enormous boulders of granite that had been polished by the floods for centuries. Mother studied the treeless surroundings of the Alcazar, then glancing towards the fertile valleys below, she beckoned Felipe to move onward.

The bumpy roads to the Alcazar continued to slow our progress. Felipe had to prod and coax our exhausted mule to pull the wagon over paths now overgrown with weeds. It had been a long, long time since my father, King Juan II, had lived at Arevalo.

Our wagon creaked and groaned as it lumbered along. I heard mother utter a few kind words of encouragement to Felipe who had been so patient in coping with all the adversities we had encountered. Finally the over-burdened mule pulled our wagon into the long neglected courtyard, its paths now overgrown with weeds. We came to a stop at Arevalo's entrance.

Felipe helped mother down from the wagon. Standing in front of the Alcazar she paused for a few minutes studying all the open doors and noting the missing window shutters. She heaved a sigh of resignation as she gathered Alfonso into her arms, took my hand and together we pushed the big main door open. The rusty hinges caused it to sag and as we swung it open, the scraping sound of the stone floor etched into my memory. As we walked across the entranceway into the great hall, the echo of our footsteps reminded us that our future was indeed bleak. Mother inspected every empty room, making a mental note of how many window shutters were missing, how many hinges were needed for the sagging doors, how drab the mud-spattered walls looked, and then she chose an area of rooms which were to become our home.

Beckoning to Felipe to pull a mop from the bottom of the wagon, Mother pulled a straw broom from the heap. She began sweeping the dust, dried leaves, and debris which had collected over the years in the entranceway and great hall. Felipe discovered some rainwater in some pottery and followed behind her mopping the grey, stone-tiled floors. Then they pulled our belongings off the wagon and placed them in the clean hall. Next, mother tackled the kitchen, located to the back and side of the Alcazar. A heavy wooden rough-hewn table, and a few odd chairs remained. The hearth was filled with ashes and partially burned logs, and the chimney was clogged with soot. Felipe discovered an old water well and began to splash clear water over the kitchen floor mopping away the scars of neglect.

The next morning, promptly at 10 o'clock, a distinguished gentleman presented himself at the Alcazar. Felipe beckoned him to enter and lead him to the new quarters mother had chosen to receive her guest.

Our visitor was quite tall, with broad shoulders and thick black hair. He was wearing a long brown cape which covered a brown shirt tucked into smooth fitting brown trousers. His high-top brown boots were gleaming, as if they had just been polished. The gold buckle at his waist and large gold cross worn around his neck were fascinating. He stepped before mother now seated on her Throne Chair. Bowing from his waist, he looked her straight in the face and declaimed: "I am Pedro de Bobadilla, Governor of the province of Avila. Your Highness, I do ask that you accept my most humble apology for the rundown state that this Alcazar is in. This is a very dangerous area for there are robbers and thieves everywhere. A few years ago they invaded our kingdom and Arevalo and stole everything that could be removed."

Mother's gaze never wavered. I knew she was silently hoping the Governor would assist her in providing money and furnishings she so desperately needed to make the Alcazar a proper home for a Queen, small Infanta and baby Infante. Before she could respond by asking for tapestries, candles, drapes, bedding, chairs and fine cabinetry, he said, "Please, your Highness, rest assured that I will do all that I can to help you to make this Alcazar a home for you and your two children." As he again bowed before her, mother knew that he was taking his leave.

A few days later the Governor arrived with some pieces of furniture, a few chairs, a new door for the kitchen and window shutters. I could see that mother didn't like the style of furniture. As she sat down on one of the chairs, she grimaced then motioned for Pedro to follow her to her quarters.

Settling into her Throne Chair, she invited the Governor to be seated and then asked, "How far is your headquarters from Arevalo?" The Governor's deep baritone voice was warm and friendly as he commented, "It is nearly ten leagues to the south from Arevalo, but the roads are well traveled and the bridges have all been repaired. We can urge our horses to canter at a quick pace taking a short time to cover the distance."

Mother studied her guest for a few seconds and then asked, "Tell me about your family. How many children do you have?"

Smiling and nodding the Governor eagerly responded. "I have a lovely wife and one beautiful, dark haired daughter, Beatriz, who is three years old. She's the same age as the Infanta Ysabella."

A look of approval crossed mother's face as she countered with, "Beatriz and Ysabella must become the best of friends."

Felipe's energy was boundless. As soon as the sun rose, he took a scythe and began hacking away at the weeds which had grown over the paths around the Alcazar. Then he would hitch the mule up to the wagon and lumber off in search of wood, more shutters, hinges, and other things needed to repair the Alcazar. His gentle demeanor surely touched many hearts as he made his plea, "Para la Madre Riena" for he would return with several much needed items. Every afternoon one could hear the pounding of a hammer, the shavings of wood from a door that needed to be fitted, or watch him fit a window shutter. Every day mother and I would walk around and inspect the work as it progressed. Governor Pedro de Bobadilla continued to gather together a few discarded pieces of furniture, and some thread-bare rugs. One day he brought some green satin drapes with gold cord tiebacks. Mother immediately decided these drapes belonged in the small room she had chosen for her gold-leafed Throne Chair and where she had begun to receive her distinguished guests.

The large, empty cavernous rooms presented a perfect play area for me. When I shouted and laughed, a fascinating echo immediately returned. Beatriz and I raced throughout the Alcazar shouting at the top of our voices, laughing, playing and listening to the echoes. As the rooms gradually filled with furniture, my play areas disappeared. Alfonso was soon walking and running with me. We explored everything together. The water well, the sentry towers, and when given permission, we would ride on the mule into the small town. It was a lonely childhood because I was not allowed to make friends with the common children.

After my birth, mother oftentimes experienced deep depressions and after my father's death the depressions increased. She was never free from anxiety. Her allowance from Enrique, who had never liked her, came so irregularly that we were reduced to the bare necessities, almost to actual want.

To mother, everything seemed hopeless, and as the people who once were her friends now neglected her, she turned to the solace of religion and dedicated what remained of her superb strength toward the welfare of Alfonso and me. I remember her lying in bed, ill, in white mourning garments, weeping for the King and at other times in the chapel in the Alcazar kneeling in reverence before the uplifted Host.

Beatriz and I were inseparable playmates often running through the enclosed garden of the Alcazar. We learned to read by mother's bedside. We approached the altar in the chapel together to receive our first Holy Communion. Sometimes we rode with Beatriz's father and his troops into the flat country, where fields of wheat extended as far as my eyes could see. Beatriz and I were taught to ride on mules. The mules were slow. No matter how much I coaxed, mine stubbornly refused to move faster.

Sometimes we would ride as far as Medina del Campo where the great fairs were held three times a year. The merchants came from all over southern Europe to buy choice Castilian wools and grains, cattle, horses and mules for Andalusia. There were cavaliers from Aragon, sailors from Catalonia, mountaineers from the north, turbaned Moors from Granada, blue-eyed Castilian farmers, bearded Jews in gabardines, peasants from Provence and Languedoc.

I was fascinated as I watched this colorful array of people. A thousand questions raced through my mind. I wanted to know all about everything and everyone. Pedro was too preoccupied to answer my questions and I soon learned it was not wise to ask.

My first true love was horses. I would race Alfonso to the very top floor of the Alcazar and then look out over the vast territory watching the horsemen gallop across the bleak plains.

By my ninth birthday, I decided that riding a mule was definitely not right for me. I wanted a real horse, one that could race with the wind, climb hills, and change directions with just the quick movement of my wrist. I coaxed and cajoled Pedro until he allowed me to mount a small spirited pony. I could tug on the reins and we would race toward Medina del Campo.

It was my eleventh birthday that I will always remember. Birthdays were never celebrated at Arevalo because there was never enough money to purchase a gift or invite a few guests. Mother would give us a very big hug and reassure us that she loved us very much. Pedro had been watching me manage his pony, and on this eventful day he arrived quite early in the morning, asking mother for permission to take Alfonso and me out for a short ride. He pulled up at his stables and whistled a short signal. A stable hand appeared leading a sorrel Arabian purebred with a blond mane and tail. I had never seen such a beautiful horse. I looked up at Pedro and he said, "Yes, Dona Ysabella, he is yours!"

Pedro helped me to mount. I just barely lifted the reins when he started off with a trot. I lifted the reins a little higher and we raced with the wind! I whirled him around and cantered back to Pedro, too excited to speak.

Alfonso rushed up to pet him and asked, "What is the horse's name?" Pedro answered with a nod to me saying, "Dona Ysabella must give the horse a name." I looked at that perfectly formed, beautiful Arabian horse and promptly said, "Pascha."

The days I spent in the saddle riding Pascha were training sessions which later in life enabled me to become resourceful, fearless, indifferent to fatigue and contemptuous of pain. It was a valuable training period which helped me through many difficult situations later in life.

My education was not neglected. Alfonso and I were taught at the local convent with priests and tutors coming to us from a parish thirty two leagues away. I studied grammar and rhetoric, painting, poetry, history and philosophy. For a time I lived at the Convent of Santa Ana in that wonderful ancient city. I was taught to embroider the intricate Moorish designs on velours and cloth of gold, and I printed prayers in Gothic characters on leaves of parchment. From my father I had inherited a great love for music and poetry.

Protocol forbade my making friends with the children in the townships. Alfonso and Beatriz were my only companions.

Mother insisted that we tell her all about what we had learned in our lessons. She wanted to be sure that the Infante and Infanta were being instructed in all the things that a Royal Infante and Infanta must know. After we had recited our lessons, she would tell us about her childhood at Court in Portugal. Her colorful descriptions and stories of the pomp and pageantry at her Grandfather's Court were fascinating. Alfonso and I sat spellbound as she wove the tapestry of life at a "proper" Royal Court. Warm and affectionate with us always, she taught us our manners and etiquette. Very rarely did she dress to go out, preferring to remain behind the walls of Arevalo.

As we grew older her depressions seemed to increase. She talked incessantly about her happy childhood, and then she would come to that fateful day, her sixteenth birthday, when her Grandfather told her she was to marry King Juan II of Castile. She was to become a Queen. It wasn't becoming a Queen that mother resented, it was her disapproval of King Juan's aide who had arranged it, Don Alvaro de Luna, Constable of Castile and Grand Master of the Order of Santiago.

Don Alvaro de Luna was a name the Castilians whispered and wrote ballads about for decades to come. It was to be many years later before I fully understood the role he had played in my mother's life, and to understand why it probably was the major cause for her deep depressions which eventually drove her mad.

Don Alvaro de Luna came to my father's Court as a young page. He was the illegitimate descendant of an Aragon noble. He was brilliant, funny and outstanding in everything he did. He had a quick wit, was fast with his sword, and out-surpassed everyone else with his competency. Suddenly he was accepted into the inner circle of my father's aides, and very soon he was my father's only advisor. He was a gentleman, charming and gifted, lean, dark and sinister. He dressed in exquisite silk and adorned his fingers with magnificent jewels. As the Constable of Castile he wielded great power often acting as though he were the King and my father a mere puppet. Alvaro de Luna made all the decisions and father signed his name to the papers. For thirty years de Luna was the intimate friend, as well as Prime Minister, dominating my father completely, even telling him what to wear and what to eat. Father was not troubled by gossip, he wanted only to be spared the boredom of administration which left him free to indulge in his passion for Latin, poetry and music.

De Luna became the wealthiest man in Castile, far wealthier than the King since all the money was collected by him and dispensed at his own pleasure. For thirty years de Luna was the absolute master of my father and all of Castile.

Don Alvaro looted the Crown making himself fabulously rich. He corrupted the Church by naming incompetents to religious offices which gave them an income. His insolence and arrogance alienated the nobles. He infuriated the people when he gave the high office appointments and special privileges to Jews and Moors. He sowed the seeds of discord in Aragon, Navarre, France and Italy for his own grandiose plans.

De Luna's thirty years of corruption established the pattern for the government to be run by the whims of a nobleman. It created the foundation for the ensuing fifty years of moral decay of the Castilian Court.

In 1447 my mother was welcomed with magnificent celebrations when she became my father's new bride. There were dances, banquets, speeches, bull fights, tourneys and glittering processions. Don Alvaro had arranged everything.

Mother was pretty, charming and bright. Brought up by a strong Monarch, she had very clear and concise ideas about how Kings should rule their subjects. As she observed her husband's total domination by de Luna, she was appalled. Her husband the slave of such a haughty subject? This was an intolerable situation.

Every time the smiling Don Alvaro bowed and kissed her hand, she looked into his sinister eyes and shuddered. This man with the soft, cultured voice and grand manners was in truth a dangerous enemy.

I, Ysabella de Trastamara, was mother's first child, and three years later Alfonso was born. It was during mother's pregnancy with Alfonso that she seized upon the opportunity to destroy Alvaro. She had encouraged a friendship with my father's messenger, Don Alfonso Perez de Vivero, who brought her bits and snatches of Don Alvaro's business activities with the King. Don Alvaro was so angry at Vivero, he ordered him to be thrown out of a window on Good Friday afternoon in 1453.

Mother promptly issued the command to have Don Alvaro arrested and imprisoned in Valladolid where a council of his enemies was waiting to pass judgment.

This was not the first time Don Alvaro's enemies had outwitted him. He had been in difficult situations before and the King always came to his rescue. To his detractors he appeared totally unruffled and confident, displaying no strain or worry, only the utmost bravado. He was certain that as soon as he had a few words with the King everything would change. Already he was planning his revenge!

My father was frustrated and distraught. His close friend and adviser, the Prime Minister, his right hand was imprisoned at the command of his young wife. Twice he was ready to sign a pardon, only to be confronted with mother's strong iron will.

The preparations for the execution in Valladolid went forward in great haste. Early on a June morning a crowd of peasants, cattle herders, and gaily dressed hidalgos began to gather in the main plaza. A huge scaffold had been erected and covered in black velvet. Its only adornment was a block and a crucifix. The anxious crowd watched as the tall masked executioner, wrapped in robes of scarlet and displaying the great sword of the King of Castile, took his place.

A trumpet sounded, the muffled kettle-drums beat, and soon there came into view a small procession. Marching at the head was a herald wearing a jaunty, gaudy cap and tabard shouting out in his booming voice the crimes of Don Alvaro de Luna. Behind him strode two ranks of men-at-arms wearing leather jerkins and cuirasses and directly behind them Alvaro.

Don Alvaro, the supreme master of emotions, dismounted and nonchalantly looked out at the brilliant assembly of foes and idly curious. He smiled and with a firm step turned toward the man in scarlet. Still totally in control, he raised his head and gazed out over the heads of the crowded plaza, placing his hand over his heart he gallantly bowed. Quickly stepping toward his confessor, he exchanged a few words, then untied the tassel cord at the neck of his blue, fox fur-lined camlet and handed it to his page, Morales. Beneath the camlet he wore the emblem of a great Crusade, the breast sword and cockleshell of Santiago. Calmly he removed a ring from his finger, then his hat, and handed the keepsakes to his page. With noble gestures he turned again to the crowd, his deep bass voice echoing across the plaza as he wished prosperity to the King and his people.

The speechless crowd looked at this calm man with jewels at his waist and feet; they stared at the polished sword of justice he wore, and looked on in silence as Don Alvaro casually examined the block and the sword. Taking a black ribbon from his jacket pocket, he handed it to the executioner. Holding out his hands in front of him he calmly permitted them to be bound, then moving before the crucifix he knelt in prayer.

His nerves of steel never failed him. His long steps toward the executioner never wavered. He held his head high and placed his bound wrists over his heart. A great hush fell over the plaza. The Grand Master placed his head on the block. A swift, quick movement, and Don Alvaro de Luna was dead.

Mother had won!

CHAPTER II
An Invitation to Study at the Royal Court

Mother was loving, caring, and very firm with Alfonso and me. She studied our progress and listened to our recitations. When she was a little girl she loved her history lessons, and history was my favorite subject, too.

When I was studying at the Convent, a wonderful priest traveled from a distant parish to teach our history lessons. He was a spell-binding storyteller, weaving stories about the powerful Moors. I sat very straight in my small chair listening to my teacher tell stories about murder, cruelty, destruction and theft of property and slavery the Islamics inflicted over every people they conquered. I would comment to my teacher, "What a difference it would make if our civilization and religion were to replace the Moor's barbaric practices." My teacher shared the grim possibility that soon all of Christendom might become just another page in history.

The Turks were coming! They had ravaged eastern Europe, stealing, killing, raping and kidnapping. They were encamped in the lower part of the eastern border of the Holy Roman Empire and had enslaved the greater part of the Balkans. They had reached the banks of the Danube. The ancient Greek capitol of Constantinople was theirs. They were the undisputed masters of Greece.

Was Europe concerned? The Kings and other leaders continued squabbling among themselves and the Christians ignored the plight of the captured Christians who were subjugated to the awesome heavy hand of the Ottoman rulers. It was true the Popes had been making a limited attempt to mobilize the Christian rulers, but the powerful Emperor Frederick III of Germany was too occupied with catching exotic birds and planting flowers. In Denmark the King stole the money that had been raised when he looted the sacred treasury of the cathedral Roskilde.

My teacher impressed upon my mind the fierceness and lust for power of the Moorish people. They were endowed with high courage, inexhaustible energy, a unique gift for leadership, and an obvious supreme military genius. As the history lessons unfolded, I was aware of the obsessiveness of my teacher's crusading talks. Being young and vulnerable, my emotions were aroused as I learned about the hundreds of Christians that were being buried alive and the horrible plight of the women and children taken into captivity. The memory of the endangered innocent Christians lived with me all of my life.

As the history lessons continued, I learned that more pressing than the Turkish army advances had been the Mohammedan Arabs who had subdued and organized the Berbers of North Africa in the century. When they had gained strength, they were invited by the Spanish Jews to cross the nine-mile strip of water at Gibraltar and occupy the southern part of the Peninsula. The plot was discovered and the Jews were sternly punished. Time passed and the Spanish monarchy eventually weakened. As the Visigoth Monarchy lost control, the Jews threw open the gates of the principal cities to the Moors. Within an incredibly short time the Africans were masters of all Spain.

The priest spread a large map of the Peninsula out and attached it to the wall. Alfonso and I paid strict attention as he pointed all the kingdoms and cities the Moors had occupied for nearly eight hundred years. Only the tiny northern kingdom of Asturias had remained under Castilian control. By the middle of the 1400's we had regained all of our lost territories except Granada. Castile must again reign over Granada! Those unforgettable history lessons shaped my destiny.

I was a King's daughter and my half-brother was now the King of Castile. Mother would listen to Alfonso and me as we talked about our studies, then she would embellish her stories about her exciting life at the Portuguese Court. Alfonso and I would ask her to tell us about Castile's Court. What kind of a man was Enrique? I couldn't even remember what he looked like. Why didn't he come to see us? And father -- what about him? Didn't he love Alfonso and me? Why were we so poor? Why didn't he provide for us as a King should? What was our half-brother doing to bring back the glories of Saint Fernando and Alfonso the Wise?

Beatriz's father was the most important official in the kingdom of Avila. Alfonso and I often saw envoys looking very official riding into his courtyard, dismounting and quickly disappearing into Pedro's quarters. Mother was always anxious about those visits. She would send Felipe around to Pedro's servants' quarters to see if there was some gossip to be heard.

One hot afternoon the silence of our quiet courtyard was broken by a clatter of thundering hooves. The

King had come! I'll never forget the excitement I felt when I saw those beautiful horses and the bright royal banners carried by Enrique's aides. He arrived with two of his aides, the Marquis de Villena and his older brother Don Pedro Giron. These two gentlemen, mother whispered to me, were Enrique's closest companions who advised him in everything. These were the most powerful two men in the realm. I studied both of them. The two aides wore beautiful clothes made of pure silk bordered with gold cloth. Brilliant large jewels gleamed on their fingers and belt buckles. Around their necks they wore heavy gold chains that had been designed by the artisans of Cordoba.

Enrique approached my mother, greeting her as he bowed and kissed her hand. He looked rather shabby. His rather long wind-blown dark brown hair was covered with a stylish Moorish hat and his small brown eyes shifted as he looked over at Alfonso and me standing beside mother. Enrique was tall, loose-jointed, and looked slovenly and awkward in his long grey woolen cloak. Instead of boots his small delicate feet were encased in buskins, like those worn by the Moors. I stared at Enrique's muddy feet and almost had to stifle a giggle as I thought how peculiar those buskins looked at the end of those long spindly legs. But his face was even more peculiar. His nose was wide and flat. It was his eyes that fascinated me. They roved and glittered.

Enrique was not a man who spoke easily. He shifted his weight from side to side as he nervously stood before mother. Suddenly he blurted, "I've come to extend a personal invitation to Ysabella and Alfonso. I want them to live at the Alcazar in Madrid, where I have moved my Court, and continue their studies there.

They will be provided with their own living quarters and servants."

The smiling Marquis and Don Pedro Giron's heads bobbed up and down in approval. Mother looked at this trio and hesitated for a moment. Enrique took a step forward and a frightened look crossed mother's face. Quickly she uttered, "I will let you know very soon. I must talk it over with the children. They are so young and they will be very far away." She hesitated a moment then she added, "I love them both very much and it will be very lonely with them gone."

In his decisive manner Villena asked, "How soon will we know?" Mother looked steadily into his dark, swarthy face and said, "I'll send you my answer within three days." And with a wave of her hand, she indicated they were free to go.

Alfonso and I ran to the windows and watched them mount their horses and canter out of the courtyard. Then we raced to the top floor of the Alcazar and watched as they disappeared over the horizon.

CHAPTER III
My Brother's Keeper

My father's reign was a social and political disaster. Enrique's was a disgrace! Undeniably there were extenuating circumstances allowed my father because of his love for music, poetry, and he was greatly admired as a brilliant Latin scholar. People were exceptionally tolerant in their attitude toward his total reluctance to become directly involved with the business affairs of his realm.

In contrast, Enrique's friends and enemies found him spiteful, spineless, a homosexual, smelly, deformed, abominable, blind to his people's feelings and needs, and at times even imbecilic.

On his ascension to the throne in 1454 his aides urged the populace to look upon their new King as the liberator. Enrique the Liberal, they repeatedly assured the people, was now their ruler. Liberal he was, but not in ways which benefitted the people. He had a great contempt for all practical and mercenary considerations. A low-ranking favorite had only to ask him for money or land belonging to the Crown and he graciously acquiesced. To his friends he gave orders on the exchequer, making it out to the payee but leaving the amount blank for them to fill in to suit themselves. If his conscientious treasurer objected, Enrique retorted, "Instead of accumulating treasures like private persons, a

King ought to spend for the welfare of his subjects. I give to my enemies to make them my friends, and give to my friends to keep them from becoming my enemies." It was simple, very simple.

The Marquis de Villena would prepare a schedule or an important state paper and present it to him for his signature. With a great flourish Enrique would bend over the parchment and sign it without ever reading its contents.

His fanciful, imbecilic mind would furtively capture an image of Alcazars, monuments and monasteries being built, and with great fanfare and ceremony he would order construction to begin.

Enrique was far from orthodox in his opinions and conduct. He chose for his companions Moors, Jews and Christian renegades. Any man who ridiculed the Christian religion was sure of at least a smile from his Majesty, if not a pension. One of the favorite daily pastimes at the King's table was the invention of new and original blasphemies; obscene jokes were made about the Blessed Virgin and the Saints. The King attended Mass but never confessed or received Communion.

Enrique abhorred bloodshed. The Castilian tradition of waging savage blood-baths against the Moors was an abominable disgrace! Campaigns were waged against the Moors, but more often it was the staging of a chivalrous rivalry. His Moor guards were in constant attendance.

For the criminal he had great sympathy and affection. He would conduct them to safety if armed, outraged citizens cornered them. Politically and privately he held little regard for rank. He was notorious in choosing men of humble birth, even the menial servants, for his close companions. To the low castes he presented grants or titles and even appointed them to high offices.

Enrique had very little regard for the upright citizens. Three honest artisans were hanged in Sevilla merely because in a peevish moment he had given his word to do so. He appointed officials who used their office to spread tyranny over the people and made themselves rich in the process. Taxes were collected by the wealthy Rabbi Jusef of Segovia. Diego Aria de Avila, a converted Jew, was given plenary powers which included the right to exile citizens or put them to death without a hearing for non-payment of taxes.

Robber barons and highwaymen preyed on farmers, laborers, and merchants who, in turn, eventually had to become criminals to survive. There was hardly a corner of Castile where a man was safe from robbery and murder, hardly a road where a girl or a woman was safe from rape and mutilation.

The nobles considered themselves petty kings in their own jurisdiction. When they had a dispute with a neighbor, they went to war. Enrique permitted them to coin their own money.

The King seemed impervious to all this for the order of decay pleased him. He found horse skulls and leather burning delightful. He disliked sunlight, the broad clean horizons, preferring instead the gloom of the dark forests around Madrid and Segovia where he loved to chase wild animals with the Moors, rustics and criminals.

Alvaro de Luna had been my father's closest confidant, ruling Castile by the crafty manipulation of the nobles. My half-brother disliked the responsibilities of ruling as much as my father, and moving into the vacuum, ever alert and eager to please the new King, was Juan Pacheco, a crafty, scheming and dangerous man. He was the scion of a noble Portuguese family and although he professed to be a Christian, he was one of the many with Jewish blood who owed his rise to power to de Luna, the great Constable of Castile. He was a descendant of the Jew Ruy Capon on both sides of his family. Along with other conversos in my father's Court, he conspired to dethrone de Luna.

Alvaro de Luna invited Pacheco to my father's Court at the age of ten to be a page. From that wily master Pacheco learned his craft. My father was so impressed with this bright young page he soon became Enrique's tutor. From that day forward Pacheco was my half-brother's closest friend and most intimate advisor. Father was so fascinated with this bright young man he rewarded him generously by bestowing upon him the title of Marquis de Villena along with great estates that legally belonged to the Crown of Aragon.

Pacheco was an amiable, likable young man. His shrewd eyes twinkled as he spoke with a slight tremble in his high-pitched voice. He doused himself liberally with a perfume made of ambergris, a secret oil removed from the intestines of whales. He had a long aquiline nose, quite hooked in the middle and pointed at the tip. He had a narrow mouth with full lips. His moustache dominated his swarthy face. Dark and full, it drooped down at the corners of his lips, then with careful grooming Pacheco applied just the right amount of wax to twist the ends to turn out and up into two jaunty devil-may-care points nearly reaching his ears. He was small in build and stature, but he mastered his craft creating an imposing presence by carefully choosing his clothes, horses and aides which made lasting impressions on everyone.

His older brother, Don Pedro Giron, gained prominence when he attained the appointment as Grand Master of the powerful and illustrious military Order of Calatrava, an order founded by two Cistercian monks and consecrated to the rule of St. Benedict. Giron was a sleek, sensual and passionate man. He, too, was Enrique's close friend and advisor. Together, the two brothers conspired to hold the power of Castile in their hands.

Enrique had divorced his first wife, Blanche of Navarre, because she had not given him an heir. Blanche was sent home in disgrace. Now the King needed an heir, and the Marquis de Villena, virtually the ruler of the kingdom, volunteered to select a suitable bride. He chose Infanta Juana, sister of King Alfonso V of Portugal. Juana was a pretty, witty girl of fifteen. She arrived at Badajoz in 1455 with twelve pretty maids of honor and a long retinue of cavaliers. They were met at the border by the young blades of the Castilian Court, who conducted them in triumph to Cordoba, where the Archbishop of Tours performed the marriage.

Enrique wanted an heir, not a wife. In his brusque, regal manner, he promptly commanded Juana to become pregnant by one of his intimate male friends. Juana was horrified. She adamantly refused. Enrique decided her punishment should be virtual imprisonment, no money, and he embarrassed her before the people as he snubbed her in public. Juana had a strong will and she was determined to resist and ignore her husband's revolting commands.

The wary eyes of the Court watched Enrique cavorting with his favorites. His intimate relations with various men and young boys became common knowledge and scurrilous rumors abounded throughout Castile.

A scandal was beginning to brew and from his pulpit the outspoken Don Francisco de Toledo, Dean of the Toledo Cathedral, began denouncing the King. The powerful Alonso Carrillo, Archbishop of Toledo and Primate of Spain reproved the King first in private and then in public for the evil life and the torrid, unsavory scandals of his Court and his inability to govern.

The storm clouds around Enrique were gathering. Alonso Carrillo was a different kind of man to deal with. Even his worst enemies declared Carrillo never lacked courage. The Archbishop now began to attack Enrique with all the thunderous gravity and majesty for which he was noted.

The Court chronicler, Don Gonzalo de Guzman, wrote in his diary, "There are three things that I will not lower myself to take up; the pompous drawl of the Marquis de Villena, the gravity of the Archbishop of Toledo, and the virility of Don Enrique."

Alonso Carrillo, Archbishop of Toledo was the Marquis de Villena's uncle. As the Archbishop of Toledo he wielded tremendous power, and in his dealings he was as open and obvious as Villena was crafty and subtle. Nothing suited his basic nature better than to suit up, don his famous scarlet cape emblazoned with its white cross, mount his great horse and charge into the skirmishes of battle. In the great wars and conflicts that were to come, this vicar of Christ became a familiar sight flashing his sword and charging wildly into the carnage.

Carrillo was a crude, vindictive and violent man. He was exactly what a vicar of Christ should not be. If things did not go his way, he either erupted in pompous braggadocio or went away sulking. His crude outspo-kenness was abrupt in delivery, sometimes verging on infantile mentality. Never was he to be trusted with secrets for invariably he attempted to take advantage of the situation by turning them into an opportunity for his personal welfare. Enrique paid no attention to him as he huffed and puffed with his rhetoric, and in later years, the manner in which I handled him was a masterpiece of diplomacy.

Enrique and the Archbishop shared a common interest in alchemy. Enrique confined his curiosity to the intellectual aspects and its application; whereas Carrillo raced across the plains and climbed mountains searching for buried treasure with his elaborately con-ceived divining rods.

It was Carrillo's massive power that caused people to put up with him. He was the Primate of Spain as well as the Chancellor of Castile. His enormous holdings included fifteen large fiefdoms, providing an income far greater than the Crown's. He had more vassals than anyone in the realm. Power he had cleverly accumulated in abundance.

In 1461 a handsome, dashing knight-of-arms suddenly appeared in Enrique's midst. Don Beltran de la Cueva moved into the inner circle and immediately became Enrique and Juana's closest friend. The trio were seen everywhere together. Don Beltran was tall, robust, expert with his sword and lance, always ready to quarrel over a delicate point of honor. It was all too obvious. Enrique and Juana were captivated by this young nobleman. The Monarch would clap his hands and laugh loudly if Beltran flew into a paroxysm of rage against him. His amusing friend was funny. The King permitted his temperamental confidant to act as though he were the lord of the Alcazar, fascinated as he watched Beltran, kick, shove and pelt a porter who had failed to open a door quickly enough. Don Beltran was exciting! This sensual, dashing hero soon electrified Juana's romantic longings.

The nobles were cautious, quiet and thoughtful. They fervently detested Beltran for his arrogance and insolence. Villena shook his head in wonderment when he realized he had been replaced in the King's affection by Don Beltran. Secretly he began to devise a scheme to destroy his rival.

Suddenly Enrique made the bold announcement the Queen was pregnant. An heir to the throne would soon be born and in March of 1462, Juana gave birth to a little girl. Enrique was exuberant and in the excitement of his daughter's birth, he rewarded Beltran with the title Count de Ledesma. Tiny Juana was proudly proclaimed the heir to Castile's crown.

The Archbishop of Toledo baptized her with all the great pomp and pageantry befitting an Infanta. The distinctive noblemen lent their enormous prestige by their attendance and the church bells rang throughout the land as the nation rejoiced.

Enrique convened the Cortes to declare his little daughter the legitimate heir to the throne. The Cortes issued the declaration but within a matter of weeks they met again to review some new facts presented to them. Enrique was not Juana's father. From that day forward, the little infanta was known as 'La Beltraneja,' as if to establish her true parentage as Beltran's daughter.

The Marquis de Villena and Don Pedro Giron had almost forgotten about King Juan's two children. Perhaps they could use Ysabel's young children as pawns in the struggle for complete dominance and power in the troubled realm. The crafty and cunningly devised scheme began to take shape in their minds, and soon Enrique was convinced that he owed it to his father's great memory to bring Ysabella and Alfonso to be educated at his Majesty's Court.

The struggle for power had begun.

CHAPTER IV
Ysabella and Alfonso's Departure

My mother was a remarkable woman, but life at stony Arevalo was not easy. After the luxury of both the Portuguese and Castilian Courts, her uneventful days were lonely and drab. Money was always so scarce we were reduced to virtual poverty. At times mother gathered up her courage and with great dignity sent word to Governor Pedro de Bobadilla or the local priest requesting their assistance.

Alfonso and I had no toys to play with, few clothes, and our shoes seemed to always be worn out. Sometimes mother would look at the two of us and her eyes would suddenly shift into a distant, far off vacant stare. I couldn't ask her what was wrong, for whenever I did she would be overcome with uncontrollable sobbing. Alfonso and I would put our arms around her and she would try to be reassuring and reminded us that we were her children, born to rule over our people. We must have courage and strength, and we were never to forget it.

Something seemed to have broken in mother's heart after Enrique's visit. The depression which was constantly with her now kept her in bed. She slept a great deal, rousing herself to give instructions to the underpaid, or probably more likely, never paid, servants. From her bedside she asked Alfonso and me whether we wanted to study at the Court in Madrid or to stay at Arevalo. There was obvious pain in her face and her voice broke as she struggled to fight back the tears. I knew that her heart was breaking.

After Enrique and his aides had cantered off, Alfonso and I chattered like magpies. We were going to live in the Alcazar in Madrid! Mother's stories loomed before us and we wanted to go study and be part of the royal household. Mother tried to be brave when we answered that we wanted to continue our studies at Court.

The next day mother sent for a young, inexperienced seamstress to prepare our royal wardrobes. There was no money to purchase material for our new clothes. Hanging in mother's closet were the beautiful silk, satin and brocade gowns from her days at Court. She pulled them out and asked the young girl to take her scissors and cut out dresses for me and shirts and pants for Alfonso. They piled the clothes in two heaps. The silks and brocades trimmed with beads and lace were set aside for my new dresses, and the satin gowns would become shirts and trousers for Alfonso.

Mother sent for a tin smith who soon arrived with a display of tin cups, plates and various objects of art he created out of this metal. Mother studied them all, and then asked him if he could make two small crowns for us. A smile flashed across the short, stocky artisan's face and his head bobbed up and down. He reached into his pockets and pulled out some colored pieces of perfectly proportioned glass. The crystal, red and green pieces gleamed like jewels in his hands. Looking up at mother, he asked, "Shall I make the crowns with jewels?"

Mother stared at those colored pieces of glass, and her mind raced back to her jewels Enrique had forced her to give him at father's death. She studied the pieces in his hand, and suddenly it seemed to her that those pieces could become a diamond and emerald necklace, a ruby and diamond broach, and a ruby ring! She took a piece of paper and quickly sketched the designs for the three pieces of jewelry. As the tin smith watched mother's hand outlining the sketches, his flashing brown eyes twinkled and a broad smile evidenced his obvious interest in the drawings. Handing the sketches to him, she said, "No, don't put any gems in the crowns. Do make these up for me!"

As he prepared to depart he looked at mother's outstretched hand and stepping forward he bowed gracefully and kissed her hand uttering, "Your royal Highness, I am pleased to be of service to you."

Everything at Arevalo suddenly seemed exciting. People were coming and going, bustling about in a flurry of activity. Alfonso and I spent most of our days with Beatriz. How I would miss my dear friend. I asked mother if Beatriz could come to the Court and study with me. Mother said she would give it some thought, but in the end, she said, "No. Pedro has already made plans for his daughter's future. He is sorry but that is the way it must be." I think I must have cried alone that day, and even though I was only twelve years old, it seemed terribly important that Beatriz and I be friends forever.

Pascha and I had become great friends. I was glad that I would be taking him with me. Over the past year Pedro and his attendants worked with me and Pascha in training him to prance, trot, and gallop as a horse of noble birth should. Pascha was an intelligent pony, responding to the commands of the reins or my voice. He was my proudest possession.

I watched the seamstress at work on my dresses. She was adding lace and sewing some beading decoratively around the collars, and in her girlish voice she proclaimed that I was certain to be the most beautiful young lady at the King's Court. I had never worn such beautiful dresses. The plain dresses and jumpers I had were very different from those I saw being made for me. Life would be very different at Court, of that I was very sure.

Mother tried to oversee the activities from her bed. Suddenly I realized that she had difficulty making decisions. She was very unsure of herself. As the time came nearer for Alfonso and me to leave, she became more distant than ever.

Finally all the preparations were finished and Felipe and one of Pedro's men worked feverishly packing our new belongings and hoisting them up on the backs of the mules, securing them with ropes and twine, ready for the long trek to Madrid.

The eventful day arrived and mother gathered up enough strength to sit up very straight in her Throne Chair to bid us goodbye. She was wearing a sparkling necklace that resembled emeralds and diamonds, a glittering broach inset with a pattern of red, and a new ring on her finger. Alfonso and I stood before her. She looked at our bright smiling faces and then she reached down into her little knapsack and pulled out the two new crowns. They sparkled and shone as bright as silver. Mother placed them on our heads and gave us a royal command. "Alfonso, you are to look after your sister as every courageous knight should. And you Ysabella, must be very watchful that Alfonso does not fall into the hands of Enrique's notorious renegades. You are of royal birth. You are the Infante and Infanta, and your conduct at Court must be representative of your great Portuguese and Castilian heritages. Now go my blessed ones, remember always that I love you with all my heart and I will miss you so. One thing you must promise me -- that you will write and tell me all about your studies, new friends, and Enrique's Court. Your niece, Juana, is almost two years old. In a few years she will become your companion, too. Treat her with respect for she, too, is apparently of royal birth. Now go quickly and God be with you."

Alfonso and I rushed into her outstretched arms, tears were streaming down our cheeks, we hugged each other, and then we said our tearful goodbyes. That was the last time that my mother embraced me with a sense of knowing that I was her child. Soon she was to slip farther and farther, ever more deeply into her depressions suffering from a mild but incurable form of insanity.

Pedro and his aides were waiting for us as the great Alcazar door swung open and then closed with such finality behind us. We mounted our horses and Pedro unfurled his banners, the servants swung the large gates open and we urged our horses onto the road. There was a clatter of hoofs, a flurry of dust and shouts ringing in the air, the King had sent his men-at-arms to escort us making sure of our safety.

Alfonso and I were very quiet as we rode across the unfamiliar terrain. Our lives were soon to change, and change very dramatically. Each of our fates was in God's hands.

CHAPTER V
Rebellion Foments

The great iron gate of the old Moorish Alcazar at Madrid swung open and before us was a massive courtyard. Alfonso and I looked around at the hoards of active people. There were at least a dozen Moors mounted on small mules elaborately festooned with ribbons of red, silver and gold. They came galloping toward us, their banners held high and blowing in the soft breeze. They cantered up and lowered their banners in acknowledgment of our royal presence. Pivoting around, they urged their mules forward forming a small procession up to the Alcazar's great wide steps.

An aide stepped from the shadows and rushed up to Pascha. Holding the bridle firmly with his left hand, he reached up to help me dismount. I looked over at Alfonso and with the help of another servant, his feet hit the ground with a thud. Together, and all alone, we walked up those steps. The great hand-carved wooden doors opened, and a page suddenly appeared to announce our arrival. Quickly other servants appeared, and we were taken to our new living quarters. I tried to hide my nervous apprehension. The Alcazar was so big, the rooms so enormous, the tapestries hanging on the wall so beautiful, the stained glass windows were magnificent. The small, neat rooms assigned to Alfonso and me were near the servants quarters. The closets were just large enough to hold our few belongings. We were told to sit down and wait. Soon someone would be with us.

The door opened without a sound, and a tall, lanky man entered. His strange, piercing brown eyes gazed out from behind heavy eyeglasses. He had bushy eyebrows, a thick brown beard, and strange, unusual clothes. He introduced himself as Master Jorge Geraldo. He was to oversee our studies, show us through the Alcazar, tell us where we were to eat our meals, how to find our way to the class room and the area where we were to play. Alfonso looked up and said to him, "But the King promised us private tutors. We will not be going to classes with other children."

The strange man looked down at my nine year old brother and said, "No, Don Alfonso, you will not be having private tutors. You are to be treated just like everyone else living at the Alcazar. You and Dona Ysabella will attend classes with the other children of the King's Court." Alfonso looked at me, and I shrugged my shoulder as if to say, "Be quiet. Don't say anything more."

I was glad that our rooms looked out over the courtyard. From the high elevation of our quarters, I could watch everything going on. The arrival of distinguished visitors, the envoys of foreign governments, and boisterous renegades who were Enrique's comrades.

Alfonso and I were totally unprepared for the life style we were suddenly thrown into. Our childhood years in the quietude and austerity of Arevalo and mother's dominant influence did not prepare us for this sudden change. There were balls, tourneys, pageants, comedies, bullfights, intrigues and scandals. Our class-mates would squeal with laughter as someone would tell a new joke about Don Beltran. They whispered about Queen Juana and her indiscretions, and then there was the never ending jokes about the King's virility.

Alfonso and I were somewhat isolated from all the outside activities. Master Jorge was considerate and kind, and often asked us what we had learned in our classrooms. Alfonso learned the accomplishments of a cavalier, and I studied music, painting, poetry, sewing and grammar. I had several free hours each day to spend in quiet prayer.

I tried to understand the attitudes of the people. It seemed that the nobles were constantly warring against each other but their quarrels and continuous conflicts seemed not to bother the King. There were the struggles between the Christians and Mohammedans, between Castile and Portugal, between Castile and Aragon. Human life was very cheap. The Moslem influence encouraged polygamy. The clergy flaunted their mis-tresses and children born out of wedlock. The morality of the Court was abominable. I wanted to hide from all the debauchery.

The political atmosphere of the Court began to shift. At the birth of Juana, Enrique had forced the grandees to swear loyalty to her as heir to the Crown. Many denied the oath as soon as it was made. There were several who grumbled at the greed and dishonesty of Villena, but were not ready to actually take up arms against the swaggering, insolent, egotistical and over-bearing Don Beltran de la Cueva. The Archbishop of Toledo thought he had no real grievance against Don Beltran. The Admiral and others, even though they hated Beltran, were willing to make a truce. Villena wavered between both factions.

Villena had wheedled vast possessions from Enrique, but he was never content and he never would be. He wanted the Grand Mastership of the Order of Santiago, an office of such power and revenues that it was traditionally bestowed upon the royal family. The Order had been founded as the result of one of the fiercest battles between the Mahometans and the Christians. The two factions had met on the battlefield when suddenly a devastating storm with lashing winds, lightning flashing throughout the heavens, followed by deafening claps and rolls of thunder stopped the battle. Frightened Christians falling to the ground suddenly looked up to see an apparition of Santiago mounted on a pure white horse, holding high the banner of the Cross. The weary soldiers rallied to their great Christian cause, reassembled their broken squadrons, and became victorious as they drove the enemy from their midst. Thus the first religious order, the Order of Santiago, was founded. Now, by the voice of the Order, the exalted honor was conferred upon my brother, Don Alfonso, son of King Juan II of Castile and Leon.

It seemed to the ambitious Marquis de Villena that my eleven year old brother was much too young to assume such heavy responsibilities. He made a quiet appeal to Queen Juana. Suddenly King Enrique IV announced that Don Alfonso had "resigned" the Mastership of the Order. Pacheco looked over the huge assemblage and smiled with satisfaction at his quiet triumph.

Juana had helped the Marquis to this extent; however, she had her own views for the new appointment of the Master of the Order. She had not thought it necessary to trouble Villena with the worry that he had a rival for the Mastership. The first indication the Marquis had of this unthinkable situation was the day the King, on the eve of departing for a hunting trip in the woods north of Madrid, announced Don Beltran de la Cueva was the new Master of the Order of Santiago.

The news fell upon Villena like a thunderclap. One of his greatest ambitions was to be the Grand Master of the Order of Santiago. He almost had it within his grasp. He thought he had made it very clear to Queen Juana that he was the only person qualified to undertake the leadership of this illustrious institution. Juana had tricked him and now he was angry -- very angry. He would show the King and Queen, as well as Beltran, who truly held all the power of the realm.

Power! Villena and Carrillo would have done anything to achieve it and once achieved, keep it. They had ruled Enrique for a long time. When Beltran de la Cueva appeared, they were alarmed. As Beltran's star rose, they grew desperate. But Villena and Carrillo were not the only malcontents. The whole country was seething at Enrique's incompetence. The disgusted nobles began addressing petitions to the King ordering him to observe the laws of the land, enforce justice, clean up his Court and bring decency into his private life.

Enrique threw the petitions away, but they continued to come. Every month they grew more insolent, more recriminatory. The people, disturbed by many wild rumors, became restless, surly, afraid -- whatever happened it could not be worse for them. The great nobles took sides. Many who despised Enrique were drawn to him by loyalty to the ideal of legitimate succession.

Don Pedro Gonzales de Mendoza, Bishop of Calahorra, continued to support Enrique. He resisted the urgent appeals of the conspirators who valued his character and the influence of his illustrious family. The Bishop was a scholar and a statesman whose powerful house was allied by the blood ties to most of the great families of the north. Little as Mendoza respected the character of the King, he was under no illusions as to the unselfishness of Villena and the cool judgment of Carrillo.

Meanwhile everyone was asking, "What will Villena do?" With his usual caution and cunning he attempted to solve his dilemma by his own method before taking up arms. He tried several times to have Don Beltran assassinated, and on one occasion the lucky knight barely escaped. That was the turning point for Pacheco. Suddenly he joined with the rebels. His disreputable brother, Don Pedro Giron, Grand Master of the Order of Calatrava soon joined him.

Some of the proudest nobles of the land, the Marquis de Santillana, the Counts de Alba, Haro and Paredes, along with the great Admiral of Castile, Don Fadrique de Hernandes, all aligned themselves against the King. When this powerful group joined Villena and Carrillo, each and every one of them angry at his position being superseded by Beltran, the mood was ripe for open rebellion to flare. The country was in imminent danger of a civil war.

The insurgents gathered at Burgos. From there they sent Enrique a stunning ultimatum which became the *"Representations of Burgos,"* a document which did not mince matters. In language so bold it was directly insulting, the nobles laid down their demands. Enrique was to repent his abominable sins, get rid of his odious Moorish bodyguards, and his oppressive power exercised over him by Beltran de la Cueva, the Count de Ledesma. Beltran must be stripped of his Mastership of the Order of Santiago, which would then be transferred back to the eleven year old Don Alfonso. The pretense of Dona Juana's legitimacy as his daughter was to be stopped. And Don Alfonso, son of Juan II of Castile and Leon, was to immediately be sworn as heir to the Throne.

Enrique rushed off to seek the advice of his old tutor, the warlike Bishop of Cuenca, who advised him to put up a determined resistance to the rebels. The distracted King, suddenly enraged, stood up and blurted, "You priests who are not called upon to fight are very well ready to shed the blood of others!" and stormed out of the Bishop's quarters.

The two opposing sides met at the town of Cigales in December, 1464. The King yielded to every particular. Eleven year old Alfonso would be placed in the hands of his opponents and declared the heir to Castile on the condition that he marry his infant niece, Dona Juana. In the royal document drawn up at Cabezon, Enrique acknowledged, "Know ye that to avoid any kind of scandal I declare that the legitimate succession to this kingdom belongs to my brother, the Infante Don Alfonso, and to no other person whatsoever; and I beg and command all of the prelates and nobles by these present, that three days from now they make oath of loyalty and homage to the said Infante Don Alfonso, my brother, in the manner and form in which it was made to me, the King, in the life of King Juan II, my Lord and father."

Three days later the ceremony took place. Alfonso was brought to Cabezon surrounded by the Archbishops of Toledo and Sevilla, Villena and other prelates and grandees. After the ceremony the factions parted again. Enrique agreed to let Villena take complete charge of my brother.

Then Enrique changed his mind. He was unable to get along without Beltran. He denied everything he had signed. He recalled Don Beltran but it was too late to rescue the Mastership of Santiago for it had quickly been conferred upon Alfonso. To compensate, Enrique raised Don Beltran from Count de Ledesma and conferred upon him a new title, the Duke de Albuquerque giving him the towns of Cuellar, Roa, Colmenar de Arenas and El Andrade, plus extensive lands in southern Andalucia.

Soon Enrique and Beltran were plotting to raise an army and within a matter of weeks, they had conscripted eighty-four thousand men.

CHAPTER VI
Rebellion and Deception

The defection of some of the most powerful nobles to the rebels' side, and the general support of the people to them, forced the King into facing the gravity of his situation. His reactions to bad news found him rushing off to bring the disturbing facts to the Queen and Don Beltran, the Duke de Albuquerque. The Duke would swear while Juana listened in contemptuous silence. Enrique wailed in one breath that he was lost and betrayed, he would be killed! He must surrender! In the next breath he swore that he would cut off the heads of all the rebels. Then he thought of fleeing to Portugal. The distasteful thought of giving battle for his kingdom flashed through his mind. Why was there no one to advise with him? Where was Villena? Why had he ever let him get away?

Juana listened to his ranting and raving and when that was spent, she persuaded him to now listen to reason. She was pregnant and soon she would give birth to a son. A new king would change their fortunes by restoring and securing their Crown. The new baby would rob the conspirators of their rejection of 'La Beltraneja,' as Juana, the little Infanta, was now called.

The rebels needed the support of Don Pedro Gonzalez de Mendoza. Villena and Carrillo composed a persuasive letter setting forth all the increased privileges and power that would be his once he joined forces with them. Mendoza read the letter and settling back in his chair, his brilliant mind began to formulate his reply. He reached for some paper and quickly replied. "It is well known, gentlemen, that every kingdom is like a body, of which we have the King for a head. If the head is sick, it seems more sensible to endure the pains rather than cut it off. Holy scripture forbids rebellion and commands obedience. We ought to preserve the welfare of the greatest number, even if some are unhappy, rather than plunge all into the evils of civil war and anarchy. Infante Alfonso, being only eleven years old, cannot reign for some years yet. Admitting that Don Enrique is weak and vicious, Castile will be no better off under a boy..." and one might imagine that Mendoza thought to himself, "and controlled by men like Pacheco."

Villena read the Bishop's reply and disturbing questions began to formulate in his mind. Suppose Enrique won the struggle? Juana's pregnancy clouded his position. If she had a son, what would become of the rebels and their estates, or their lives? Villena's crafty mind chose never to be on the losing side of anything. His cagey thinking began to develop another plot. He rushed to Valladolid to present a little program that he assured Enrique would benefit both of them.

Villena knew the King desperately needed money. He would give him an ample sum. The rebels were ravaging the estates of Enrique's supporters in Andalusia and Villena offered to supply Enrique with three thousand lances which would provide the equivalent protection of ten thousand men. Villena would place Alfonso under the King's protection. He pledged the influential Pacheco family allegiance to him. This left Carrillo and the Admiral isolated and totally at the mercy of the

King. Villena concluded his plans assuring the King that if he would arrange for my marriage to his older brother Don Pedro Giron, this would swing all of the royal power back under the King's domain.

Enrique's shifty eyes studied Villena as he outlined his cunning plans. Giving his sister in marriage to Don Pedro Giron was brilliant! The fact that Giron was not a member of any royal household never crossed his mind. He saw it as an immediate solution to all of his difficulties. He agreed to sacrifice me to retain his Throne. Soon, any day now, the Queen would bring forth a new heir. It was a jubilant King who clapped his old friend on the shoulders and with renewed confidence escorted him to his waiting horse.

Juana's son was prematurely born dead. The rebels stepped up their pressure and gained new support from the kingdoms. Enrique flew into a panic. He rushed around issuing orders for his Council to convene. He needed their advice.

In the opinion of some, the King still held the whip hand, but only if he acted immediately and with a firm show of strength.

The aged Bishop of Cuenca, who had been a counselor to my father, declared there were no two sides to any question. Pounding his fist on the table he cried out, "A King who hopes to preserve his royal authority can have no dealings with rebels who defy him, except offer them battle!"

Enrique looked over at the Bishop, his flabby mouth curling into a sneer, solemnly said, "Need I again remind you Bishop, men of God who need not fight nor lay their hands on swords seem to be very free with the lives of others."

There was a moment of eloquent silence. The King had spoken. The old Bishop rose, and with a firmness of strength he shot back, "Henceforth you will be called the most unworthy King Castile has ever known; and you will repent of it, Sir, when it is too late!"

Villena left the meeting in haste. He was weighing the pros and cons of the still delicate situation. He rushed forth to meet with Carrillo and the Admiral. Villena tried to persuade his co-conspirators that it would be unwise, dishonorable and even disloyal to lead their rebel troops into battle before every peaceful plan had been explored. He convinced the Archbishop and Admiral they should allow him to negotiate a plan with Enrique and wrench the most favorable terms from him.

The Archbishop and Admiral didn't trust Villena but they knew he was the only one who could manage the King. Reluctantly they agreed to wait and see what the Marquis would gain for them. In his eagerness for more power Toledo had failed to note that when Alfonso was placed under Villena's supervision and the arrangement of a marriage between Don Pedro and me was concluded, the struggle for power ended. The only one left to benefit from the situation was the Marquis. The weightiness of this deceitful plan infuriated the diminutive but explosive Don Fadrique. The Marquis had made fools of them all!

Villena eloquently drew on his soft gloves, picked up his riding whip, bowed to his uncle, Alonso Carrillo, then nodded to the Admiral and left the room. His horse was saddled and waiting, his aides were ready to hear the unfolding plans. They cantered off in search of a safe place to keep my brother.

Don Fadrique and Toledo signaled for their horses to be immediately saddled and ready for a long ride. Mounting their steeds they raced toward Madrid. It was late in the evening when they arrived, and they wasted no time in sending immediate word to the King requesting an audience with him. Enrique was charming and polite as the rebellious twosome humbly stood before him professing they had now seen the error of their ways. They assured the King they were mortified at the very thought of the treachery into which they had been inveigled by Pacheco. They now came before him to repudiate it and to pledge their loyalty to his Majesty.

They denounced Villena as an unscrupulous traitor who had betrayed the King and the entire country. Don Fadrique spoke eloquently pointing out that with Alfonso in the Marquis' custody, Castile virtually had two kings. Whenever it pleased Villena to raise the flag of revolt for either side, he would not hesitate to do so. Toledo and Fadrique knew it was their duty to come to the King's assistance. They advised him to publicly revoke the *"Representations of Burgos"* and promptly demand Alfonso be returned to Madrid.

Enrique was flattered at first and then he suddenly looked frightened. Don Fadrique spoke so eloquently as he urged Enrique to place himself in their hands. Enrique looked into the faces of his old adversaries and in a weak moment decided to show his gratitude. He called for an aide and demanded he bring to him the deeds of certain valuable properties which he knew his detractors had long coveted. With a great flourish he signed the deeds and handed them over to the Admiral and Archbishop. With another flourish he concluded their audience with him. The next day the Archbishop and Admiral quietly departed from the city going in their different directions to take possession of their new estates.

The King convened the Cortes and repudiated the *"Representations of Burgos"* and issued a sharp command to Villena to return my brother to Court immediately.

Villena and his friends doubled over in laughter when the news reached them. Villena sent word to Enrique that he was confused. Since the Infante had been placed in Villena's care by the power of the nobles, Alfonso would remain with him.

The King sent an urgent appeal to the Archbishop asking him to return to Madrid acknowledging the Admiral and Archbishop had been correct -- Villena had tricked the King.

Meanwhile, the Archbishop and the Admiral had gotten the estates they had wanted for many years and decided there was nothing more the King could do for them, so they rejoined the rebel forces. The news of the Archbishop and Admiral's betrayal left Enrique devastated. Now he had no one to advise him. The Queen was ill and Don Beltran had left for his new estates at Cuellar.

Enrique's deep gloom permeated the atmosphere of the Alcazar. Everyone was afraid. They spoke in soft voices, almost whispering. The watchful and eager observations of all of the activities by my personal maid, Maria, were shared with me every day. The gloom was spreading and it seemed that I was beholding the unfolding of history. This could be the beginning of the end for Enrique's reign. In his despondent mood Enrique would mutter, "Naked came I out of my mother's womb, and naked shall I return thither." He shut himself up, strummed his lute and sang some sad songs. Why had he ever offended the Marquis of Villena?

Maria and Master Jorge followed the changing political winds, and I learned of all the plots and counter plots through them. Alfonso had sent a few notes to me, but I was still refused permission to travel outside the city. The rumors were spreading that they were planning to declare my brother the King and a large assembly of insurgent Lords would soon be arriving at Avila. Master Jorge brought the news that the Archbishop of Toledo had been seen everywhere in his gleaming mail, armed cap-a-pie, mounted on his huge black horse, and over his curlass fluttered the crimson cloak with the great white cross emblazoned on it. Couriers were seen racing over the roads from one end of the kingdom to the other. The feudal retainers of the Admiral were on the march northward.

One afternoon, a secret courier arrived and asked Master Jorge if he might see me. Master Jorge smuggled the courier into the Alcazar and brought him to my quarters. I was anxious about Alfonso's safety and the courier assured me he was safe and well as he handed me an invitation to attend my brother's coronation. The awesome responsibility of the Crown being transferred to my eleven year old brother, and the news the King had agreed to my marriage to that disgraceful old Don Pedro Giron suddenly engulfed me. I read the note carefully and with haste, I quickly picked up a pen and sent back my regrets. I could not lend my support to Alfonso. Enrique was the King of Castile.

My faithful maid, Maria, brought me snatches and pieces of the unfolding drama. I was fearful that Alfonso was much too young to become the king. He was now merely a pawn in the struggle between the nobles positioning themselves to either retain or regain property and the coveted appointment of offices. I asked Master Jorge to secure permission for me to visit Alfonso. Sending his regrets, Enrique rejected my plea.

I shuddered at the thought of marrying Giron. Being pledged to marry a complete stranger was not new. Although I was fourteen years old, there had been negotiations for my hand for Ferdinand of Aragon, Carlos of Viana, Alfonso V of Portugal, a brother of Edward IV of England, and probably the Earl of Gloucester who later became notorious as Richard III. But they all had royal blood. Don Pedro Giron had no royal blood, and he was reputed to be a scoundrel with many vices. Marry that man? Never! "God will not permit it, and neither will I."

CHAPTER VII

A Young King is Crowned

The rebels were not idle. They had possession of my eleven year old brother and in his name they hurriedly began their subversion. Burgos, Toledo, Sevilla, and Cordoba were persuaded to rise up against Enrique. In a secret conclave at the Monastery of San Pedro de la Duenas, they plotted to take the King a prisoner.

Enrique discovered their plot and barricaded himself in the Alcazar situated high on the northern cliffs of Segovia. He sent a messenger to Archbishop Toledo reminding him of all the past favors he and his father had pledged to him and urged him to return to the fold. Carrillo promptly came back with his famous retort, "Go tell your King that I am sick of him and his affairs, and now we shall see who is the real King of Castile!"

The rebels decided upon a de facto ceremony dethroning Enrique followed directly with a coronation of Alfonso as their new King.

Avila was the chosen site for the public humiliation of Enrique and the crowning of Alfonso. An effigy of King Enrique IV was royally clad in a mantle lined with miniver thrown over a black mourning robe. There was a jeweled collar, a gold chain around his neck, pearls, rubies and emeralds at his girdle, and the slovenly Moorish buskins. Nothing was left out of his natural attire. The royal banner of Castile swaying in the wind was placed over the head. And around the platform, as if guarding the mock king, stood knights, men-at-arms, crossbowmen and lancers.

Word of the dethronement of their King quickly spread and a teeming crowd surged around the scaffolding and platform. The brightly colored capes of all of the crafts and guilds signaled this group was well represented. The brown cowls of the Franciscans and the black and white of the Dominican Orders indicated the Church was taking a definite interest in the ceremony. The Moorish sheiks in elaborate turbans had arrived and the whiskered Jews wearing little circular badges on their chests were sprinkled liberally throughout the crowd. Students from as far away as Salamanca University, anxious to observe the spectacular event, milled around the scaffolding. The arrival of the cavaliers wearing the insignias of three military Orders created a murmuring of voices and heads began nodding up and down as each perceived the gravity of the ceremonies about to be witnessed. The peasants from the countryside, wearing their long woolen mantles, stood side by side with the Castilian Lords.

The Archbishop of Toledo had removed his armor and put on his vestments of red and white glimmering with touches of gold. Other noblemen solemnly stood militarily erect as the ceremony began.

At the signal of Villena, the trumpeters raised their trumpets to sound the call, and the kettle-drums broke the stillness in the noon day sun. A bell rang out and the Archbishop made the sign of the cross. The Mass began. The crowd knelt as the Host was held high. A great murmuring echoed throughout as the Mass ended. The crowd pressed nearer to the platform. They wanted to hear every word and see every action taken in the dethronement of their King. The uncertain course of their nation's future was on their minds.

The Archbishop in his gruff, booming voice read a long list of grievances and accusations against the King. As his voice rang out with accusation after accusation, howls and yells went up from the titillated rabble.

The Archbishop, his ruddy face very grave, stepped toward the effigy of Enrique, and with slow deliberate movements, he removed the crown from the head saying "Thus lose the royal dignity which you have guarded so ill."

The Count de Benavente stepped forward and seized the scepter which had been placed in the effigy's right hand exclaiming, "Thus lose the government of the realms, as you deserve."

Diego Lopez de Zuniga now cried out, "Lose also the throne and the reverence due Kings!" Then he rushed forward and kicked the stuffed image off the seat sending it tumbling to the dusty ground.

The trumpets sounded again and the roll of the kettle-drums concluded the first part of the ceremonies.

Shrieks, groans and loud sobs of horror from the crowd quickly filled the air. The emotional ceremony had ended but the people were ever mindful that in Castile, a King, whatever he may be as a man, represents the sovereignty of the people, which comes from God.

Suddenly a shout of triumph from the partisans for Alfonso reverberated throughout the valley dimming the sounds of those who shrieked and sobbed. The rebels pressed onward with the declaration of their new King. Alfonso meekly approached the empty throne and now seated, the crown was placed upon his head, the scepter in his hands, and his oath was given. The gravity of the nation was now upon his young shoulders.

Shouts of glee and merriment of the men followed and raising their voices they shouted, "Castile, Castile for the King Don Alfonso." The trumpets burst upon the summer air, the royal standard was unfurled, and the sounds of the kettle-drums resounded through the valleys. The grandees stepped forward and kissed his hand, and as Alfonso stood up, the ecstatic crowd threw their hats into the air. Joyously they lifted their voices in song as the rays of the bright June sun played upon the gleaming jewels of the crown, sword, and scepter of their new King.

Today was a new day. The sweet promise of a new era was beginning.

CHAPTER VIII
Nobles Foment Rebellion
The Lesson of Alhamar

The mood of everybody at the Alcazar was gloomy. The atmosphere of fear and anxiety was everywhere. The Queen bustled about in a flurry of activities trying to create the impression that Enrique was the King, still in command of Castile. She gave small parties, afternoon teas, and entertainments for her guests. Suddenly she began to include me in all of these activities.

I had disciplined myself to become accustomed to solitude. My days were filled with reading, embroidery and daily rides on Pascha. Everyone was suspicious of everyone else. Juana now decided she should join me every day in riding. I was free to wander anywhere in the Alcazar, but if I decided to go for a walk in the sunshine, I knew a hundred eyes watched every step I took. I was a prisoner in my brother's care.

Master Jorge and Maria were my protectors and friends. Master Jorge brought me stacks of books. He piled them in a corner of my small quarters, and I browsed through them choosing those that interested me. Master Jorge and I had many serious discussions about history. He was a historian who taught me much about the folly of kings and rulers. Among the books he brought to me were several volumes outlining the Ottomans' rise to power. I read those books from cover to cover, and then I read them again. How had they become so powerful? I thought I had discerned a glimmer of what had helped them to succeed. They had Sultans who understood the importance of making government appointments to capable administrators.

The Ottomans proved their uniqueness as their warriors marched forth transforming the fruits of their military conquest into an effective political organism. By the end of the 14th century they ruled over an empire which extended eastward to the Great Wall of China, northward into the steppes of Russia, southward to the River Ganges and the Persian Gulf, westward into Persia, Armenia and the upper waters of the Euphrates and the Tigris. The Sultan's instincts for the proper mix of political and administrative appointments had brought them tremendous power. When I reflected upon my father's reign and now observing Enrique's, I decided their weaknesses in both of these areas had created the great problems Castile was facing today.

One morning a smiling Master Jorge arrived earlier than usual with a thick volume in his hands. I knew he had found a book that would fascinate me, and I reached out for it asking, "Master Jorge, you have brought me another book to help pass the day. Tell me, is it history or short essays?"

Master Jorge's eyes gleamed and his smile still lingered as he spoke, "Infanta, I have discovered the most wonderful historical account of Muhamed Ibm-l-Ahmar!"

I tried to quickly refresh my memory to remember who Muhamed Ibm-l-Ahmar was. Master Jorge seemed to sense I was trying to place him and he went on to say, "No, Infanta, I'm sure you don't remember him as Muhamed Ibm-l-Ahmar because his people simply called him Alhamar."

As Master Jorge sat down, I was still trying to place this Emir of the Moors in my history lessons. Lifting the book in his hands, he said, "This book is written in their language, and from my own memory I do not believe it was ever translated into Castilian. Since I read and speak the Moor's language fluently, let me tell you all about this remarkable man."

A Granada Moor remarkable? As that thought crossed my mind, my face must have registered an inquisitiveness, for Master Jorge went on to say, "Yes, here in this book is a most remarkable story. I know that you will find many things within its pages that you will remember for years to come. Let me tell you all about him. You know that we do have a lot of time to spare these days, so let us spend the next day or so discussing Alhamar. To begin with, it was Alhamar who designed and built the Alhambra in Granada."

Thoughts of that magnificent structure of buildings that everyone talked about flashed through my mind, and I exclaimed, "Of course, and they named that great ediface the Alhambra after him!"

Master Jorge was beaming and nodding his head up and down as he adjusted his sitting posture, and then he said, "Alhamar's people always thought he dealt in magic because he could produce immense sums of gold which he would spend on the buildings at the Alhambra. But, Infanta, it wasn't magic, the secret was he lived an exemplary life."

My mind raced backward remembering all the Kings of Castile and other European Kings and the only King I could think of that I thought was remarkable was my grandfather, Enrique III, who died at the age of twenty eight. Since he had died so young, he didn't reign long enough to become an example for his people.

Then Master Jorge began to tell me about Alhamar. He was of the rich and noble family of Beni Nasar, born in Arjona in 1195. His father sent him to the best schools and before he had reached the age of twenty-one, encouraged him to take part in those military skirmishes which Moors mounted against each other.

I was thinking out loud as I interrupted my teacher saying, "The Moors fought each other just like the Castilians do now?" Master Jorge nodded his head and went on saying, "There were two major leaders who ruled over the split territory, Alhamar was the general and leader of the Beni Nasar faction, and he was opposed by an ambitious Aben Hud who ruled Murcia and Granada. When Aban Hud died in 1238, Alhamar became the sovereign of all the territories."

I burst out with, "That was a simple solution. I wonder how it happened so easily." Master Jorge thought that question over and said, "Well, the book states that it was the multitude of the people who supported him. Remember, Infanta, any time a ruler gains the support of the people, that establishes a firm base for the ruler's power and Alhamar understood this. As soon as he became the ruler he took immediate steps to do many things those former Moor Emirs had never done. First, he reinforced his nation's major fortresses along the northern Christian borders. Then he began to repair and strengthen all of the frontier posts and later refortified his city of Granada. He recognized the need to organize an army to fortify his strongholds. Every soldier assigned to serve at the outposts was given a horse and a small plot of land to farm. They were permitted to have their families live with them, too."

That last remark really caught my attention. "Master Jorge, did I understand you correctly? Alhamar gave every soldier at the outpost areas a horse and land. That's incredible! Our rulers would never have done that for any of our soldiers. Yes, I'm beginning to think you are quite correct. Alhamar was a very unique leader."

"Those precautions which he took were very wise," Master Jorge said, "for the northern Christians had pledged to regain their lands. James the Conqueror had conquered all of Valencia and King Ferdinand had regained Jaen!" I was beginning to smile at that last remark. My ancestors had been successful and when Ferdinand reconquered Jaen, he became a real threat to the Moors. I had remembered that from my earlier discussions with Master Jorge. I nodded my head as his signal to go ahead with the story, and with his usual expressive hand gestures he continued.

"Alhamar wanted desperately to regroup and charge into another battle for Jaen, but Ferdinand had defeated him and he knew he did not have the money to organize another military campaign against the formidable Ferdinand, so he quickly decided to appear privately in King Ferdinand's camp. Standing before Ferdinand he said, 'I come confiding in your good faith to put myself under your protection. Take all I possess and receive me as your vassal.'"

I remembered my history lessons and now recalled the story very well. Ferdinand, ever the gallant warrior, embraced Alhamar as a friend, refused Alhamar's wealth, allowed him to go home and rule over his people, but first he extracted a promise from Alhamar that the Moors would pay a yearly tribute to Castile. Now my history lesson about this unique Moor was beginning to focus in my mind.

Master Jorge motioned for me to be quiet, but I burst out with the exclamation, "So that is why the Moors pay Castile a yearly tribute!" My teacher nodded his head affirmatively and then said, "But listen to this. In addition to allowing him to return to his people, Ferdinand also invited him to attend the Cortes as one of the nobles of the empire."

I think my face expressed a slight shadow of a frown. That was a most unusual gesture for a Castilian King to make. Master Jorge noted my slight agitation and said, "Then Ferdinand knighted Alhamar."

This was beginning to sound a little like our present King, but the story was becoming very interesting. One of my ancestors had actually knighted a Moor! Master Jorge picked up the book and opened it to another page, and commented, "Soon after Alhamar was knighted, King Ferdinand asked him to gather his soldiers and join him in his siege against the Moors at Sevilla. Gallant soldier that he was, Alhamar and his troops joined Ferdinand drawing their swords against their fellow Moslems. When Sevilla finally surrendered to Ferdinand in 1248, a saddened Alhamar returned to Granada."

"Yes," I said, "I can understand Alhamar's feelings. It was a very serious position to have been placed in. How did his people respond to the role he played in that siege?"

Master Jorge shook his head and glancing at another page in the book said, "When Alhamar returned to Granada his people greeted him by building great arches which lined all the streets. From every section of the city the people came in throngs with shouts and cheers echoing through the city as they welcomed him home." Alhamar was not only their great leader, but their hero as well.

That was almost unbelievable. I tried to imagine any Castilian welcoming Enrique home after he had lost a major city in our realm. That would never happen here, of that I was quite certain. I motioned for Master Jorge to go on.

"Alhamar realized that the differences between the Moors and Christians were so deep and ancient there never would be harmony between the lands. So again he fortified all the fortresses. He knew he must protect his people. Then he directed his energies toward reorganizing the administration of the cities by appointing Moors who had distinguished themselves when they encountered danger with firmness and used their good judgment, mindful always that those he appointed must also be accepted by the people." I really liked that idea. I had overheard much gossip in the Alcazar about this or that favorite of Enrique totally incapable of administration being given very high and important appointments, and sometimes even placed in charge of important cities. I made a mental note to always remember Alhamar's wisdom in that aspect of governing.

"Alhamar," Master Jorge said, "decided an efficient police force would help him carry out the rigid rules he made for the administration of justice." What a unique idea! I thought once again of my grandfather, Enrique III, who had organized the Santa Hermandad, a group of dedicated men who had effectively curbed the spread of crimes against the people. I wondered if my grandfather had read this book and had known all about Alhamar.

According to the book in Master Jorge's hands, the poor and distressed didn't find it difficult to be admitted to Alhamar's presence. He personally listened to their stories and gave his assistance to remedy unjustness. "Yes," I thought, "That's what my grandfather did, too!"

Master Jorge's eyes seemed to take on a special gleam as he spoke of Alhamar's next exploits. "He built hospitals for the blind, the very sick and for the old people, and provided places to live for his subjects who were not able to work and earn a living." Master Jorge raised his expressive hands with his familiar gesture, saying, "Alhamar visited them often and not on a specifically appointed day. He would arrive suddenly and unexpectedly because he wanted to actually see and inquire about the treatment of the sick and to observe the manner in which they were treated."

My green eyes must have registered approval, for I could not help but smile at the thought of this great leader arriving unannounced at a hospital checking to make certain his people were getting the best of care. I liked that idea.

I motioned for my teacher to go on, and as he turned to another chapter he exclaimed, "Alhamar founded schools and colleges which he often visited, arriving unannounced to listen to the teachers and watch the students. He took a very personal interest in the instruction of young Moors.

"He did not want any of his subjects to be hungry so he built butcheries and public ovens so the poor people could purchase good food at affordable prices." I was beginning to really develop an admiration for this Moor. I needed to hear more.

"He searched for clever engineers to reroute the streams so that water would flow into the cities. He built baths and beautiful tinkling fountains. He constructed water aqueducts and great canals which would irrigate and fertilize the valleys surrounding Granada. His engineers devised a means whereby the sun would heat the water to be used in the baths in the Alhambra. The city's warehouses were filled with grains, luxuries and merchandise from everywhere. And," said Master Jorge, "that is why the city of Granada has been so prosperous for centuries."

I tried to visualize those great aqueducts and canals bringing water to the parched plains and valleys. Truly, Alhamar was a great man. I silently wished that my father and Enrique could have been leaders who would have done the same for Castile.

Maria cautiously opened the door, and asked if we would like to have some fresh fruit and hot bread. We both were hungry and motioned for her to bring it to us because I was anxious to hear more about Alhamar.

After we had finished eating, Master Jorge continued his recitation of Alhamar's life. "Alhamar loved the artisans and believed in giving premiums and privileges to the best ones. He admired beautiful horses and became involved in improving the breeds. He encouraged the growth and fabrication of silk, until the looms of Granada produced the superb quality and beauty unmatched by those imported from Persia. He ordered new equipment which mined the silver, gold and all the other metals found in the mountains of Granada."

I thought of Master Jorge's remark earlier that his people thought he was a magician because he could produce great quantities of gold so quickly, and when I heard that last remark, I knew that was the way he obtained his gold. The gold came forth from the mines in great quantities because of the new equipment he had provided.

"When did he build the Alhambra?" I asked.

Master Jorge thought for a short while and said, "It was about the middle of the 13th century, just after he returned from the siege of Sevilla. He superintended the construction and personally directed the artists and workmen." Then Master Jorge's eyes started to gleam again and he was smiling. I wondered what Alhamar had done next.

Master Jorge cleared his throat and looked at me and said, "All of Alhamar's works were magnificent and many were astoundingly impressive enterprises. But he enjoyed a very simple life style. He always dressed very plain because he didn't want to distinguish himself as different from his people."

I thought of the lavish wardrobe Queen Juana had. Seamstresses were always scurrying in and out of her quarters with exquisite bright satins and brocades. Of course Enrique didn't seem to care at all about clothes, but Don Beltran de la Cueva and the Marquis de Villena made up for him with their extravagant tastes. Thinking it over, I decided a simple style of dress was more important than the expensive outlay of precious money for clothes.

I asked, "He was so busy and active, did he ever have the opportunity to take time to enjoy his Alhambra?"

"Oh, yes," my teacher responded, "he passed many, many hours in the gardens which he had planted with the rarest of plants which still bloom with beautiful flowers all year long."

"And he remained a loyal subject to King Ferdinand?" I asked.

"Indeed he did. When King Ferdinand died in Sevilla in 1254, Alhamar sent his ambassadors to console Alfonso X. Ahead of him he also sent a gallant train of a hundred Moor cavaliers from very distinguished families who lighted tapers and surrounded the bier of the Castile King." It seemed to me that I had heard that story, but I had not been certain that it was true. And I commented, "I think I have learned that Alhamar respected our King Ferdinand so much that every year after our King's death, Alhamar and his cavaliers traveled from Granada to Sevilla to stand with lighted tapers in their hands in the very center of the beautiful cathedral where Ferdinand was buried."

Again my teacher was nodding his head affirmatively saying, "Those are true stories. He held Ferdinand in very high esteem and he wanted Ferdinand's people to remember their King and to respect him as he did. Alhamar was a very kind, gentle and thoughtful man who used his power with brilliance and cared about all of his people."

As my teacher stood up to leave, I was very quiet. I looked up at him and nodded my head which he understood was my thanks. It was a lesson I remembered every day for the rest of my life.

I missed my mother very much and wrote to her every week, but I seldom heard from her. The letters between Beatriz and me flowed back and forth and I looked forward to my only contact with the outside world. From time to time Beatriz would mention that she had visited mother, and alluded to mother's inability to overcome her difficulties. I knew that she was trying to tell me that mother was going insane and in my daily prayers I asked God to restore mother's health.

I was frightened for Alfonso for even though he had now been declared the King, I felt he was in grave danger. As for my own future I was asking God daily to intervene. The wedding date for my marriage to Don Pedro Giron had not been set because a special dispensation from the Pope was needed before the wedding could take place. Don Pedro was the Master of the religious Order of Calavatara and before he could marry, he needed to have the Pope's consent.

Juana sent her seamstress to me to design my new dresses. There were not to be too many she said, just enough to make the right impressions because my soon to be husband was so very rich he would provide me with fabulous gowns, jewels and horses. I permitted Juana and the seamstress to choose the fabrics and colors for I had observed Juana's temper when she did not get her way, and I wanted her to believe that she was my friend.

During the four years that Alfonso and I lived at Court, there were some anxious moments. I will never forget our first audience with Enrique and Juana. We had just arrived at Court and a summons was brought that the King and Queen would welcome us to the Alcazar. Alfonso and I talked about what we would wear. He decided upon an ill-fitting white satin shirt and blue satin trousers. I had never worn any of the dresses mother had prepared for me, and I chose a light blue dress trimmed with tiny pearl beading and delicate lace. I put the dress on and noticed one sleeve was shorter than the other. The lace was sewn on crooked, and the beading didn't seem to be right either. I heaved a sigh and declared that I would wear it anyway. I looked at my scruffy brown shoes, and silently wished there had been enough money to buy me some proper slippers. But never mind, the dress would cover the shoes, except when I curtsied and maybe no one would notice. When Alfonso and I were dressed, I opened a drawer and took out our tin crowns and we put them on. We were ready to meet the King! Now there were to be new dresses for my uncertain future.

While Juana was busy planning the wedding festivities, I was on my knees in prayer talking to God for I was frightened and all alone. Giron had the worst reputation in Castile. He was as treacherous and turbulent as his brother Pacheco and his depraved morals were shocking. My flesh crawled at the very thought of marrying this middle-aged debauchee.

Enrique received the Pope's dispension freeing Giron from celibacy, and with the document now in his hand, he and Juana began making final plans for my future.

Don Pedro Giron mounted his horse to begin his journey to Madrid. He had planned his trip with great care and was traveling in great splendor. He wanted all the common people to know he was going to Madrid to marry the Infanta.

On his way Giron stopped for the night at the castle El Burreco near Jaen. Just at the hour of Vespers, a great flock of white storks suddenly appeared in the sky. They flew straight across the wasted plain toward El Burreco, hiding the setting sun which now caused the castle to grow dark. Making strange sounds, the storks hovered low over the castle until the sun had set. A disturbed Giron asked his aides if they thought there could be some sinister meaning to the storks' strange behavior. No one answered. Silently they watched the storks finally begin their northward flight.

The next morning Don Pedro awoke with a sore throat and pain in his upper chest. He called for a doctor who told him he believed that he had a mild case of quinsy and it would be best for him if he remained at El

Burreco until he was well enough to travel. Giron soon sank into a stupor gasping for breath. The doctor could do nothing and within three days he was dead, blaspheming God and refusing to take the last holy sacraments or say Christian prayers.

In the meantime word had been brought to me that Don Pedro would soon be arriving and in desperation I turned to my only solace, God. I rushed to the church and kept an all night vigil in prayer. The priest arrived the next morning and found me still kneeling at the altar. As he helped me to my feet he brought the news that Don Pedro was dead. My prayers were answered!

CHAPTER IX

August 1467 - The Battle of Olmedo

The news of the absentee dethronement of Enrique and the crowning of an eleven year old boy echoed throughout the country and Europe. Some were shocked and others jubilant.

The state of Castile was deplorable beyond words. No man dared venture beyond the walls of his city without an armed escort for other nobles would come down from their estates like beasts of prey and the defenseless traveler had no choice but to redeem his liberty by paying a ransom.

The rebellious nobles who dethroned the King had done their deed too thoroughly. Something was stirring throughout the land. Enrique was being looked upon as a martyr. True, the rebels had certainly wounded the Castilian reverence for the idea of kingship, but the Moors, the Jews and the large class of office-seekers who had obtained favors from their deposed King were now indignant and began to foment unrest.

With the death of his brother Pedro Giron, Villena's house of cards fell and he openly joined his forces with his uncle, the Archbishop of Toledo and Admiral Fadrique.

Enrique had no choice but to either abdicate or prepare for battle. His future was not entirely hopeless for he could still count upon the strong support of

Mendoza. The royal forces numbered at least seventy thousand infantry and nearly fourteen thousand cavalry. He made up his mind to fight.

Frenzy spread over the countryside. Some of the people were declaring for Enrique and others for Alfonso. There were attacks and counter-attacks in many cities with nothing to calm the troubled waters of the land.

Villena, the Admiral and Archbishop Toledo decided to mount their horses, and placing their new King dressed in shining armor on his horse, they started south for Toledo.

Enrique's scouts sent word to him that Villena and Toledo were now marching. He rushed to Beltran's quarters and urged him to gather the forces together and march north and intercept the rebels. Beltran dressed with great care. Summoning the troops, he struck the Duke de Albuquerque banners and began the northern march.

Toledo's advance scouts observed Beltran and his troops just outside Olmedo and cautiously approaching him, they pulled their horses to a stop.

Toledo's senior officer called out, "Sir, we ask permission for an audience with his Highness." Beltran was silent for a moment, and then he said, "His Highness? I believe that you dethroned him and have declared that he is no longer King! Now you request an audience? The answer is no!"

Toledo's scouts were not prepared for this defiant answer and promptly snapped back at Beltran saying, "The Marquis de Villena, the Archbishop of Toledo and Admiral Fadrique have assembled a mighty array of troops far outnumbering yours. We have come to warn you. Turn back. If you do not heed our warnings, you will be dead before sunset!"

Beltran remained calm as he listened to their threats. Then in a firm voice he countered with, "Our battle ready troops far outnumber Toledo's. I ask you, would your Archbishop dare attack us when our might is obviously so much stronger?"

The senior officer bravely replied, "Toledo's strength is far superior to yours and he will place every soldier on the battlefield and fight to the finish!"

Beltran looked into the faces of the enemy and with his voice still very controlled, he retorted, "I will wager 50,000 maravedies that Toledo will lose! Return to your camp and tell your Archbishop that I am wearing a red and gold armor emblazoned with the crest of the Duke de Albuquerque. I will be wearing a royal blue jacket with bright purple trousers, and a gold shirt. Your good Archbishop will have no trouble locating me on the battlefield. Now go back to your traitors!"

The officers raced toward Olmedo to give their report of their encounter with Beltran. Toledo listened to their briefing and turning, he donned his coat. Over his coat of mail he tossed his flaming red cape with the white cross emblazoned on it. He was ready to charge into the foray of battle once again.

It was a Thursday morning in August, 1467, when my young, inexperienced King-brother was awakened by his confederates. They had pitched their tents for battle just outside Olmedo and Alfonso was told he must prepare to lead his troops into battle. Within minutes trumpets were blaring and battle lines were drawn. Suddenly there was a charge of calvary and the shattering of lances. Rapidly and inexorably the rival factions began their skirmishes. The horses were cut down and the riders dismounted, fighting to the death with their swords. The pitched battle raged on through out the entire day. By nightfall both sides were claiming victory with each faction pulling backward.

Enrique remained with a small guard in Olmedo where the Queen and her daughter 'La Beltraneja' joined him. He was a pathetic figure, bewildered, penitent, and suddenly not without noble sentiments. There was a crucifix placed inside the entrance hall, and as Enrique was walking back and forth waiting to receive the news of battles won, he suddenly dropped to his knees before the crucifix and cried, "Thine aid I implore, my Lord, Christ the son of God, by whom kings reign; to Thee I commend my person and dignity. I beg that this punishment which is less than I deserve, may be for the good of my soul. Lord, give me patience to endure it, and permit not the people to suffer for my sins."

Enrique's forces took the banners of the Archbishop de Sevilla, Count de Plasencia and the Count de Banalcazar. Seven banners were taken by the rebels. Velascos, two of the Marquis de Santillana, two of Don Beltran's, even Enrique's royal pennon. Enrique had not permitted his pennon to be unfurled and it remained in the box. With darkness falling, Beltran's forces withdrew leaving the field in Villena and Toledo's hands. They regrouped their forces, struck their banners, and marched triumphantly back into Olmedo. Victory was theirs!

Enrique fled into a nearby field, taking refuge for the night in the village of Pozaldez. The next morning he borrowed some clothes and now in disguise he mounted a mule that was lent to him. He didn't stop to look back until he reached Madrid.

Enrique's star was setting. Alba deserted him. So did the Marquis de Santillana, the head of the powerful Mendozas. And worst of all, Segovia opened its gates to Alfonso!

CHAPTER X
Death of Alfonso - 1468

J uana and Don Beltran fled from the battle zone at Olmedo and rushed back to Madrid. Panic and mayhem were spreading like wildfire! Everyone was concerned with their own safety and welfare, determined to hold their properties. Enrique closeted himself again with his lute and sang his sad songs, saying his advisors left him and he had no one.

The Queen decided she must leave Madrid and move her residence to the Alcazar at Segovia, taking her six year old daughter 'La Beltraneja' with her. The Alcazar at Segovia was one of the loveliest structures built for Monarchs in all of Castile. It had been built by the Moors when they had occupied the area. They built this imposing Alcazar on a high hilltop surrounded by forest of tall, stately black pine trees. Juana urged me to come with her reasoning that since the Alcazar was perched on the hilltop, protected by high walls with tall, silent watchtowers and sentries posted inside protecting the Monarch and his family, it would provide us with a safe haven.

I hesitated wondering if that was a wise decision for me to make. In my heart, I acknowledged Enrique was the legitimate King, but I had never openly expressed my view. Should I flee with Juana to Segovia? I decided to ask God to help me solve my dilemma. As

I knelt in prayer, a small voice within me seemed to say, "Travel to Segovia, for all is well with you."

We arrived at the Alcazar in Segovia early in September, and as I walked through this great ediface for the first time in my life, I knew it was here that I truly belonged. Some of the floors were inlaid with pink alabaster and the glinty walls sparkled with plated silver. I gazed up at the vaulted ceiling in the Hall of Pineapples. There were almost four hundred gilded stalactites hanging from the ceiling creating a spectacular opulent room. I wandered into the throne room and gazed in awe as I looked up at the great dome and the friezes ablaze in intricate arabesques. I wandered on and came upon the lovely small chapel where our Kings had worshiped. I gazed at the altar, and then at the hand carved choir chairs. I wondered, "Who would be worshiping in this chapel as the king -- Enrique or Alfonso?"

My father loved the art gallery. He had a special wall built for a cherished painting which entirely covered it. I stood before that painting and silently wondered if my father, from his angelic realm, was able to perceive Castile's tragic future.

Several years earlier Enrique had skilled craftsmen design statues of all the Kings of Castile which were placed in the Sala de los Reyes. There were thirty-four statues beginning with Pelayo and ending with our father, John II. The gifted artisans had combined gilt and polychrome which created an effect of a solid gold likeness. I stood before my ancestors, some great and some not so great, and wondered what our nation's future held for Alfonso, me and its people.

The rebels had not been idle. Learning that Segovia had declared for Alfonso, they gathered their forces and cantered southward. As they entered the city the cries went up, "Castile! Castile! for Don Alfonso!" As the cries echoed throughout the city, Juana grew frightened and suddenly decided to flee with her daughter, 'La Beltraneja.'

Once again I needed to make a decision. Flee with Juana or wait for Alfonso to rescue me. Suddenly it seemed "right" to wait for Alfonso to make his grand entrance into Segovia and join with him at his side.

He was only thirteen years old when the battle at Olmedo was fought, and it was with great pride his closest aides spoke of his bravery and calmness in the thick of the battle. His life had been in danger on the battlefield but his soldiers had kept him from being harmed. When the battle was over and the rebels declared they had won, Alfonso, dressed in his battle armor, unfurled the banners and led his rebellious countrymen into the city proclaiming the defeat of Beltran and the now deposed King Enrique. It was a heady experience for him and he shared the excitement of those moments with me at the Segovian Alcazar.

Alfonso's fourteenth birthday was soon to be celebrated and we made plans to travel to Arevalo to visit mother. It had been four years since we had left that lonely ediface to live at the Court in Madrid. We discussed our concern about her mental well being. Alfonso had heard that mother was having difficulty coping with day to day activities, often slipping into deep gloom, staring vacantly into space, and mumbling to herself.

We arrived at Arevalo the day before Alfonso's birthday eager to embrace our mother. I don't think either of us were prepared for the shock as we greeted her. She looked so pathetic and frail sitting up in bed, a rosary in her hands and still wearing the glass beaded necklace, broach and ring. Her servants told me she would not let anyone touch them for they were hers. "Mine, mine, mine," she would utter.

That November 15th was not the happy birthday celebration Alfonso and I had anticipated. We both fell into a light depression after speaking with mother's doctor. He told us mother was suffering from an incurable light form of insanity. He was sorry but there was nothing more that could be done for her.

They were having a fair at Medina del Campo and to relieve our gloomy thoughts, we mounted our horses and trotted off to speak with the people, relive the past and now compare it with our future.

My childhood friend Beatriz and I chatted late into the night. She wanted to hear all about the Court in Madrid and I needed to hear about Avila. Beatriz's aunt had arranged her marriage to a brilliant, handsome young man from Segovia, and her hand in marriage was promised as soon as she became eighteen. She wanted to know all about the city that would become her home.

Segovia was a city that haunted me, and I decided to return. I felt the need to enter a convent to spend my days in conversation with the priests and nuns, contemplation and prayer. I thought about choosing my confessor and upon my arrival in Segovia I met Fray Tomas de Torquemada, prior of the Dominican Abbey. For the next several years, it was Fray Torquemada that I turned to for religious solace and to hear my confessions.

It was early in the morning on the 5th of July, 1468 when a courier called at the sequestered convent asking me to come quickly. Alfonso was very ill.

Pascha was quickly saddled and we galloped over the winding dusty roads to Cardenosa. As I was dismounting, the Archbishop of Toledo rushed to greet me. I looked into his face and I knew that Alfonso was dead.

CHAPTER XI
Ysabella Refuses the Crown

Alfonso was buried beside our father with a service befitting a King. The funeral was over. I watched as they lowered his casket into the new grave and thought to myself. "Two Kings buried side by side in Valladolid. Why wasn't a tomb prepared for my father and placed in a chapel as we had done for other Kings?" That thought continued to haunt me. Within my heart I knew that I was the legitimate heir to the Throne, and I vowed before the altar in the chapel at Valladolid that someday there would be a proper resting place for our Kings.

Riding back to Arevalo on Pascha, I thought about my future. What had happened that caused Alfonso to suddenly become ill? Some had whispered, "Poisoned fish!" I thought about Villena. I knew he still coveted the office of the Grand Master of the Order of Santiago. Did he murder my brother to pave the way for his ambitious appointment? I was confused. I was now seventeen years old, my father and brother were dead, my mother insane. I was totally alone. Where should I go and what should I do? Live again at Enrique and Juana's Court? No, I would not go back to Madrid or Segovia. The shock of Alfonso's death left me feeling almost numb. Alfonso had always been so energetic and healthy, I couldn't remember that he had ever really been sick. I asked his doctor what caused his death, and was told that, "Probably Alfonso had eaten a piece of fish that might have been poisoned."

I wanted to spend a few quiet days with mother, even though she didn't recognize me. I needed to be with her now for she was all the family I had left. Enrique was indisputably the King. What should I do? I was so totally disenchanted with Queen Juana and Enrique's escapades I felt that I could never return to their Court. I needed some time to myself to think about my future, and I asked the Sisters at the Cistercian convent of Saint Ann if I might be sequestered there to read, pray and fast.

The powerful rebel nobles who had deposed Enrique gathered together to plot their new strategies against Enrique and Don Beltran. In unison they decided to offer their dead King's crown, the great crown of Castile, to me.

The morning quiet was broken as the clatter of horses' hooves broke the silence. The noblemen with their unfurled banners cantered along the crooked streets as the townspeople peeped out of their grey, flat-roofed houses. Riding at the head of the group of nobles and cavaliers they saw the Archbishop of Toledo dressed with his official red mantle cape and white cross emblazoned upon it, pulling up abruptly at the gates of the Convent of Saint Ann. Carrillo leaped off his horse, adjusted his red cape and lifted the hilt of his sword knocking on the gates breaking the silence of our morning prayers. The Archbishop of Toledo was begging for an audience with the Infanta Dona Ysabella!

I was kneeling at the chapel altar in prayer when a nun lightly tapped me on the shoulder, and as I looked up I saw a smiling, beaming face with eyes gleaming in excitement. The powerful Prelate of Spain was asking to see the Infanta Dona Ysabella! I was wearing a simple white mourning woolen robe, and decided to receive them in this simple statement of dress. One after another they stepped forward, knelt and kissed my hand. I waited for them to speak.

Carrillo stepped forward and spoke of the sadness he felt about Alfonso's death. It was a national calamity! The hope of the nation now rested on my shoulders. He and his fellow noblemen had come to declare their allegiance and recognize me their Queen after placing the great crown of Castile upon my head.

My stomach was churning and my head was spinning. In truth it was a dazzling proposition. There was no question in my mind but that I, Ysabella de Trastamara, was the legal heir to the Crown, but God had placed Enrique upon the Throne and until his death I could not claim the realms.

I studied that white-haired warrior standing before me, and without the slightest hesitation I responded. "Return to the kingdom, to Don Enrique, my brother, and thus you will restore peace to Castile. Enrique is the lawful King, for he received the scepter from my father, King Juan II. And as kings reign by the permission of God and are responsible to Him for the authority they hold, no lawful power in Castile may take it from Enrique without his consent so long as he lives." I paused to catch my breath, looking into the eyes of Carrillo and his attending nobles standing in the room, and then went on to say, "I shall never seek power by unconventional means, for in doing this I will lose the grace and blessing of God. As long as Enrique lives, I pledge my obedience and loyalty. If I should gain the throne by disobedience to him, how could I blame anyone who might raise his hand in disobedience against me?"

I looked around at those men. My words had caught them off guard. They were stunned into abject silence. I had only one thing to ask of each of them, "If you hold me daughter of King Don Juan, my Lord and father, and worthy of the name, by the King, my brother, and the nobles and prelates after his life -- and may that be long -- declare me the successor to the realm. This I will take as the greatest service you can do me."

Carrillo, almost in tears, pleaded with me. "Your Highness, you must think of our nation's future. How can any nation survive without leadership? If you refuse this Crown it will create grave problems and injustice for many. Friends who rallied to your dead brother's cause will now be ruined! The wrath and vengeance of Enrique and Juana will be upon us. You, Dona Ysabella de Trastamara, are making a very grave mistake for the very fate of Castile hangs in the delicate balance of your hands."

I could only shake my head and say, "Go make your peace with our King."

Villena was cautious and calculating. He was afraid Carrillo might gain too much influence over me because he was the Primate of Spain and the Archbishop of Toledo. He quickly stepped forward saying, "Yes, you have the absolute right to refuse the Crown!" Silently he was reminding himself that a new Grand Master of the Order of Santiago must soon be elected, and this time he would make it very clear to Enrique. The price of peace was simple. Elect him the new Grand Master and Enrique's power would be restored.

CHAPTER XII

1468 - Royal Reconciliation

The days that followed at the convent were filled with an air of anxiety. I could feel it when I spoke with the nuns. There was an uncertainty about everyone's future. I felt their love and concern for me, but I also knew they did not totally understand my decision. As I knelt in prayer, I asked for guidance and direction. Somehow I thought God was nudging me to call upon the Archbishop of Toledo to arrange a meeting with Enrique suggesting we put our differences behind us.

I sent word to the Archbishop that I would like to speak with him and in haste he arrived at the convent, beaming and smiling for he was certain I had changed my mind.

As I outlined to him my request, he started to shake his head no, then he looked into my eyes. "Yes," he said, "I will discuss this with Enrique, but I will have to find just the right opportunity when Villena is away." He bowed, kissed my hand and departed.

It was just a week or so later when he arranged for his audience with the King, and Enrique agreed to enter into negotiations to adjust our differences.

The exuberant Archbishop jumped on his horse and raced to Alcala de Henres, his palatial home. There he sequestered himself and began to draw up his lengthy declarations for Enrique's signature. Finished, he rolled the parchment up and wrapped it in a soft leather pouch, saddled his great horse and raced northward to the kingdom of Avila.

The Sister brought word to me the Archbishop had returned. I was excited, nervous, anxious and a little squeamish inside. What if Enrique had refused? I gathered up my courage and sat down to speak with my friend. He was nodding, smiling and triumphant. The King was willing to negotiate our differences, and Toledo informed me he had prepared all the proper papers setting forth our position and conditions for reconciliation. All that was needed was my signature on them. Everything was then finished.

He handed me a thick sheaf of papers, and I tried not to look surprised. I glanced through the first few pages of his scrawling, childish handwriting, and politely asked to have a little time to read them carefully before signing them. I suggested he come back in two days for the signed papers. Frowning, he reluctantly left.

I sat down in the garden and began to read page after page of his lengthy stipulations and declarations. The good Prelate of Spain had put forth his own position, listing all of the items which Enrique must recognize as points won in favor of Dona Ysabella.

Placing Toledo's sheaf of papers at my side, I pulled out a quill and some paper and began writing. The first point I wanted recognized was for the King to grant a general amnesty to noblemen and citizens alike for all past offenses. If Enrique would agree to the first point, I felt there could be peace throughout the land

Next was Queen Juana. For four years I had watched her flirtatious gestures toward nobles and cavaliers, listened to her notorious lies and decided her conduct so deplorable something must be done. The second point on my paper was: "The Queen, whose conduct was admitted to be a matter of notoriety, should be divorced from Enrique and sent back to Portugal."

In my father's Will he had stipulated that the income from the city of Cuellar was to be mine. All during my childhood and teenage years at the Court, the income from Cuellar was collected by others. After the *"Representations of Burgos"* declaration, Enrique had given the city of Cuellar to Beltran. I thought back to my childhood history lessons. I decided my next point would be: "The kingdom of Asturias to be settled on me, together with a specific provision suitable of my rank."

I was the daughter of a king, and I now must be recognized as heir to the Crown. The next item on my paper requested: "I be immediately recognized heir to the Crown of Castile and Leon."

And in keeping with the previous point, my succession to the throne should be acknowledged. My next request was: "The Cortes to be convened within forty days for the purpose of bestowing a legal sanction to my title."

I thought about all the abuses the government forced upon the people and I wanted something done about it. So I wrote down: "There would be a reforming of the various abuses of government."

The painful memory of my brother arranging a marriage for me and my having to marry against my will was another point I wanted to clearly define. My last stipulation was: "I should not be constrained to marry in opposition to my wishes, nor would I marry without the consent of Enrique."

The Archbishop carried the new stipulations I had written out to Enrique, and still in a jovial mood and with his usual flourish and bravado, Enrique signed consenting to each point. It was decided that a special ceremony should be held publicly to announce and seal the reconciliation.

Two months after Alfonso's death, Archbishop Toledo and I mounted our horses, and accompanied by two hundred lancers, we traveled toward Toros de Guisando. Enrique arrived with a guard of over one thousand along with nobles and prelates that included Antonio de Veneirs the Papal Nuncio established in nearby Cadalso.

The ceremony began with the Marquis de Villena stepping before the King, dressed as the newly elected Grand Master of the Order of Santiago, bowing and asking the King's pardon. The King publicly forgave him and reassured Villena of his full support. The Archbishop was holding the bridle of my horse, and after Pacheco had been forgiven he tugged on Pascha's reins and led me forward. He helped me to dismount and I stepped toward my brother and bent to kiss his hand. Enrique waved me away with a jest and high-pitched laughter. If Enrique seemed to be at his best, the Archbishop was at his mulish worst. He stood by my side somber, sulky and scowling, not even recognizing the King. In a quiet voice I urged him to step forward and acknowledge Enrique. Toledo snapped back, "I will not!" The Nuncio finally succeeded in urging him to kiss Enrique's hand. Then the Papal Nuncio read a solemn letter absolving everyone from an oath of loyalty to Juana de la Beltraneja. Then taking Enrique's hands in his he swore, "Ysabella de Trastamara, daughter of King Juan II and sister of King Enrique IV is the one true successor to the Crown of Castile and Leon."

CHAPTER XIII
Enrique's Deception

E verything had moved along so quickly and smoothly I was elated. I allowed my emotions to soar and when Enrique suggested that I accompany him to Ocana and live at Court, I had no reason to decline.

It was not long before I became aware that it was as though the ceremony at Toros de Guisando had never taken place. Enrique immediately began to hedge and renege on every point I had won. He refused to give me Asturias saying that since I was living at his Court there was no need for me to have an income. He refused to divorce Juana. He did summon the Cortes to approve my succession, then he tried to dismiss them before they convened. The Cortes is an independent body of elected individuals representing the populace and they refused the King's order to disband. Instead, they met to acknowledge me as the heir to the Throne.

Those were anxious winter months for me. With the exception of the convening of the Cortes, everything I had won had slipped through my fingers. Enrique was determined to choose a husband for me. He had in mind Portugal's Alfonso V. The Portuguese embassy arrived and Enrique tried to force me to accept the King's proposal. I was about to be trapped into marrying another fat old man and I would have to live in Portugal. No, that could never be! If I had to live in Portugal as the wife of Alfonso V, Enrique could give the Crown to 'La Beltraneja.' I refused. Enrique was furious.

The most powerful nobles attached to Enrique were the families of Mendoza and Villena. Mendoza had left in disgust after the convention of Toros de Guisando. He had openly supported the ascension of Queen Juana's daughter to the Throne. Mendoza's meddling caused Enrique to ignore our reconciliation agreement.

I thought about my future and it seemed bleaker with each passing day. I was compelled to look at the disaster which my carefully worded agreement with Enrique was becoming. I felt I had no choice but to secretly enter into my own negotiations for my husband.

Archbishop Toledo, the Admiral Don Frederick Enriques, the maternal grandfather of Ferdinand of Aragon, and I had become friends and I felt comfortable trusting them. The Admiral's open support of me presented a most favorable situation. I asked the Archbishop and the Admiral to travel to Aragon and begin quiet inquiries offering my hand in marriage.

King Juan of Aragon had dreamed that one day his son would rule over Castile and Leon. They responded very promptly. Archbishop Toledo was in a jovial mood when he brought the good news to me. He had thought it all carefully through. There needed to be certain negotiations and clear understandings between the two nations. He pulled a thick sheaf of papers out of his pocket and in an off-handed, casual way suggested that he had prepared all the paperwork and it was ready for my signature.

I was beginning to understand the Archbishop. He was going to become my closest aide, confidant and advisor. He would wield the power after Enrique's death. This was to be my marriage and I wanted to carefully present a pre-nuptial agreement that would protect me and Castile. There was a rather strange expression that crossed his face as I promised to read it through very carefully. He picked up his riding whip, adjusted his red cape and did his best not to make a retort to my reaction to his outline for a successful marriage contract.

As the door closed behind him, I thought to myself, "The Archbishop is a powerful man and very valuable to me. I will have to learn now to keep my dignity, hold on to my power, and keep him my friend."

Deciding what to put into my pre-nuptial agreement seemed to automatically flow into my mind and my hand raced across the paper as I set down my requests. First, I asked Ferdinand to faithfully respect the laws and usages of Castile. As I thought that point over, I realized that Aragon had laws that would not apply to Castile and Leon and I felt that by making this request first, it would establish the rules for conduct. I had watched my native noblemen make up laws on the spot to satisfy their own greedy situations, and I thought it was an abhorrent practice. A new groom by my side might have the same reaction as he established his power and position.

I knew that Villena would always be my enemy. When my father had given him the title of Marquis he also gave him large tracts of land that legally belonged to Aragon. King Juan of Aragon had borrowed money from Castile using that property as collateral for his loan. Before he had time to repay his debt, de Luna and father had confiscated it to give to Villena. I knew that Villena would be livid if he knew that I was entering into secret negotiations with Aragon because his property might be taken away from him. I wanted to avoid any confiscation of Castile's property so I wrote down, "Ferdinand may not alienate any property belonging to the Castilian Crown." I thought that would be sufficient to protect everyone's financial interests.

Next I stipulated that Ferdinand may not make any appointments of a civil or military nature without my consent. I wanted this point clearly established because I had been observing that appointments made to the Moors and others who were not citizens of Castile, were serving foreign interests very conveniently. My mind was firmly made up about governmental appointments of either a military or civilian nature being specifically awarded to Castilians.

Next I wanted to exercise the full authority over the appointment of ecclesiastic benefices. The practice for the past several years of allowing foreign clerics to be appointed to positions of power within the church was to be abandoned.

I wanted Ferdinand to enjoy the prestige as a monarch, even if he was not reigning. So I stated that all ordinances of a public nature would be signed by both. That, I decided, would satisfy any male's ego.

It was true. Enrique was a disaster -- politically and personally. Still he was the King and I asked Ferdinand to respect King Enrique.

I wanted to be certain that Villena's property would remain his, and I sat down, "Aragon could not demand restitution of the domains and property formerly owned by Aragon's King Juan II which now belongs to Castile." That should satisfy Villena!

I had heard rumors that Ferdinand had quite a temper and frequently exercised it to get his way. That was a problem I knew I would have to confront. I thought for some time on my next point, then decided it was appropriate and wrote: "Ferdinand may not return to Aragon without my consent."

Now for the dowry. I had been penniless all my life. I needed everything! The ladies at Enrique's Court dressed in magnificent gold, silver, ivory, white, soft pastels and bright glorious silks, satins and brocades. Their feet were encased in satin slippers, their stockings were silk, their cloaks were made of ermine and soft furs. Item by item, I listed the dresses, cloaks, coverlets, shoes that would make up the dowry. I glanced over the seven pages listing all of my needs making certain I had not left out anything. For just a moment I wondered if I was asking for too much. I decided if it was unreasonable I would allow for negotiations on this point. I signed the last page, took out my wax, placed my seal and put it in a soft leather pouch.

I sent for Don Frederick Enriques, Ferdinand's grandfather, and handed him the leather pouch containing my sealed pre-nuptial demands. I asked him to accompany the good Archbishop of Toledo to Aragon and present the document to King Juan and Ferdinand and return with their signatures. I was very matter of fact, pretending as though there would be no bargaining back and forth. The Admiral took the pouch and within a matter of hours he and Carrillo, wearing his flaming red cape, were seen racing along the quiet countryside headed toward Aragon.

The next day a messenger brought me an invitation to be the house guest of the Bishop of Burgos in Madrigal. I knew the Bishop was Villena's nephew and I was certain the Marquis had urged him to send the invitation. I needed to escape from Enrique's Court and decided there would be some advantages for me to be in that particular area because Madrigal was located in the northern central part of Castile, making it easier for me to complete my secret negotiations and wedding plans. I decided to wait for the return of the Archbishop of Toledo and Don Enriques with word from Aragon and then I would depart for Madrigal.

It was just a short ten days later when I looked out my window and saw the big black warhorse with the Archbishop of Toledo mounted upon it. He wasn't wearing his usual red cape, just a jaunty colorful hat and his banners were unfurled. The Admiral was cantering confidently alongside him. They explained to Enrique's aides they had come to pay Dona Ysabella their respects.

They were jubilant! They had anticipated that King Juan and Ferdinand would want to renegotiate my pre-nuptial requests. Instead, they were surprised that the document was signed by Ferdinand, sealed with his royal seal and handed back to his grandfather for safekeeping and delivery to me. The Admiral handed me the pouch. I took out the sheaf of nine pages I had written and noted that Ferdinand indeed had agreed to every point.

Toledo's demeanor was rather downcast and surly and I was aware this was because I had cast his paperwork aside and wrote out my own pre-nuptials. I had observed that in his churlish, childish deportment, something new could come along which would catch his interests and he apparently soon forgot about all situations that had not gone his way. I was later to discover Carrillo never overlooked or forgave an indiscretion he considered aimed at him.

As they were taking their leave I told them about my invitation from the Bishop of Burgos explaining to them why I had accepted. They both nodded in agreement and promised to stay in touch with me at Madrigal.

The next morning Juanito, Pascha's groom, had saddled my horse and strapped my few belongings on the back of some mules and I was off to Madrigal. The Bishop of Burgos lived in baronial splendor. He graciously received me and escorted me to very elegant quarters. He assured me that I was very welcome and he wanted me to be comfortable, to come and go as I pleased. In fact, my every wish was but his command.

The Bishop of Burgo's servants were very curious about Dona Ysabella's affairs and questioned my servants in such a clever way the secret of my wedding plans leaked out and the good Bishop sent a messenger racing through the countryside to notify Villena in Madrid of my plans. Villena's notorious temper erupted and he went screaming to Enrique. They decided they must kidnap me and hold me in Madrid until I was married to the King of Portugal.

Maria was still traveling with me and she overheard the messenger bring the news to the Bishop. Quickly she rushed to my quarters to tell me about the planned kidnapping. I knew that I was in immediate, grave danger. I immediately dispatched a note to Admiral Enriques and the Archbishop and explained the emergency, asking them to quickly come to my rescue. Maria passed the notes and instructions to Juanito who mounted a little slow moving mule and meandered out of the courtyard, its rider staring absently into space. As soon as he was out of the sight of the Bishop's people, Juanito urged his mule into a quick canter arriving safely first at the Admiral's and then he pushed on to see Toledo.

For the next twenty-four hours my heart was in my throat. I didn't think I panicked easily, but I was frightened. If Enrique and Villena arrived with their troops first I had visions of remaining imprisoned until another fat, old man would be my husband.

Late the next afternoon I looked out the window and saw the Admiral and Toledo with a gallant array of cavaliers and banners billowing in the breeze cantering into the courtyard. They made such a dramatic entrance the Bishop dashed out to welcome them. In his booming voice, Toledo boldly announced, "We have come to pay our respects to Dona Ysabella."

By this time I had given urgent instructions to Maria to jam my things into the cloth bags and I hastily departed from my quarters, walked down the stairs and out into the courtyard. I bowed before the Bishop, thanked him for his gracious hospitality, mounted a horse and in unison the Admiral, Archbishop and I, along with their small army, triumphantly swept out of the courtyard traveling to the friendly city of Valladolid.

There was no time to lose. My life would remain in danger until I was safely married to Ferdinand. Archbishop Toledo and the Admiral agreed with me that a messenger must be quickly sent to Aragon explaining the urgency and asking Ferdinand to consider traveling immediately to Valladolid for the marriage ceremony.

The Admiral chose Gutierre de Cardenas and Alonso de Palencia to travel to Aragon. When the envoys arrived in Zaragosa that September morning, King Juan's affairs looked desperate. Ferdinand's marriage to me was his only real hope to keep his life-long foe, Louis XI, out of the Pyrenees. To send Ferdinand to Castile now might prove a disastrous move for his political stability at home. They were confronted with this precarious situation in Aragon coupled with a watch in northern Castile now being kept by the Bishop of Burgos, and along Aragon's border a patrol by the Mendozas. There was the lack of money. They had not prepared my dowry.

Ferdinand decided to travel in disguise. He would ride with five of his men, all dressed as salesmen going to Castile to market their wares. He would care for the horses and serve the men their meals. Two of the Admiral's aides would ride ahead of them and two would ride at the rear acting as lookouts. The two that were to ride in front were entrusted to carry Ferdinand's wedding gift to me.

My situation was still very precarious. Word had been received that Villena and Enrique, marching with four hundred lances and all the cavalry that could be spared were expected any day from Estremadura. I sat in my quarters with my needlework, outwardly reflecting calm, but inwardly apprehensive and even frightened.

As Enrique and his calvary was traveling north a small caravan of merchants left Tarazona in Aragon. The inconspicuous caravan with the heavily laden, slow moving mules and asses were traveling as quickly as they could. They were cautious to create their outward impressions because they didn't want to be questioned by troops racing through that territory. They traveled at night along trails not commonly used, moving through the small villages and sleeping during the day.

Working their way along the river Douro to Soria, they followed a rocky trail across the mountains. Late the second night of the journey they came to Burgos de Osma arriving at the estate of one of my staunchest supporters, Count Trevino. Cold and hungry, anxious to get a good night's rest, Ferdinand and his companions stood outside the gate and knocked. Trevino's sentry responded to their knock with a volley of stones from his battlement. One of the stones grazed Ferdinand's head.

Ferdinand called out in the name of King Juan of Aragon, that he, Ferdinand, had come for the hand in marriage to Dona Ysabella. When Trevino's men were satisfied that it was the heir to Aragon's Throne standing at the gate, the trumpets were assembled proclaiming his arrival and with shouts of joy and open festivity, Ferdinand was welcomed to Castile. The next morning the Count ordered his banners struck and with a small envoy of a well-armed escort, Ferdinand and his tired aides were conducted through the countryside in safety.

On October 9th, he reached Duenas in the Kingdom of Leon where the Castilian nobles and cavaliers eagerly thronged to render him the homage of his rank.

CHAPTER XIV
Marriage - 1468

The quietness of the mid-morning was broken by the clatter of hooves and shouts from the townspeople. I looked out my window and saw the Admiral and the Archbishop racing toward my host's home accompanied by Guiterre Cardenas. Anxious for the latest news I moved quickly down the stairs. Standing before me the beaming trio bowed from their waists, and then the Admiral spoke. "Ferdinand has arrived safely at Burgos de Osma. He is now safe in friendly territory."

The tension that I had felt since I had learned that I was about to be kidnapped was immediately released, and my first thought was, "I must go to the church to give thanks for my prayers once again being answered." There were many questions that I wanted to ask but I knew this was not the time and I graciously thanked Cardenas for successfully outwitting my brother's forces.

Knowing that Enrique must be told immediately of Ferdinand's presence in Castile, I had already written my letter to him. Don Frederick volunteered to personally deliver it to the King. In the note to Enrique I apologized for the course of action that I had been forced to take expressing my great disappointment, embarrassment, humiliation and concern that possible harm could have come to me by Villena and Mendoza. Then I added the political advantages Castile would have by connecting Castile and Aragon. I closed the letter noting that my forthcoming marriage was sanctioned by the Castilian nobles. I asked Enrique for his approval and blessing reassuring him that Ferdinand and I dutifully submitted to his regency.

I was nineteen years old and planning my wedding to the future king of Aragon. I knew that God had been protecting Ferdinand and me, and that our marriage was sanctioned by Him. I wondered, "What will Ferdinand think when he meets me?" I was eleven months older than Ferdinand and about an inch taller. My height had reached five feet six inches and as I looked into the mirror I saw in its reflection my forehead was not as broad as I wished it to be, green eyes rimmed with deep blue, a fair complexion, brown hair with copper and red highlights, a rather pretty nose, but my cheeks were too plump. I had a natural grace when I moved and my voice was low and distinct. I was a descendant of the English House of Lancaster, and my red hair, green blue eyes and fair complexion could be attributed to that ancestry; however, as I thought about it, mother had red hair and a light complexion, too.

I thought about mother and whether she should be brought to my wedding. I wanted her to be here, but I was afraid that her mental stability might be too fragile. I sent a note to Governor Pedro de Bobadillo and asked him to convey the news of my marriage to Ferdinand to her and to let me know if she was well enough to travel. Pedro hastily penned a note back that it would be impossible for mother to travel. He accepted the invitation on behalf of his wife and daughter Beatriz, promising to be at my wedding.

The seamstress was busy making my wedding gown. I chose a beautiful ivory brocade with small seed pearls sewn at the neckline. As the fitting progressed, I looked at the neckline and it seemed to be too high. The seamstress was reluctant to change the design, but I insisted until it was lowered at least an inch.

I had no money for a proper royal wedding and feast and I asked the Archbishop to loan me the necessary funds. I sent up a grateful prayer of thanks to God for Toledo's loan. Now I could attend to the guest list.

As soon as word was brought to me that Ferdinand and his four attendants had arrived safely at Duenas, I sent word to the Archbishop to welcome him and to please escort him to my host's, Juan de Vivero, palace.

Amidst the sound of trumpets and the roll of drums, Ferdinand arrived with banners unfurled, escorted by the Archbishop wearing his red cape. Ferdinand was escorted to my quarters by Toledo, and as they entered the doorway, I looked up to gaze in the warm brown eyes of my future husband. After the introductions, Toledo bowed to each of us and took his leave. Ferdinand had dressed carefully for this occasion, wearing a gold waistcoat and bright emerald green trousers. His ivory colored shirt had touches of delicate lace at the collar and wrists. His black leather boots had been polished to a high gloss and in his hand he held a velvet oval-shaped box.

I motioned for him to be seated, but he chose to stand as he presented to me his wedding gift. Opening the box, he placed it in my hands and I looked down to gaze upon the most beautiful ruby and pearl necklace I had ever seen. I was so overcome with emotion I could not think of a word to express my grateful appreciation. Ferdinand understood and lifting the necklace from the box, he placed it around my neck, then he kissed me lightly, but firmly on my lips. For the first time since I had left Arevalo and my mother's loving arms, I felt that surge of happiness and experienced the profound feeling of knowing that my marriage to Ferdinand would be a union of heart, mind and soul.

Ferdinand and I chatted for nearly two hours. It seemed as though I had known him all my life. He really was about an inch shorter than I, but his hair was a rich dark brown, and his high forehead and sparkling brown eyes allowed him to appear quite handsome in my eyes. He walked with a panther-like grace and his rich baritone voice was a wonderful contrast to Enrique's high-pitched sounds and Villena's raspy tones. As he rose to take his leave, I managed to acknowledge a proper thanks for his lavish gift, saying it would always be my proudest possession. Bending low over my hand, he kissed it and wished me good health. Then he was gone and I did not see him again until we spoke our wedding vows.

The preliminaries for the marriage were quickly adjusted and on the morning of October 19, 1469, in the palace of Juan de Vivero, we were married. The wedding ceremony was conducted by Ferdinand's grandfather, the Admiral of Castile, Don Frederick Enriques and the Archbishop of Toledo. Attending also were a multitude of guests of royal rank and nearly two thousand commoners who witnessed this great event -- the momentous occasion of our marriage. It was a grand affair.

CHAPTER XV
Anarchy Reigns, 1469 - 1473

There were profound differences in the characters of Ferdinand and myself. Ferdinand was superb in developing the craft of politics. He was devious, wily, mercenary and crass. There were occasions when his astuteness turned into actual dishonesty which at times was so well camouflaged it was hard to make a distinction. Ferdinand's political commitments were mere conveniences. His treaties scraps of paper. His methods were, at times, less than commendable. If guile could properly serve him, he rarely resorted to anything else. But he also had his merits -- vast merits. His strong male vigor was reflected in a forceful and tireless leader.

For my part I chose to develop my character to reflect the great art of statesmanship. It was on the level of Ferdinand's crafty political skills and my statesmanship that the foundation of our marriage and historical reign blended in perfect accord. All of our problems, the differences in our character, education and points of view dissolved in our ambitious dream for Castile and Aragon. It was the rock on which we based our thirty-five years of marriage. It was one of the most remarkable concordances in history. A partnership so firm and unbreakable that it became impossible not to link our names and speak of one without the other.

Unbreakable that partnership had to be for we

faced enormous dangers. I knew that it would be only in the perfect unison of purpose that we could ever hope to steer our difficult course. Our adversaries and our friends were soon to realize from the beginning that we functioned as one body -- one power.

As soon as our vows were taken and I had a moment to myself, I dispatched a letter to Enrique telling him of my marriage to Ferdinand and asking for his blessing. When the note was delivered, he read it through and then his beady eyes roved around the room looking into the faces of his aides. Out of the corner of his mouth, he sneered, "I must advise with my ministers."

I had to smile to myself when that comment was brought back to me. I never really got to know Enrique and I was just as glad that I didn't. His actions and reactions to everything were so different from mine.

Ferdinand and I held our little court at Duenas. We had nothing to reign over during the first four years of our marriage. We were very poor and many times had no funds to purchase food. At times Ferdinand found it necessary to write to his father asking for funds to pay his aides. It was a very difficult and precarious time for us, but we grew to understand and love each other and with the birth of our tiny daughter, Ysabel, on October 1, 1470, life seemed good.

The Archbishop of Toledo called upon us regularly. He was a crafty churchman, and I felt he was not really an ally I could trust. True though it was, he rescued me when I was about to be kidnapped and he loaned me the money for our wedding ceremony and reception.

In his subtle way, Toledo phrased his words to remind me that he was my benefactor. Ferdinand and

I assumed he was attempting to extract from us repayment of this indebtedness by placing himself exclusively by our side. He looked with a jealous eye toward my friend Beatriz who had married Andres de Cabrera. Andres was quickly gaining power in Enrique's inner circle. Toledo thought Andres was too bright and his ties were too close to me.

There were times when he would complain directly and openly to Ferdinand and me, insisting that neither of us deferred to him properly nor did we seek his wisdom and council. He habitually ranted, raved and acted like a tyrant in our presence. I would watch him and decided he thought we should both shrink back and meekly submit to his power and overbearing demeanor.

It was hard to conceal my disgust, and I admit that my statesmanship was put to the test many times when I didn't always respond with the most diplomatic replies. I was learning to develop the ability to express myself as earnest and meaningful. Toledo gave me a lot of practice. Ferdinand listened and kept his counsel. Once Toledo accused him of being tone deaf and in an outburst of frustration Ferdinand shouted, "I, Ferdinand, am not to be put in leading-strings like so many of the sovereigns both now dead and still alive in Castile!"

Throughout the country frightful anarchy prevailed. The nation was foundering and Enrique's shameless Court was consumed with corruption and frivolous pleasures. The administration of justice was neglected. Crimes were committed with such frequency and scale that it menaced the very foundations of all Castilian society.

The noblemen were busy with their own fiefdoms, still squabbling among themselves, each struggling for power and control. Within twenty-four hours the Duke de Infantado, the head of the House of Mendoza, could quickly assemble ten thousand soldiers and one thousand lances. Battles raged between my supporters and Enrique's.

In one particular area, the kingdom of Andalusia, there were continuous battles between the Duke de Medina Sidonia supporting me and Ponce de Leon, the Marquis de Cadiz, the second most powerful family in that kingdom.

This was the state of affairs among the church and noblemen of Castile. Each one acted like a statesman attempting to carve out, or grab, more power. For the commoner the result was bloodshed, destruction and hardship. Men were stripped of their harvests and driven from their fields. These wandering and homeless displaced commoners abandoned themselves to idleness and plunder. Food was scarce. Prices were excessive.

I prayed daily that God would help me to impress them with a sense of my character, integrity and justice knowing that I truly cared about their welfare. I hoped upstanding and articulate Castilians would convey this to noblemen and commoners alike throughout the land. If this happened I felt it would strengthen my position everywhere. When in my presence they discussed their fears and dangers, I remained calm. My small court was a definite contrast to the bawdy frivolity and sensuousness which disgraced the Court of Enrique, Juana and 'La Beltraneja.'

Thinking Castilians who were concerned about their future determined to support a government which would perpetuate their own wealth and self-importance. They studied me and many began to shift their allegiances. They reasoned if Juana's daughter 'La Beltraneja' were to succeed to the throne, those corrupt ministers directing the councils of Enrique would continue to direct the destiny of Castile and Leon.

Among those powerful noblemen concerned with retaining power and fortune was one of Enrique's advisors, Pedro Gonzales de Mendoza, Archbishop of Sevilla and Cardinal of Castile. His watchful eye noted the shifting of allegiance among the nobles. As he quietly discussed and assessed the political storms brewing and listened to nobles speaking their minds and shifting sides, he decided to desert Enrique. It was true, he had been a co-conspirator with Pacheco earlier when they decided to kidnap me to prevent me from marrying Ferdinand. His powerful status in the Church, his brilliance and great talents made Mendoza a giant among men. Like Toledo, he had a restless political ambition.

Ferdinand's father, King Juan, continued to mount skirmish after skirmish against his testy northern neighbor, Louis XI, of France. King Juan needed troops quickly. He sent an urgent message to Ferdinand asking if he could help. Ferdinand brought the disturbing news to me. We had no money, no soldiers, no lances, no horses. I sent for Archbishop Toledo.

Toledo arrived and promised to send seven thousand soldiers and thirteen hundred lancers. Ferdinand was anxious to see his father and his small son, born out of wedlock in Aragon before our pre-nuptial papers had been sealed. He left with his contingency of men and arrived safely in Aragon, with dignity, to fight by his father's side.

The confidential letter I received from Mendoza arrived after Ferdinand had left for Aragon. In his carefully worded letter, the Cardinal suggested he was entertaining the possibility of supporting my succession to the Throne. To have this powerful man's support gave me an extra-ordinary edge in the struggle for power beginning to emerge. I acknowledged his letter and suggested when Ferdinand returned from Aragon they could meet in secret to solidify positions. I knew that Mendoza's secret communication to me signaled he was continuing to keep his options open with Enrique. When Ferdinand returned to Castile he met secretly with the Duke de Infantado, the head of the Mendoza family, securing their support.

The Marquis de Villena, the Grand Master of Santiago, and still Enrique's closest aide, was craftily developing other schemes. He knew he must continue to control Enrique and to do this he needed to solidify his grip over all of Castile. Ferdinand seemed to be a foe, one not to bend to Villena's demands.

The Basque and Andalucia kingdoms had swung their support to me, as had the cities of Sevilla, Jaen and Baeza. The Constable of Leon, Don Miguel Lucias, boldly worked for my interests in spite of Enrique's threats. The mighty Duke de Medina Sidonia put himself at my disposition. The best minds of Castile were finding Ferdinand and me an irresistible attraction. We were young and vigorous demonstrating sound judgment. We represented justice and stability for people who had endured unending poverty and oppression for nearly a century.

CHAPTER XVI
1473 - Attempted Reconciliation with Enrique

Segovia, my favorite city at that time, had moved through storms of discontent and was now tranquil compared to many other cities. In 1473 Beatriz and Andres de Cabrera, the King's Chamberlain, were married. Cabrera was a tireless counterpoise to Pacheco, for he never failed to speak up to Enrique for my cause. He was also the Governor of the Alcazar of Segovia. In December, choosing a time when Pacheco was away, he suggested to Enrique that we meet again for a family reunion. When Villena was absent, Enrique was easy to manipulate and he agreed.

I was holding my small court at Aranda de Duero. Beatriz decided she would travel to Aranda to become my traveling companion to Segovia. In the dark of the night, disguised as a peasant traveling on a slow moving donkey, Beatriz slowly made her way north. I had spoken with Archbishop Toledo about the plan and he was waiting astride his big black horse ready to escort Beatriz, Ferdinand and me to Segovia. On December 28th, Day of the Holy Innocents, I returned to Segovia. I wasn't certain about Enrique's eagerness to meet his new brother-in-law and cautiously I decided that Ferdinand remain at the castle of Turengo just in case there was some trouble.

Enrique could be quite charming when Pacheco's

influence was not around. He arrived the next day at the appointed hour and sat down in the patio of the Governor's Palace as we renewed our family ties. In my conversation with him I defended my past conduct and then asked Enrique to sanction my marriage to Ferdinand. Enrique was in an amiable mood. He didn't explode with his temperamental tantrums. Instead he looked a little whimsical, disinterested and at times withdrawn. I wasn't sure how he would react to my next suggestion, but decided to explore it suggesting we appear together in public to demonstrate family unity requesting that Ferdinand appear by my side. Enrique's head nodded up and down and on New Year's eve we moved along the chilly winding streets of the city with Ferdinand and the Archbishop riding behind us. Enrique walked along beside Pascha holding the bridle which represented to the people that we were a united family. It was a public acknowledgment of his position toward me.

Andres and Beatriz hosted a succession of parties in our honor with splendid entertainment and much laughter and gaiety everywhere. I had a favorable impression that finally all the past was buried.

On January 6th, Enrique and I participated in another state procession through the city, and Cabrera again celebrated the great occasion with a magnificent banquet given in a house owned by the Archbishop of Toledo.

The following day, Enrique suddenly doubled over with violent sharp pains in his right side. Frightened, he immediately sent his aides off to find Pacheco. Within a matter of hours the Marquis was galloping toward Segovia. He lost no time convincing Enrique that Andres, Beatriz, Ferdinand and his sister had attempted to poison him. He urged Enrique to kidnap me and keep me isolated. Cardinal Mendoza arrived and alarmed when he heard the plan emphatically said, "No!" squelching Pacheco's treachery. In anger and haste, Enrique and Pacheco saddled their horses and departed for Estremadura.

CHAPTER XVII

1468 - Death of Marquis de Villena and Enrique IV

Segovia was my city! The people were warm, responsive, and passionately loyal to me. Beatriz and Andres invited us to remain at their Palace. Ferdinand was very jovial because he was participating in sports and other activities. He was an excellent horseman and enjoyed the hunts staged by our Segovia hosts. I savored the heady experience of being constantly courted by foreign powers.

Those ten months Ferdinand and I spent with our little daughter at the Cabrera Palace were some of the happiest of my life. Time moved quickly and events were soon to bring profound changes to Castile. Word was brought to me that on October 4th, Pacheco, the Marquis de Villena, Grand Master of the Order of Santiago, had died in Estremadura. While death always brings sadness to those who respect and love the departed, I do admit that I heaved a sigh of relief for my worst enemy was gone.

Ferdinand received another urgent note from King Juan asking him to return to Aragon to help with yet another skirmish at the Aragon border with France. He and his aides saddled their horses and departed. As I stood in the courtyard of the Palace in Segovia that brisk morning in October saying goodbye to my husband and his aides, my heart was full and overflowing.

Ferdinand looked quite handsome as he mounted his horse to begin the five day journey.

Upon Ferdinand's arrival in Zaragosa, several citizens of the city requested a private meeting with him. Ferdinand noted expressions of anxiety and fear in their faces as he beckoned them into his quarters. The men informed Ferdinand that a member of a noble family, Ximenis Gordo, had relinquished the privileges of his rank in order to qualify himself for a municipal office. After receiving the appointment, Gordo then began to wield personal power which alarmed the people. Gordo took over the most important positions of the city government for himself, and then proceeded to pack his appointments with relatives and close friends. He abused authority, perverted justice, and perpetrated flagrant abuse and crime. Everyone knew Gordo was responsible for all that was happening; however, everyone was powerless to act against him. This group of citizens asked for his help. They insisted Gordo could not be brought to justice in the usual manner because he held too much power over every municipal appointment.

Ferdinand decided to invite Gordo to his private quarters to discuss a "business matter." He extended a courteous invitation, properly deferring to Gordo to make him feel the Prince of Aragon was going to convey upon him a great opportunity for wealth and power.

At the appointed hour a smiling, jubilant Gordo arrived to keep his appointment with Ferdinand. As he entered the chambers his face registered surprise as he stared in disbelief at the public executioner and the noose hanging from the ceiling. A priest was standing nearby. Gordo immediately knew that his life now hung in a delicate balance.

Gordo was charged with multiple crimes. He was found guilty and sentenced to death. Babbling to Ferdinand, he reminded him of the services he had performed for King Juan. Ferdinand assured him these actions would be gratefully remembered to his children. Then it was time for him to make his confession to the priest and hand him over to the hangman. Gordo's body was hung in the marketplace. His death was a signal that lawlessness in Aragon would no longer be tolerated.

The last years of Enrique's reign were the very worst, if that could be possible. Enrique was cynical and an irresponsible degenerate ruling in the midst of chaos and confusion. The Court had sunk in disgusting debauchery. Enrique had totally abandoned the reigns of government to his unscrupulous favorites, Villena and the Duke de Albuquerque. His tall figure now stooped and his eyes that once glittered seemed to convey a sense of blankness. He spent his days glowering in moody silence or rushing off to hunt wild boars in the forests around Madrid and Segovia.

I had no personal contact with him and from time to time word was brought to me that his health was failing but that was all.

Enrique spent most of that time in Estremadura. Once more he decided he wanted to see the wild animals of the forest of El Pardo, and early in December he returned to Madrid. Suddenly he was seized with a violent flux of blood, followed by a pain so unbearable he collapsed upon his bed.

The doctors rushed to his side and after examining him said nothing could be done. His kidneys had failed. A priest arrived to give him the last sacrament and hear his confession. An altar was set up before him to induce him to take the sacrament. He paid no attention. The doctors and priest began to heckle and badger him and as they raised their voices he grew more obstinate. His arms flailed this way and that as he lay writhing in pain on the bed. All of his life he had been at ease in the company of menials and ruffians, so the priest now handed to these low castes standing close by the responsibility of tending to their dying King.

They laid out the corpse, still in his Moorish buskins, on some old boards. Callously, abjectly, the ruffians trundled it off.

Madrid was located forty-five leagues from Segovia. The courier, Rodrigo de Ulloa, galloping over the difficult terrain and near exhaustion, arrived at the Palace in Segovia to bring me the news of my brother's death.

A thousand thoughts raced through my mind. Ferdinand was still in Aragon. It would take time to notify the councilors and prelates. There were people that I must consult. I thought of Villena's sons and Don Beltran. The courier told me that Juana's daughter was now in the custody of the Villenas. I reasoned that I must move quickly.

I sent messages by courier to all the members of the Cortes asking them to convene immediately to determine and declare publicly my legal ascension to the Throne.

The couriers spread across the land to bring the Cortes together. I had urged each of them to ride quickly and return with the elected member of the Cortes. Next I must send an emissary to Aragon. Ferdinand must be told. I sent for Don Frederick Enriques asking him to send one of his aides and to especially choose a horse that was quick on its feet. Don Frederick cleared his throat and in a quiet voice said, "Ferdinand's aide, Palencia, left immediately for Aragon when word reached us of Enrique's demise."

I lowered my eyes and moved some papers on my desk so the Admiral wouldn't notice my reaction to that news. I quickly gathered my thoughts and said, "It is proper protocol for me to send official word to Ferdinand through Castile's couriers." Don Frederick nodded his head in agreement, bowing, he kissed my hand and departed.

There were the notices to be sent to all the councilors and prelates, the officials in every city, the church officials, and the people. I worked far into that first night dictating letters and sending couriers off with official dispatchs. I caught an hour or so of sleep but awakened early refreshed, my mind clear and alert.

Beatriz asked if her seamstress and assistant could make my coronation gown. I had been so busy the day before there was no time to think about a dress. Dear Beatriz, how I treasured her friendship. She always seemed to be at my side at just the moment I needed something. We chose a beautiful white brocade that Beatriz had intended to use in a dress designed for herself. She quickly assured me she could easily replace the fabric for her dress later. I wanted an elegant long train, inset sleeves that puffed out with a lot of fullness, and a properly cut neckline because I would be wearing the ruby and pearl necklace.

Enrique had never officially severed his ties with Andres. When he left so hurriedly eleven months earlier, he left behind Castile's Crown jewels. Beatriz asked him to bring the jewel chest for me to choose the jewels I would wear for the coronation. As I opened the lid, a quick rush of excitement flashed through my body as I gazed at a magnificent array of precious stones set in gold and silver. I lifted one or two items, and then my eye caught a familiar looking necklace, a broach and a ruby ring. My eyes filled with tears and I had to stifle my sobs. My mother -- I had forgotten to send a courier for her! I looked up at Beatriz. She was reading my thoughts and shook her head, "No!" I had known in my heart that mother would never again leave Arevalo, but I did so want her to be by my side when I was crowned the Queen. I mentally told myself that as soon as I could, I would take her three pieces of jewelry and travel to Arevalo and give them back to her. Maybe that would help her to get well.

Word was received the Cortes was meeting at Ocana to decide my future. I had some anxious moments as I patiently waited to hear from them. A group of three members of the Cortes was chosen to pay their respects and officially inform me that once again they had debated the circumstances of 'La Beltranejas' birth, declared her not to be Enrique IV's daughter, and unanimously agreed: "For the first time in the history of the Peninsula, a Queen would rule the land." Ysabella de Trastamara, daughter of King Juan II and Ysabel of Portugal was the Queen of Castile and Leon!

PART II

**Ysabella's Coronation,
War with Portugal
and Reconstruction of Government**

CHAPTER XVIII
The Coronation

The bright winter sun in Segovia displayed its golden rays from the high heavens that brisk, chilly morning on the 13th day of December, 1474. The procession for my coronation ceremony was beginning to form in the courtyard. The Mass for my brother was said in the small chapel of the Alcazar, and in my fervent prayers I asked God to be patient with Enrique. Time was moving so quickly. The Mass was over and I looked out into the courtyard to see swarms of people arriving. Word was brought to me that workmen had worked far into the night building the platform in the main plaza for my coronation.

As I left the chapel, Beatriz stepped to my side and we hurried toward my daughter's quarters. I wanted to oversee the preparations for Ysabel's first appearance before the people as the Infanta, and since she was our only child, she was heir to the Throne. Beatriz had given the seamstress instructions to make a new white dress and a matching white coat for her. As we entered Ysabel's rooms my excited daughter rushed towards us exclaiming, "Aunt Beatriz, mother -- look! Look at my beautiful white dress and coat. And they've brought me new white slippers with shiny silver buckles!"

I reached out to my daughter to give her a warm hug and as she squirmed to free herself, she looked at Beatriz saying, "Are you going to help me get dressed?" Beatriz looked at me and I said, "Ysabel, I am going to help you dress. Today is a very important day for both of us and I'm going to help you put on your lovely new dress, pull on your white stockings and buckle your new shoes."

Ysabel looked at Beatriz, then at me, and asked, "And will my father be here to see me in my new clothes?"

I took a deep breath and my voice quivered a little as I quietly answered, "No, Ysabel. Your father is still in Aragon. He cannot be here today." A fleeting shadow of disappointment crossed her little face and I stooped down to hug her once more. I needed Ferdinand by my side, too.

Ysabel was quiet as I helped her dress and then I brushed her long red hair. As I stepped back to look at my daughter, I thought to myself, "She's a perfect Infanta!" I stooped to give her a final hug and then rushed out of the room hurrying towards my own quarters.

Maria and the seamstresses had my white coronation gown ready and the jewels I had chosen were carefully placed in a small chest. My white slippers gleamed with the special diamonds Beatriz and I had decided to pin in place on each shoe. The dress slipped over my head and someone brushed my long brown, copper-toned hair. Beatriz entered the room wearing a spectacular red velvet dress. Around her neck she wore the pearls Andres had given her as a wedding gift. I looked towards this tall, stately, perfectly groomed lady with her long, thick black hair pulled back from her face and piled high at the back of her head and smiled with approval. Stepping forward, she fastened the ruby and pearl necklace around my neck. As I stood up, a long ermine cape was placed around my shoulders. I wanted to appear calm and dignified to them and as I turned to look at my dearest friends, I noted each face wreathed in smiles of pride and approval. I embraced them one by one and then the entrance of my private chambers opened and standing in wait for me were Alonso Carrillo, the Archbishop of Toledo, and Admiral Don Frederick Enriques, Ferdinand's grandfather.

As the great door of the Alcazar swung open to the courtyard, I looked out over the plaza and saw the narrow streets full of people. From the four gates of the Alcazar courtyard to the stern, silent walls surrounding it, a sea of humanity milled. I could hear the rumble of murmurs, singing, shouts of joy and the expectant choruses of "Castile! Castile! for Don Fernando and Dona Ysabella!" echoing throughout all of the city.

Merchants who had gotten up before dawn were thronging into the market place searching for a proper site to display their wares. They expected business would be brisk today. From the east, south, west and north, through the four gates of the city of Segovia, troops were arriving and men armed cap-a-pie were escorting this or that nobleman flourishing their colorful pennons. The air was filled with the sounds of the deep booming sackbuts, blaring of the trumpets, shrill notes of the flagelots and the rumble of kettle drums. The horses were ablaze with the brilliant colors of the noblemens' family crests gleaming with polished silver and precious gold. Glittering burnished steel flashed in the bright morning sun. Segovia was ready to celebrate the historic coronation of Castile's first Queen!

All was ready. The white palfrey caparisoned in gold, precious inlaid gems sparkling on the bridle in the bright sunlight, was waiting for me as I stepped into the courtyard. An aide, dressed in colorful splendor, stepped forward to help me mount. I motioned to an attendant to place my little daughter on the small white pony saddled for her, then I lifted my head and nodded to the gate attendants. I was ready.

The massive gate swung open. Two officers dressed in archaic splendor cupped their hands around the jeweled bridle of my white horse to lead me through the crowded streets. Andres de Cabrera, the Alcayde, took his place beside me and on the other side rode the Archbishop of Toledo wearing purple and gold vestments over his breastplate of Toledo steel. A few cavaliers in doublet and hose followed wearing jaunty little velvet hats. The entire clergy of Segovia joined in the line of march, ablaze in their stiff medieval vestments.

Before me, astride a great black horse, rode Gutierre de Cardenas, holding point upward the naked Castilian sword of justice, catching the bright Segovia sunlight, flashing to the people its symbol for change. Behind Cardenas strode two pages bearing on a pillow the gold, ruby and diamond Crown of King Fernando the Saint.

As we wound our way through the streets, the shouts of "Viva la Reina!" echoed throughout the city. The shouts from those thousands of throats swelled echoing and re-echoing as we slowly inched along the stony main streets. It was a gorgeous procession. The magnificent array of prelates and priests in their chasubles worked in gold thread over purple silk were walking, two by two, and chanting "Te Deum

Laudamas!" Nobles in bright velours. glistening with precious stones and gold chains rode on their finest horses. The councilmen of Segovia displayed their ancient heraldic costumes, followed by spearmen, crossbowmen, men-at-arms, flag-bearers, and musicians.

The platform the faithful workmen had erected during the night was draped with bright, colorful rich cloth. Except for the throne chair placed in the very center, the starkness of the platform depicted the solemnity of the occasion. An aide stepped forward to help me dismount. I steadied my balance, lifted my head high and slowly ascended the steps to the platform. I seated myself on the Throne with the greatest of deliberation, confident in purpose and composure. The clamor and noise was deafening!

Suddenly the crowd became quiet. The stillness of the bright morning air was broken as the trumpets sounded and the heralds stepped forward and dramatically unfurled the royal pennons. Then the traditional ancient cry of the heralds, "Castile! Castile! for King Don Fernando and the Queen Dona Ysabella, Proprietress of these realms," went up.

Archbishop Toledo stood before me and placed the great Crown of Saint Fernando on my head, and as the jeweled scepter was placed in my hand, I faithfully promised to lead and protect the people of my kingdom.

The Archbishop stepped to the side and Andres de Cabrera knelt before me placing in my hands the keys to Segovia and the Alcazar.

In a loud voice the herald cried, "Castile! Castile! Castile for King Don Fernando and his wife Dona Ysabella, Queen Proprietress of this kingdom!" Shouts went up from the crowd, "Viva la Reina Ysabella!" The royal flags and pennons of the cities, hidalgos, and military Orders suddenly snapped in the wind. The bells of the churches and convents pealed throughout the city. Muskets and arquebusses were fired from the keep of the Alcazar. The heavier bombards thundered from the city walls. I was the Queen of Castile and Leon!

The dignitaries, prelates and nobles began to take their places to kneel before me and pledge their allegiance. The first magnate to present himself was the great surly warrior-priest Alonso Carrillo, Archbishop of Toledo, who knelt before me. Then Gutierre de Cardenas, followed by the capable Alonso de Cardenas and the Prince of Youth, Gonsalvo de Cordoba. Then the Cardinal-Archbishop Mendoza of Sevilla, the remarkable prelate and great secular potentate who managed to combine his two roles very effectively. His contemporaries respected his spiritual stance and feared his power and political skills. The Count de Benavente who had gained in many ways through the unrest was now anxious to defend his domains stepped forward. From this day forward he continued to remain one of my staunchest supporters.

Next Ferdinand's grandfather, Admiral Don Frederick Enriques, my faithful supporters Pedro Fernandes de Velasco and the Count de Haro, Constable of Castile stepped forward to kiss my hand.

The Duke de Infantada, head of the powerful Mendoza family and brother to the Cardinal-Archbishop of Sevilla stepped forward, along with another member of the family, Diego Hurtado de Mendoza, the Marquis de Santillana. I knew Santillana would soon be supporting Cardinal Mendoza's wish for the appointment to the Chancellorship of Castile as well as for his own Dukedom.

The powerful Manrique clan who had always been my loyal supporters were represented by Don Pedro, Count de Trevino and Don Juan, Count de Castaneda.

Tendering their loyalty were the hereditary Admirals of Castile, the honorable Enriquez de Castilla, Count de Medina Celi, and Fernandez Alvarez de Toledo, Duke de Alba.

Then the peerless knight-of-arms Don Beltran de la Cueva, Duke de Albuquerque, stepped forward and kissed my hand.

The loyal profession of the College of Bishops was amply represented. Each stepped before me and kissed my hand.

Others who might have attended but obviously missing were the sons of the now deceased Marquis de Villena, lord of so many manors and cities, Don Diego Lopez Pacheco, Master of the Order of Calavatara and the Count de Uruena.

The throne of Pelayo, of Alfonso the Wise, and my father, Juan II, was now mine. This land of Recared and El Cid Campeador, the cities of Toledo, Sevilla, Burgos, Salamanca and the green hills and valleys of Galicia, the wide expanses of La Mancha, Estremadura and Jaen, and the wave-washed Santander were mine! Granada must wait, but that, too, would come in time.

My first official act was a religious one. I stepped down from the dias and signaled for the procession to form behind me as I lead the way to the Cathedral. Crowned with the Crown of Saint Fernando, confident in myself and God's mercy, I knelt at the altar. I asked for grace to rule according to His will and to use the authority He had given me with justice and wisdom. Then I stood up and turned to stand before my people ready to reach those great heights of my destiny.

CHAPTER XIX
The Confrontation

The official ceremonies behind me, I plunged into the myriad of details that needed immediate attention. Hernando del Pulgar, secretary to Enrique, arrived and I asked to see him immediately. I had met Hernando on a number of occasions and made mental notes that he seemed mentally alert and very astute. I had observed he always had the correct information either within his immediate reach or he displayed a remarkable aptitude for instant memory recall. I had been impressed with his integrity, deportment and gracious approach toward me, Enrique and other nobles.

Hernando brought with him a wealth of knowledge about government affairs. He had carefully packed all of the important government documents and papers concerned with every aspect of governing -- domestic and foreign -- and presented them to me. As we sat and talked, I studied him. I asked what were his plans for his future. Del Pulgar acknowledged that because the King's death was so sudden and unexpected, he had made no firm commitments or new plans. I asked him to consider becoming my First Secretary handling my appointment book and the most "confidential of communications" that needed to be dealt with. His affirmative nod prompted us to plunge immediately into the paperwork.

I wanted to make certain the city of Segovia was secured. Villena, Jr. had remained in Madrid, and although he had not had time to consolidate power as his father had, I was reminded that he, too, could become a dangerous enemy if provoked. I missed Ferdinand and desperately wished that his father had not called him back to Aragon.

Ferdinand's aides had ridden fast and hard to arrive at the King's Alcazar in Aragon in three short days. When the news was received in the Royal Alcazar, Ferdinand and King Juan were jubilant. Ferdinand would be crowned King of Castile and Leon which would permit them to now play a powerful role in foreign affairs as well as regain their land stolen during King Juan II's reign. Ferdinand's father had already retained a jeweler to design the crown his son would wear when he would be crowned King of Castile and going to his locked jewel chest he brought it forth. Ferdinand looked at the perfectly crafted crown of diamonds, emeralds and sapphires, then he took it in his hands and placed it upon his head. It felt "just right." His aides were waiting in King Juan's antechamber when my official envoy arrived from Segovia.

King Juan urged Ferdinand to return to Castile immediately for there was no time to waste. Racing against time they galloped over the dusty roads urging their horses almost beyond their endurance to reach Segovia quickly.

Arriving at the outskirts of the city, Ferdinand commented in wonderment that there was no royal escort riding out to meet him to conduct him into the city. They slowed their horses and quietly cantered along the streets. They sensed a difference. No longer were the poor lazy and surly, frowning and suspicious.

People were active, some even singing, smiling and industrious. As they rode through the city, they saw bouquets of flowers attached to windows, doorways and posts. The people were beaming. Recognizing Ferdinand, they smiled, waved and shouted, "Long live Don Fernando!" Ferdinand, obviously savoring the attention, slowed his horse to a walk, tipping his head in acknowledgment of their salutes to him.

Rounding the corner in the town square where the workers were dismantling the scaffolding which had been built for my coronation, they gaped in disbelief at the frenzied activity. Ferdinand stared at the workers, who never looked up to acknowledge his presence, then he looked at the ground where large bouquets of flowers with ribbons still tied and blowing in the breeze were cast aside and left to wilt.

He motioned to two of his aides to find out what was happening. The aides rode up and were told my coronation was Saturday and they had been ordered to dismantle the platform. The aides circled around to join Ferdinand, and in a hushed voice, Alonso de Palencia described the past Saturday's event to Ferdinand.

Ferdinand's temper flared. The news that I had permitted a sword of justice to be carried before me was unthinkable! Things were not done that way in Aragon. In Ferdinand's mind he was now the legal heir to the Throne of Castile. I had absolutely usurped the male privilege when I allowed the sword of justice carried before me.

He spun his horse around and galloped at breakneck speed to the Alcazar. Arriving there, he quickly dismounted, adjusted his royal purple velvet cloak and his red sash with the jeweled sword in place, ready to enter the Alcazar. As he walked into my outer chamber he saw several familiar faces, and as he set foot in the anteroom he observed my aides scurrying around with pieces of paper, writing things down, giving instructions. Everything appeared very orderly.

Ferdinand took long, assertive strides into the room moving toward my chamber. Hernando del Pulgar put his hand up to stop him saying, "The Queen is having a private conference with Andres de Cabrera. They are studying the seriousness of Castile's nearly bankrupt finances. Your Highness must wait."

Ferdinand started to ignore the command. Hernando placed himself in the doorway. Two more aides stepped forward to bar his entrance. Ferdinand blurted out, "I should be with Ysabella to advise her."

Hernando said, "Just be patient. Just a little more time, please."

Finally Andres emerged and Hernando beckoned Ferdinand into my chambers, announcing that Ferdinand had returned.

Ferdinand strolled into the room with his usual assertive manner and self-assurance carrying his crown in his hand. Ever observant, I noted the purple cloak, red sash holding the jeweled sword, and the crown in my husband's hand. I rushed forward to give him a warm embrace, greeting him with love and affection. Standing stiff and stoic, Ferdinand held his crown in his right hand and with his left hand resting on his sword, he glared at me. I stepped backward in disbelief.

Ferdinand swaggered a few steps to the side, placed his crown on a small table, removed his purple cloak and red belt which held the jeweled sword. Then he looked at me and in icy tones announced that as soon as word reached him in Aragon he had left immediately to be with me when I was crowned. Looking over at his velvet cloak, his voice even colder, he told me, "I, too, was to have been crowned King of Castile." His voice grew louder as he went on, "Now I have arrived back and discovered you have played a treacherous trick on me. Couldn't you have waited six days? After all, I am of the Royal Trastamara House of Aragon and I promised to uphold Castilian laws and to work for better times for your people." He paused a moment to catch his breath, then continued. "I rushed home only to discover deceit, displeasure and rudeness on the part of the secretaries outside. Those menial creatures treated me as one would a commoner! Absolutely no one greeted me with proper deference as I entered that outer chamber."

Nearly speechless, I attempted to embrace him again. He pushed me back, demanding an explanation.

I asked, "Explanation? I really don't know what you mean. The Cortes met and declared me as the legal, rightful heir to the Throne. It was this declaration that..."

Ferdinand interrupted with, "It is Aragon's law that no woman can rule! Always, there must be a male heir ruling. It's Aragon law. You even permitted the sword of justice to be paraded before you in such a flagrant manner! That is absolutely the most improper action a woman can take. When the people of Aragon hear about the sword of justice displayed in such a manner and that a woman was crowned..."

I retained my quiet composure and interrupted with, "Yes, I fully understand Aragon's law. I'm ever so observant of your land's law. But this is Castile. Castile has no such law."

Ferdinand snapped back, "Am I to understand that I am not to be recognized as the King? That I must be acknowledged as the Queen's consort? Never, never, never! I'll return home to Aragon where men are men and rulers are rulers!"

Still composed, I said, "Ferdinand, when you signed the marriage contract you agreed not to return home to Aragon without my permission."

Ferdinand grimaced on that point, then quickly countered with, "And my father and I are expected to live up to every point in that document?"

I had an answer on my lips, but he shouted at me with, "What about the wedding dowry you demanded? Seven pages of demands you made upon us. Never in the history of our realm has such demands been made upon us. You demanded a dowry that even the Queens of Aragon do not receive. Was this extravagant dowry presented to you at the time of our marriage?"

Quietly I said, "No, Ferdinand. But only because of the urgency of the situation at the time. That urgency made the dowry seem not reasonable and I decided it was to be overlooked."

Sneering, Ferdinand came back with, "So you overlooked one part of the contract, but you cannot override another part?"

Ferdinand and I had never quarreled before, and I was not anxious for the conversation to continue, and I asked, "Ferdinand, please let's not quarrel. It was important that I take command of the realm immediately upon Enrique's death. I could not wait for Villena to declare Juana as the queen. I couldn't wait. It was not prudent to wait."

Ferdinand was in a quarrelsome mood and insisted, "My father and I are the true heirs to the Castilian crown. As my wife, all your rights must be deferred to me. As for your prudence, well....I don't think it's prudent for you to wear any jewels belonging to the Trastamara House of Aragon. You may return to me, now, the ruby necklace you seem to enjoy displaying at every opportunity."

I was stunned! "The ruby necklace? Ferdinand that was your wedding gift to me. How can I return a wedding gift? You presented it to me so eloquently saying that it truly represented your heart. To me, that ruby necklace is also the symbol of our struggles. And it will be the symbol of our triumphs. I cannot give it back."

I was fighting back the tears and I turned my face away, then I started to turn my back toward him. He grabbed me, spun me back around and demanded the necklace. I pulled backward, fought back my tears and gathered my strength, calmly suggesting, "Ferdinand, you have had a long ride. You are obviously very tired and your nerves are on edge. And your temper -- well, I've never experienced such an outburst of anger from you."

Ferdinand turned on his heel and stormed out of the room. I was certain my aides would immediately conclude that Ferdinand and I had quarreled. I opened the shutters and looked out the window to see him mounting his horse and disappearing beyond the walls of the Alcazar.

Meanwhile I continued with my interviews and discussions of the merits of the recommendations various people were making. I was beginning to make an outline for the formulation of laws that needed to be set in motion immediately.

Ferdinand remained silent for a few days. I had no idea where he was staying. Suddenly Palencio was asking to see me and as he entered my chambers, he bowed and then presented Ferdinand's claim to the crown of Castile and Leon. I just looked at Palencio and shook my head. I was the Queen. That could not be changed. Ferdinand was my husband, the father of our little daughter, and I loved him. I urged Palencia to convey to Ferdinand that I wanted to adjust our differences and together we must reconstruct the affairs of the government to bring peace and prosperity to the land.

Palencia countered with, "I know Ferdinand very well. He will never accept your position. But I will repeat your exact words to him." And with that statement clearly made, he departed.

I was concerned that Ferdinand really was angry enough to take the ruby necklace back to Aragon. I asked Hernando to seek out a very good woodcarver saying, "I think I'd like to have a hand carved wooden cross for my small private altar."

A few days later Pulgar introduced me to the woodcarver who showed me some samples of his work. Satisfied, I asked him to carve two identical crosses. I was specific in my instructions. They must be identical in every way, especially in dimensions. I asked him to carve out a hollowed area in the back of one of the crosses. I gave him the specific dimensions for the outer perimeters and for the area to be carved out in the back of the one cross. The little man nodded and left.

Several days later, he arrived back with the two wood carvings. I examined the front. They were lovely. I turned one cross over and noted the perfect hollow. I dropped some gold coins into his knarled hands. His eyes sparkled and his jaunty, lively step assured me his Queen was not only generous, but pleased with his artistic triumph.

As soon as he had gone, I took the ruby necklace from a drawer, placed it in the hollow of the cross, took out my wax I used to seal my official communications, and pressed the two crosses together. My wedding gift was safe.

CHAPTER XX
Reconciliation with Ferdinand
"The Concord"

My first resolution was to make a clean sweep of my brother's Court. The Moorish guard was sent scrambling south to Granada. The highwaymen, cut-throats and extortioners soon found their way to the prisons, gallows or joined the desperate robber barons who sneered at the notion that a twenty-three-year-old woman could carry out reforms. They predicted the new laws the Cortes hastily passed were devised just for the sake of appearance in my effort to subdue the unhappy throngs of people.

They were soon to admit that apparently I was going about everything in a business-like manner. First I appointed able and trustworthy men to the principal offices of the kingdom. Mendoza, the Cardinal of Spain, became Chancellor. Count Haro remained as the Constable of Castile. Fadrique de Hernandes as Admiral of Castile, and Gutierre de Cardenas became the Treasurer. These strong leaders immediately removed the impostors. Justice was dealt to thieves and murderers quickly and those found guilty were hung in the city and town squares as a reminder to the people and to those who entertained breaking the law, that punishment could be severe. I appealed to the people that with the justice with which they fulfilled their duties, everyone's property and their persons would now be protected by the Crown.

Hernando briefed me daily. He always seemed able to uncover important plots and give me incisive reports on everything happening throughout the realm. Over the years he had developed strategic contacts with various influential individuals both inside and outside the government. His lines of communication reached across the length and breadth of the land. I quickly discovered that appointing him as my First Secretary had been one of my wisest and most fortunate decisions.

Ferdinand was still an absent husband. I contacted his uncle, Admiral Fadrique Hernandes and the Archbishop. Together we decided to work out a truce. The Admiral would argue my point and Toledo would argue for Ferdinand. They were requested to look into every aspect of Ferdinand's demands and after proper deliberation and agreement between us, a written "concord" would be prepared for our signatures. I was very unhappy that I had to defer to this measure with Ferdinand. He had a strong will -- and so did I.

Del Pulgar and I pasted a large map of Castile and Leon on the wall. The map was partitioned by the principal bodies of the noblemen who supported me, and as del Pulgar so aptly put it, those who refused to recognize me as the legal heir to the Throne. Villena was powerful and destructive. His immense estates stretched from Toledo to Murcia giving him extensive influence over the southern regions of New Castile.

The Duke de Arevalo wanted to increase his land holdings and sent his troops into the frontier province of Estremadura. He had developed a friendly relationship with the Marquis de Cadiz, a bright, young handsome nobleman. The Marquis de Cadiz's brother-in-law had been elected the Grand Master of the Order of Calavatara and together the trio were preparing to challenge the Crown. I remained coolley in charge, keeping abreast of the troop movements and various situations, but concentrated upon developing reforms and attempting to restore the national treasury.

The nobles who were absent at my coronation, or who had sent their personal representatives, continued to keep their distance evaluating the government's strength.

The Manrique family were impassioned supporters of my ascension. One member of the family not attending the coronation was Don Rodrigo Manrique. The death of the elder Villena, who had held the Grand Mastership of the Order of Santiago, opened the wounds for noblemen aspiring to that powerful office. It was an enviable position, always hotly disputed because of its military and economic power. The Order's land was widely scattered throughout New Castile and farmed with immense profits going into the Order and to the Grand Master. It was an important source for patronage and direct wealth for the head of the Order. The Grand Master had the right to give part of the Order's holdings to new members. One faction of the members supported the election of Don Rodrigo Manrique as the new Grand Master. Another contender was the powerful Alfonso de Cardenas of Leon. Each were physically battling for control by laying waste to each other's lands. Their objectives were to reduce one or the other's holdings in their respective territories to the extent that when the election was held, the noble holding the largest number of members and greatest resources would be elected.

While I was making sure of my supporters in Segovia, Villena was discreetly silent in Madrid. He was preparing his own ultimatum and agenda to retain his family's power. He decided to appeal to my immediate need for paying an army and to appoint my friends to respective posts. His father had wheedled certain territories which had clouded titles and he wanted the doubts removed from Alcaraz, Trujillo, Requerna, Escaoma and Madrid insuring his legal ownership of these extensive holdings. He urged me to convey to him his father's title of Marquis. Also, he had two younger brothers, Don Pedro Puero and the Count de Uruena, making the demand that I must provide incomes for each of them. To add insult to injury, both of his younger brothers submitted their own demands with additional personal wishes.

The custody of 'La Beltraneja' apparently was given to Villena upon Enrique's death. He was certain he held the ultimate "ace" in his hand when he threatened to declare my twelve year old niece the Queen of Castile and Leon. His last stipulation was that I could easily resolve the bickering over the Grand Mastership of the Order of Santiago by giving the appointment to him. In a veiled reference, he alluded to his relationship with the Pope who might possibly intervene and support his bid for that Office.

Another private war was being waged on the upper reaches of the river of Guadalquivir in Andalucia. True, it was on a smaller scale than the Cardenas/Manriques dispute; however, the houses of Aguilar and Fernandes de Cordoba were bitter enemies. Cordoba quickly declared his support for me. His declaration barely interrupted the private feud. Within days the town of Alcaraz revolted against the rule of Villena in favor of me. Troops under the able military leadership of the young Marquis de Cadiz soon joined forces with

Villena. Suddenly the powerful Duke de Medina Sidonia of Seville stepped into the fray to take a firm command and within a matter of days he overcame the insurgents.

Ferdinand's uncle and the Archbishop were working out the details of the rift between Ferdinand and me. I reminded the Admiral when Ferdinand signed his pre-nuptial agreement, he agreed to abide by Castile's law and the first law of our land was the power of the ruling Monarch. I asked him to suggest to Toledo they request the Cortes to reconvene to study and debate my royal position. The Cortes met and emerged to declare me the sole Monarch of Castile and Leon. Ferdinand had lost that point.

I learned that Ferdinand and his father had signed the agreement thinking it was nothing more than a mere piece of paper. They had assumed that my character was just as weak and impassive as my father and Enrique's. It never occurred to them that I would dare to take an authoritative position on anything. Ferdinand would take command of the country and skillfully blend it into Aragon. It was to be simple, very simple.

A concord agreement was the only solution. I spent many sleepless nights dwelling over the situation. During the first four years of our marriage we had a very limited income. In order to conserve funds, I sewed all of Ferdinand's new shirts. During those sleepless nights, I made a vow to myself that throughout the years to come, I would always make his shirts. While the negotiations continued, the new shirts were cut and stitched, ready for Ferdinand when he came home.

The negotiations lasted six weeks. As they inched forward, I continued to appoint committees and concentrate upon the lawlessness that prevailed. Ferdinand's aides would pick up bits and pieces of gossip and he learned that I had a strength and a sense of purpose he had not counted upon.

In the end it was Ferdinand who capitulated, signing an agreement which upheld our original marriage contract and established seven more points.

• Important appointments would be made in the name of both with the advice and consent of the Queen of all municipal appointments.

• All fiscal matters and issue from the treasury were to be subject to the Queen's order.

• The commanders of the fortified places were to render homage to Ysabella alone.

• Justice was to be administered by both conjointly when we were residing in the same place, and by each independently when separate.

• The proclamations and letters patent would be subscribed with the signatures of both.

• New coins were to be minted. Both our images would be stamped on the public coin.

• The united arms of Castile and Aragon would be emblazoned with a common seal depicting the castles and lions of my Castile and Leon, and the bars and eagles of Ferdinand's Aragon and Sicily.

After studying the agreement and signing it, I attached a personal note to Ferdinand writing, "My Lord, there is no reason why you should raise these matters. Where there is the conformity which by God's grace exists between you and me, there can be no differences. Wherefore, whatever is decided here, you as my husband are still king of Castile, and what you command shall be done in the realm. And as for the governing of these kingdoms, we must remember that if God's will so pleases, the Infanta, our daughter, must marry a foreign prince, who would appropriate for himself the government of these kingdoms and would wish to place the fortresses and royal patrimony in the power of other foreigners of his nation who would not be Castilians, or it could happen that the kingdom would fall into the hands of a race of strangers, which would be a grave charge upon our consciences, a disservice to God and the utter ruin of our successors and our native subject." I read the note through and satisfied, I signed it and gave it to the Admiral to hand to Toledo to present to Ferdinand.

Ferdinand had no recourse but to accept the document. In actuality the new agreement confined him to a greater degree than did the marriage contract. He was excluded from making any appointments within the affairs of the Church or to offices in which the Crown's income was handled, and though these preferments were still to be made in the joint names of each, they were to be "at the Queen's will alone." The concord signed, we agreed to never again create problems between us over our differing opinions and from that day forward, our inevitable destinies were linked together as one body, one mind, one government.

CHAPTER XXI
Ferdinand and Ysabella

The Crown's authority had limited influence in Estremadura, Galicia, Guipuzcoa and Andalusia where battles were raging and the pillage and anarchy were shameful. The motives of the different nobles who took particular sides were mixed, varied, and in many ways were affected by local factors. Those who took my side had gained during the civil strife earning concessions of lands or offices from Enrique and were anxious to retain their new wealth carving out their powerful positions.

Families such as Mendoza, Manrique, Velascos and Fernandes Alvares de Toledo had extensive holdings of property that had formerly been royal land, inalienable in law, if not in practice, from the Monarch's patrimony. Such possessions could be vulnerable in revocations from a strong and unsympathetic Queen. Everyone was cautious and wary.

The division among the nobles gave me a great advantage for it conveyed that the forces of stability were on my side representing the best hope for future security. The nobility was divided in its loyalties but nearly all of the Crown fiefs, fortresses and towns supported me. Throughout the land the people proclaimed, "Castile! Castile! for the king Don Fernando and the Queen Dona Ysabella!"

Together we had the throne, but it was a throne

of a country in utter confusion, morally and economically exhausted, bleeding from a century of internal wounds and neglect. To heal all the nation's ills would require a well thought out plan, appointments made to capable people, and organization.

First we organized our Court surrounding ourselves with people we could trust. Old friends, and even a few old enemies, arrived daily to kiss our hands and see if there was a government appointment for them. The strict formality we established was to become the hallmark for the Spanish Court for the next one hundred years.

We determined we needed an efficient administration of justice, and I immediately introduced a plan for reform. I reasoned that the codification of our existing laws would enable justice to be evenly carried out and reasonably swift. The third problem needing my attention was to address the suppression of the wayward noblemen. The fourth recommendation would be their abdication of ecclesiastical rights which had been more or less usurped by the papal see and belonged to the Crown. The fifth item on my agenda was the regulation of trade. And the last point Ferdinand and I decided needed to be addressed was the pre-eminence of royal authority.

We were in the process of diligently pursuing the implementation of the first and second points when we had our first setback. The Archbishop of Toledo, my friend and confidant, now presented me with his demands. There were certain lands and titles which, he insisted, Ferdinand and I had promised him some time before the coronation. He strongly objected to the men we had appointed to those offices and he went on to remind us that he had been loyal to Ferdinand's father,

King Juan of Aragon, and to my husband in their skirmishes with France. If Carrillo was to remain my friend I then would have to make others my enemies and rescind their appointments. I wrote a note to Carrillo suggesting we work out a suitable compromise with posts and entreatments that were still available. I was willing to go to great lengths to satisfy him and asked him to accept gifts and offices equivalent to those he had so coveted. The churlish Toledo retorted, "I will take what I was promised and nothing else!" While I was searching for another solution, he quietly took his leave of Segovia for his palatial home, Alcala de Henares.

Within a matter of days del Pulgar brought the disturbing news that Carrillo had joined with his nephew, Villena. Why? Because I seemed to have no need for his wise advice and counsel. He insisted I was addressing questions to everyone who did not know about the affairs of the nation. Further, Toledo had supported me from the beginning, helping me to gain the powerful position I now held. Toledo deemed it proper for Ferdinand and me to elevate him to the position that had been held by de Luna in my father's reign, and Villena had held in my brother's disastrous government. Nothing else would do.

Trickery and even treachery might have been expected from anyone named Villena -- but the Archbishop of Toledo? That was another matter. His motives, although admirable, were usually childishly clear, and it was very clear he was jealous of Mendoza's elevated position and angry that he could no longer hope to lead Ferdinand and me around with strings attached.

I simply could not believe I had been betrayed and deserted by the man who had stood for me at

Olmedo; at Toros de Guisando; rescued me from being kidnapped at Madrigal; and officiated at my marriage and coronation.

It was important that I make amends with the Archbishop and I reviewed all my options with Ferdinand as well as others. In the end I decided to travel to his home at Alcala de Henares. Ferdinand and several others expressed grave misgivings as to the wisdom of such a venture. I felt driven to go and make a personal appeal to him. I had made up my mind and without further discussion, accompanied by the Duke de Infantado, Count de Haro and the Duke de Alba, I mounted my horse and took to the high road for Alcala de Henares. I decided to stop at Colmenar Viejo and asked Count de Haro to call on Carrillo at Alcala de Henares to prepare him for my unexpected visit.

Seated on a red velvet tufted chair, Carrillo received the Count in his majestic surroundings. The tapestries hanging on the walls blended perfectly with the red velvet drapes trimmed with gold fringe and inlaid pearl tiebacks. Gold candlesticks were everywhere! The floor was inlaid with a dark, rich wood that gleamed as if it had been polished with a soft leather textured cloth. Count de Haro stepped into the room and Carrillo, sitting in his comfortable chair, failed to stand up to greet his caller. With a deeply furrowed frown and glaring eyes, he motioned to Haro to speak.

Count de Haro was not prepared for this cold reception, but gathering his thoughts as he bowed to his host, he looked boldly into Carrillo's face and said, "Your Excellency, it is good that you have taken time to retreat to your beautiful home here at the Alcala de Henares. You, who have devoted your entire life to God and country, and so generous in your great concern for the welfare of our people; your loyalty and concern for the good of our nation has captured the admiration of everyone far and wide. There are many areas of government that need your wise counsel and vast experience. Everyone prays that as soon as you have rested here at your lovely estate you will be busy taking up your official duties for the Crown."

The glowering churchman's expression never changed. He was quiet for just a moment, and then said, "If you will excuse me, I must confer with a friend." Motioning for Haro to be seated he left the room. Returning an hour later, courtly in manner but in a very stern voice he informed Haro, "I am not interested in making bargains." With a wave of his hand he indicated he had terminated the meeting.

Count de Haro stood up, bowed again to Carrillo and in a quiet, firm voice, he volunteered, "The Queen is waiting at Colmenar Viejo and wishes to call upon you at any hour you choose."

Carrillo was obviously flustered with this startling statement. His face flushed to the roots of his white hair and bristling with obvious anger he shouted, "If she enters at one gate of Alcala, I shall go out the other. I took her from the distaff and gave her a scepter. And I will send her back to the distaff!"

Disappointed, Haro returned to Colmenar. I was kneeling in prayer at the church when word was brought to me that Haro had returned from his meeting. I rushed from the church anxious to receive the latest word. I listened to Haro's account of his meeting with the Archbishop and upon hearing the Count repeat Toledo's words, I turned pale with anger and disappointment. Fighting back my tears, I put my hands to my head, closed my eyes and remained silent for a moment. Gaining my composure, I looked heavenward in prayer. "My Lord Jesus Christ, in Thy hands I place all my affairs, and I implore Thy protection and aid." There was nothing more to be accomplished. I mounted Pascha and rode away greatly troubled with this turn of events, but firm in my conviction that I would never allow my subjects to make unwise demands upon the Crown.

Returning to Segovia, I reviewed the seriousness of Toledo's situation with Ferdinand. We decided upon a "wait and see" policy. I had listened to his ranting and raving for nearly seven years, and thought possibly he might change his mind. In the meantime I wanted to visit my mother at Arevalo and return to her the jewels Enrique had stolen. Ferdinand and I decided to take our little Ysabel with us. Ysabel resembled mother so much I though it might help her regain her mental stability if she had her jewels back, met her new son-in-law and held her little granddaughter in her arms.

The Count de Haro was returning to his domains in the north and traveled with us as far as the kingdom of Avila. It was early in May and the hillsides were ablaze with blooming red poppies. Everywhere I gazed there were thousands of flowers covering the hills with their brilliant flaming red blossoms. We rode along the dusty roads in the central plains of Castile, arriving at the little walled town of Madrigal which suddenly had become a famous village, for it was "the birthplace of Castile's new Queen."

Madrigal stands high on the bleak plateau. We slowed our horses as we came upon the four ancient gates in the city wall silently directing strangers along the way. The arrow pointing east lead the way to Arevalo, to the south was Penaranda, on the west one could travel to Cantalapiedra, and to the north lay Medina del Campo. I looked toward the east to see in the far off distance the defiant familiar tower of Arevalo. I remembered those carefree childhood days when Alfonso, Beatriz and I climbed to the very top of the chambers and gazed over the vast tawny, windblown plain. Here and there I could see a river lazily winding its way across the landscape, and as I looked beyond into the distance, there were the peaceful little villages with multi-colored roofs spread along the valleys.

We stopped at the ancient church of San Nicholas in Madrigal and gazed at its exquisite arches and arabasques. The octagonal cupola was still brilliant with gold and jewels of light. There was a crudely made sign which had been quickly made and stood at the font stating, "It was here the Infanta Ysabella de Trastamara was baptized."

I had sent word by a special courier to Pedro Bobadilla that Ferdinand and I would be coming to Arevalo to visit with mother and discuss business matters with him. His lookout men saw us in the distance, and soon they had mounted their horses and raced toward us to escort us to the Governor's headquarters.

I had not seen Pedro since Beatriz's wedding. His stocky body and sturdy walk hadn't changed. He greeted us with great affection and jovial laughter. How good it was to see him again. I asked about mother and a saddened look crossed his face. I knew that news wasn't good. Our conversation turned immediately to the affairs of government and Ferdinand spoke of the forthcoming changes that we were busy developing and hoped to soon be implementing. Pedro sat and quietly listened, his head nodding up and down from time to time. By nature, he was a quiet and thoughtful man.

Over the years I had realized that his mind was brilliant and his decisions were wise. Watching his response to our ideas convinced me that the winds of change Ferdinand and I were embarking upon would be successful. Bidding him a fond goodby, we mounted our horses and left for Arevalo.

Dear Felipe, now bent with age, his bald head covered with a funny little cap, greeted us at the big entrance. His smile was broad and he was obviously greatly impressed that he was escorting the "new Queen" into the Alcazar of Arevalo. He stepped forward and bowing, opened the huge doors and we stepped inside. Scurrying along the empty hall was a little old lady, who courtesied to me, nodded to Ferdinand, took our little daughter by the hand, and led the way to mother's quarters.

Mother had gotten out of bed and dressed, waiting for us in the "throne room." She looked so tiny and frail sitting with her back straight and holding her head high. She was still wearing the glass beads the little tin smith had wound into a necklace, broach, and ring. I felt mother knew she should greet me with loving affection, but as I approached her, I realized she didn't recognize me. I courtesied and Ferdinand bowed and kissed her hand. Her blank stare evidenced no emotions. I took a box out of my satchel, opened it and showed her the gleaming jewels Enrique had demanded from her. She looked at them, pushed them away and then placing her hands on her necklace she stammered, "Mine, mine, mine!"

Disappointed, I placed her jewels back in my satchel and presented our daughter, her namesake who looked exactly like her -- the same blue eyes, red hair and fair complexion. Ysabel's nose, chin and face structure were the exact image of her grandmother. Mother's vacant stare never wavered. She understood nothing we were trying to share with her. Suddenly she motioned for us to leave. She had given us the proper time and now others were waiting to see her. We must go.

Felipe appeared and whispered, "Your Highness, it is time to move along for if you don't, 'Her Highness' might become hysterical." Tears filled my eyes for I was heartbroken. I had been praying that this visit would help mother to regain her mental faculties. I had no choice but to resign myself to the realization that mother would never be well again. I stopped again at the Governor's residence and asked Pedro to continue to look after her. I assured him I would handle the financial burden of her care and promised that those funds would faithfully be sent on a regular basis.

Ferdinand and I decided to travel a little farther north to Valladolid, the city where we were married, and then on to Burgos. My father had a small Alcazar near Burgos and just before his death he had chosen this site for a new monastery to be built and it was his chosen place for his entombment. I was thinking that I should complete the buildings and place within its walls the tombs of my father and younger brother, Alfonso.

We traveled at a leisurely pace, stopping to talk with the peasants along the road and the townspeople as we rode into the villages. I made mental notes of the garrisoned fortresses, the fields of grain, the private armies of the various nobles. Moving so casually through the countryside and taking the time to speak with my people, even though they were anxious and fearful for their future, I knew they were willing to work together for change.

CHAPTER XXII
Powerful Nobles Rebel Against Ysabella

Cardinal Don Pedro Gonzales de Mendoza, the newly appointed Chancellor quickly became indispensable to me. The Crown's difficulties mounted and multiplied with the passing of each day. I found myself working far into the night, every night, sorting out paperwork, studying the reports del Pulgar, my First Secretary, was placing on my desk, making notes to myself, and attempting to gain some semblance of control over the disarranged government I had inherited. Mendoza was the son of a distinguished soldier and poet, the Marquis de Santillana, the first Castilian scholar to translate Dante into Spanish. Mendoza was well educated displaying a keen intellectual perception. He was very charming as well as extremely capable. But it was his character, even more than his talents, that drew me to him. Mendoza was one of the few men I could absolutely trust in an emergency. He was not ascetic as was Fray Tomas de Torquemada, for in his youth he had been a man of the world and had a son, as well as daughters born with two women of noble birth. He was born an illegitimate son of the Marquis and had none of the pride or vanity of the tempestuous Alonso Carrillo. His piety was sincere with a sturdy spiritual foundation. His love for his country was rooted in the pride of an honorable old family. His sense of social solidarity and responsibility was firm and sensitive.

In the crisis with the Archbishop of Toledo he agreed to ride to Alcala de Henares. Toledo received him in his study with a firm handshake. Mendoza expressed the purpose of his visit was to plead with the old warrior to lay aside his hurt feelings and support the Monarchy. He went on to say, "Give Ysabella a chance to bring peace and stability to this war-torn land. There have been too many civil wars which have led to nothing but anarchy and ruin. It would be tragic, perhaps fatal, to have another. Everyone must make some sacrifice for the public good." To disarm the Archbishop's envy of the Cardinal's new post as Chancellor, Mendoza stated, "I will disassociate myself from the role I have agreed to undertake when the reformed Cortes meets this spring in Segovia. I will volunteer to step aside and allow you to become the chief officiator at this historical conference."

In a monotone voice Carrillo replied, "I have always considered Ysabella to be the legitimate heiress, and I will gladly see the Cortes assembled." The Cardinal believed his tone was too conciliatory, and returned to Segovia expressing his concerns with the unsettling remark to me, "I feel certain Villena and Carrillo are openly switching their allegiances and aligning themselves with Alfonso V of Portugal!"

Shortly after Mendoza's visit to Alcala de Henares word was received that my sister-in-law, Queen Juana, had died in Madrid. This was good and bad news. I had been hoping that Juana would decide her daughter would be accepted at Court in her native Portugal and would pack their things and depart. Now 'La Beltraneja' would be controlled by Villena.

The contest for the Grand Mastership of the Order of Santiago was still raging between Villena, Alonso Cardenas and Don Rodrigo Manriques. The Duke de Medina Sidonia continued to support Villena. During the past three years he had acquired a rather sizeable army as his constant private war against the young Marquis de Cadiz continued in, around and about Sevilla.

Just a few days after one of their major skirmishes, del Pulgar received word of still another conflict among the nobles. He brought the information to me all written in his very legible handwriting, smiling as he placed it before me, and without a word turned and left the room.

I opened the packet, took out the papers and read that within days after our new year had begun, the Duke de Medina Sidonia was observed riding out of Sevilla at the head of two thousand calvary and two thousand infantry with every intention of seizing certain towns belonging to Alonso de Cardenas. The Duke was supporting Villena in his bid for the Grand Mastership and laying waste to some of Cardena's territory seemed quite fitting and proper. The Duke's followers dressed in their armor, trudged along the road singing gay songs with the debonair Duke leading the way. At the head of the column marched the musicians playing their lusty songs. The Duke had urged nine singers from the Cathedral of Sevilla to join him in his adventurous caper.

Meanwhile, Cardenas was away from his home front fighting some battles against the Count Feria. Feria had sided with Villena and Cardenas decided to strike against him. He swooped down upon the small town Feria was staying in, and when Feria saw the family banners of Cardenas looming over the horizon, he ran to the Church of St. Bartholomew and barricaded himself inside. Cardenas attacked, fighting from early dawn until nearly dusk. Finally the Count had a slight opening, one just right to slip through, and he fled into the countryside.

By now the Duke had arrived with his jaunty soldiers in Cardenas' undefended territory, quickly claiming the rich farm land and seizing a huge number of cattle, oxen and horses.

Cardenas was a quick thinker and a man of action. In the dead of night he gathered together three hundred fifty horsemen who galloped into Guadalcana where the jubilant Duke had stopped for the night, and failed to post a guard. Cardenas startled the sleeping victors with a blast from his trumpets and the rattle of swords to break the stillness of the night. The alarmed Duke clambered out of bed, dressed hurriedly and departed with his four thousand panicked troupers. Cardenas' victorious troops ransacked the camp taking back their cattle, oxen, mules, horses and adding silver, garments and the nine choir singers of Sevilla to their booty. In the morning the jubilant troops were seen riding home basking in their triumphant rout.

I had to smile to myself as I allowed my mind to wander visualizing the confrontations. Medina Sidonia had declared for me but I now wondered about his allegiance. I had already written Cardenas' name down in my book long ago noting his solid support for me. Old spites still rankled, especially with Villena. I was very concerned about my dying brother placing 'La Beltraneja' in his custody. Word continued to reach me that around Villena a new rebellion was forming. He was joined by his cousins, the reigning Master of Calatrava, the Count de Uruena, the Duke de Arevalo and his great uncle, the Archbishop of Toledo. It was a powerful cabal!

The idea of using Portugal as a pawn in their ploy to regain their power was beginning to germinate in their minds. Villena and the recalcitrant nobles entered into negotiation with Portugal pledging the King's niece, the thirteen year old 'La Beltranejas' hand in marriage to the divorced King. The marriage contract signed, Alfonso immediately declared himself the King of Castile and demanded that I abdicate the throne. I ignored his ultimatum, and instead, began the serious assessment of the graveness of the predicament that Villena and Toledo had fomented.

Ferdinand and I had been cautiously taking our first steps to establish control over the government. When these sudden turns of events loomed upon our cloudy horizons, we determined we must protect the Throne.

The nation was bankrupt. Enrique had allowed at least one hundred fifty nobles to mint their own money, each with different weights and measures. The nobles collected the taxes and kept the money as their wealth. The yearly income for the Crown was so minimal, there was no way we could begin to implement the changes needed for a more promising future. Ferdinand and I were ill-prepared for battle. He had been exerting his energies toward the reunification of the land, enforcing laws and attempting to gain control over the collection of taxes. Money was scarce. Our treasury was empty and we had only five hundred troops.

My first act was to dispossess the rebels of their offices and income, and within a short time I sequestered their land and began collecting their rents. In a joint communique which Ferdinand and I promptly dispatched to Villena, Carrillo and the Girons, we reproached them in feudal terms for being rebels 'against their natural lords' and denounced them as 'foes of the fatherland.'

King Alfonso continued to harass us and devised a scheme for further embarrassment when he began to mint coins depicting himself as the King of Castile. The right of coinage was a jealously guarded act of royalty. Working late into the night, Mendoza, del Pulgar and I drafted the communique that would be sent to every hamlet, town and city directing the officials to confiscate any and all fraudulent Portuguese coins.

To counteract this improper action by Portugal, we immediately embarked upon the minting of our coins with Ferdinand and my likenesses on one side and our coat of arms on the reverse side. With the value of coins fixed, coupled with our next directive forbidding the export of money and precious metals, we stabilized the economy.

I knew as long as 'La Beltraneja' remained betrothed to Alfonso, there could be no peace with Portugal, and there was no way that I could reconstruct Castile's finances nor address the problems of the people. The Portuguese forces were becoming a threat, particularly at sea. They were spoiling for a fight. We had expanded our territorial rights westward toward the Canary Islands, and the Portuguese seaworthy ships were interfering.

Ferdinand, Admiral Enriques, and I decided to strengthen our naval operations. First we sent a fleet to defend our western ports. Then we added a few more ports that were exposed to Portuguese attacks. The captains of our small armada were commanded to interrupt the Portuguese shipping lanes to Africa. We then secured Castile's southern borders by negotiating a truce with the Moors of Granada. Trade with Portugal was outlawed. We organized pirate raids from our outposts in the Canary Islands which interfered with their trade with their African colonies and commercial shipping to their mainland.

Ferdinand and I fully grasped the absolute necessity that we both must travel to the outer limits of our realm and thence to the major centers of Castile shoring up our lines of defense. We decided to ask Beatriz if we might place our little five year old Ysabel in her care until the crisis was over. True friend that she ever was, Ysabel's godmother literally became her mother for the next few turbulent years.

In our efforts to weed out the inadequate administrators in the various towns, cities and provinces, we appointed qualified commissioners to represent the Crown. These representatives helped to coordinate certain resistance from various holdouts who held control over the towns and fortresses. We were cautious not to alienate the sentiments of those citizens whose past history of local privileges and customs were important to their way of life. We urged our representatives to respect the local privileges throughout the realm. There was one area where this cautionary measure would not be realistic and that was at the frontier strongholds.

Our newly appointed representative would arrive in a town, or at a garrison, to symbolically take over the source of power. He would show the local authorities the royal writs in his favor and they, in turn, would take the writ in their hands, kiss it and place it on the top of their head. This was an ancient Castilian custom with letters that bore royal commands. Kissing the writ and placing it upon their heads was their acknowledgment that the writs were the words of the Queen and they were required to adhere to those written orders. After the symbolical acknowledgment was performed the royal nominee then took the insignia of government, the rods of justice, in their hands and dutifully replaced the municipal councils. They were empowered to make new laws and vote upon any local ordinance at will.

We immediately put aside our long-range plans. If Portugal succeeded we would not even have a country to rule let alone reform. I sought to resolve the impasse with diplomacy. I obviously had no physical resources to become embroiled in a war which could result in disaster and decided to send three embassies to Portugal. Alfonso responded with a resounding communique stating, "Alfonso considered 'La Beltraneja' Queen of Castile and he had every intention of marrying his thirteen year old niece!" I countered with the suggestion that the Pope arbitrate the matter. Alfonso sent back a curt "No!" Ferdinand's father approached him with an equal lack of success, even offering him money and financial help with Portugal's African campaigns.

Those avenues exhausted, we had no choice left but to plunge into a torrent of activity. There was no time to waste.

Throughout the first six months of 1475 we made hurried preparations, attempting to impose order and unity over the land, and develop economic reforms and experiments to try to salvage the foundering fortunes of the Crown.

Villena and his new co-conspirator, the Archbishop of Toledo expressed alarm, disgust and uneasiness in their ploy to grab Castile from me. The common people supported me and I was gaining strength. Throwing up their hands they decided, "Whatever the cost, the Queen must be stopped!"

While Alfonso continued to make threatening demands that I abdicate, I moved swiftly to fortify our ports and strongholds. Loyal supporters advanced the Crown money and we made provisions for its repayment either from our royal treasury or stipulated the repayment would be met from local revenues.

I quickly saw the need to gather food, clothing, bedding, tents, guns and ammunition. Far into the night I worked, dictating to my secretaries, and when they became exhausted I sent them off for a much needed sleep, and continued writing out my own directives sending them on their way the next morning. Some of my aides wondered aloud if I ever slept.

Ferdinand and I took full advantage of those five months. He traveled to Leon then north and west. I raced over the highways and byways of Old and New Castile. For the first time since I had been crowned, I appeared in my traditional ambiance, on horseback, in armor, galloping the long dusty roads, crisscrossing the country, persuading, commanding, raising a promised handful of men in some village, an army of a nobleman in a remote kingdom. Over the dusty roads, trails, and crumbling bridges I raced to Valladolid, Burgos, Toledo and Madrid.

Ferdinand moved from one kingdom to another at a break-neck pace asking for troops. He had little success. Finally he arrived in the northern kingdoms where he found some very inexperienced men who agreed to become a part of the motley bunch of misfits we would refer to as our army.

I visited the border areas, inspecting each garrison personally and ordering the towns to be fully garrisoned to protect the people from the invader. I drove myself to a point of near exhaustion.

My doctor was urging me to be cautious, ride slowly, gallop carefully, get proper rest, eat regularly, and don't overdo, or I would lose the tiny baby now growing in my womb. Somehow those warnings were not possible to heed, for Pascha and I raced with the wind over the countryside urging, cajoling, asking, pleading, praying for food, clothing, bedding, tents and soldiers. There was no time to lose.

The news that Alfonso had crossed our border, entering Castile at Estremadura was expected. It was not without nervous trepidations that Ferdinand and I renewed our efforts to prepare for his attack.

The official word of the invasion of Portugal's armed forces reached me in Toledo on May 28th. My health was not the best for I was having a difficult time with my pregnancy. Nevertheless, as soon as the disturbing news reached me, I ordered my horse saddled, chose my aides that would be traveling with me, and we began our race toward Avila. Three days later as we neared Cebreros, I felt the piercing, wrenching pain of an aborted fetus. Because I was clinching my teeth to bear the knife-stabbing pain, I couldn't cry out, "My baby, my baby! Dear God, I'm losing my child!" I slumped in my saddle and would have fallen to the ground had not a quick-thinking aide rushed to my side.

I don't remember those two days we were forced to remain in Cebreros. My mind must have been totally blank. Exhausted, I do remember that I slept most of that time. On the third morning I awakened feeling strong enough and determined to resume my race against time. We caught up with Ferdinand and his scouts who had been receiving sporadic reports on Alfonso's troop movement, and I was given a full report. Late that night, my husband's arms around me, the tears of sadness flowed freely for the first time. Together we found solace, and vowed that soon, very soon, we would have a son.

After entering Castile at Estremadura, Alfonso traveled with his troops taking a northerly course toward Palencia. There the Duke de Arevalo, Villena, and a confused 'La Beltraneja' joined him. The royal pair were proclaimed with the customary solemn ceremony befitting a Sovereign, and then they proceeded with the issuance of an audacious circular which was delivered in neat packets to various cities, attempting to establish 'La Beltraneja' as the legitimate heir to the throne, proclaiming her betrothal to Alfonso V of Portugal, and establishing their lawful regency over Castile.

It was a proper time for feasts, revelry, toasts, pomp and circumstance. Their ultimate destination was to travel to Arevalo, the very center of Castile, where they would set up their headquarters. The Duke de Arevalo and Villena had promised Alfonso their battle-ready troops would arrive en masse to become a formidable foe for those "impostors of Castile's Crown." Then, too, they reasoned that from the center of the kingdom they would negotiate with all the nobles from every part of the country. Holding the kingdom of Avila in their power would give Ferdinand and me no central place to assemble an army, and Villena's Castile based troops could travel freely to the Avila plateau.

During those five hectic months, we had been given verbal commitments for soldiers, lancers, horses, mules, ammunition, food, tents and supplies. Now we must marshall them all together and immediately prepare for the defense of the Crown. It was an awesome task. I was still weak, but that never deterred me from keeping my all night vigils as I worked late into the night preparing the dispatches to leave by couriers in the early morning before daybreak. To the east, west, north and south they raced against time bringing the urgency of the nation's peril to the people.

As the wheels of organization were put into motion, the vast supplies for our war with Portugal began to pour into Valladolid. It was a burden that would tax everyone's strength almost beyond endurance, but at the same time we each renewed our determination to win. Ultimately that first confrontation was to bring us to our knees when we experienced the humiliation of defeat.

CHAPTER XXIII

Defending the Realm Against Portuguese Aggression

In the midst of all the chaotic, turbulent events, I focused my concentration toward the direction of an ordered assembly of war supplies. Every day del Pulgar piled packets upon my makeshift desk. Those dispatches indicated to me Castile was in the midst of a war without a front. There were rebellions and counter-rebellions spreading like wildfire across Castile. As I studied the problems it appeared three major theaters of conflict were taking shape. In the north was Alfonso joining with the forces of the Duke de Arevalo with his soldiers poised to march on Castile. At the center of the storm, near Madrid and Toledo, Villena's men were actively fomenting unrest. In the south Villena's cousin, the Count de Uruena, was attempting to exploit the dissension and divisiveness of my supporters.

Far into the night I bent over my desk reading dispatches and dictating replies. There were times when I didn't take time to sleep. My daytime activities were devoted to riding throughout Valladolid, designated as the official supply depot, inspecting the supply centers. The city officials and I had worked out a plan to organize the supply base. Ammunition would be delivered to one area, at another space food would be stored, another for tents and bedding, another for horses, mules and carts. A disciplined pattern of organization was taking place. I made a mental note when I was personally "in their midst" there was a definite difference in attitude and cooperation. It was obvious to everyone their determination to succeed was buoyed by my presence. Some were moved to tears with my exhortations. The people believed my words and knew I trusted them.

By the end of June, Ferdinand and I determined we had made solid progress mobilizing the hidalgos, lancers, and foot soldiers. I returned to Segovia to handle some urgent affairs. There were many volunteers eager to join our cause from the Segovia area -- some rode on horses, others on mules, but most of them were foot soldiers. They were courageous patriots animated by their adventurous spirit and the unique leadership of their young Queen. I put on my armor, inspected my troops, and rode at the head of our columns. Onward we marched to Valladolid where we would rendezvous with Ferdinand's troops.

Ferdinand had traveled to the north and brought his volunteers down from the mountains. From Old Castile, Biscaya, Guipucoa and the Asturias by the Sea they flocked to Valladolid. No one came from Andalucia or Murcia.

By the first of July, our extra-ordinary exertions assembled troops for a head count of about forty thousand men who seemed to have "sprung up" in the very center of the storm clouds now gathering. There were four thousand men-at-arms, eight thousand light horsemen, and thirty thousand foot soldiers all making up our untrained, non-disciplined militia.

Alfonso's troops had been quiet for a month. They were celebrating the affiancing of their King to his child queen. At the end of June, Alfonso began his northward march toward Arevalo where he would wait for the Castilian reinforcements of the Duke de Arevalo and Villena. Arevalo and Villena were soon to learn that troops from their private armies had declined to enter into a conflict against Ferdinand and me. Alfonso's high hopes were momentarily crushed.

Villena's influence was still commanding and within a matter of days he had an agreement from the citadel of Toro to deliver that city to Alfonso. The defection of this city was a crushing blow to our morale. Toro was one of the most important cities in Leon. It was strategically important to Portugal because its location enabled troops to move freely from Portugal into Castile.

Ferdinand was determined to charge into battle against the intruder. Undaunted, we threw everything we had against them. Ferdinand marched along the river roads, and I dug in with my makeshift headquarters at Tordesillas. We had devised our battle strategies with Ferdinand striking at the very walls of Toro while I lead my division of troops around from the other side cutting off supplies and troop reinforcements destined for Alfonso.

Ferdinand arrived at the walls of Toro on the 19th of July and immediately drew his motley army up in an orderly manner ready for battle. Alfonso stayed behind the walls with his defenses. Hoping to "smoke him out," Ferdinand sent a herald into his camp challenging him to a fair field fight with his entire army. That plot failed and Ferdinand then invited Alfonso to decide their differences by a duel. Alfonso accepted the challenge of a duel, but neither side could agree upon the guarantee of the performance of the duel. The episode faded into an empty boast of chivalry.

The disturbing news that the ancient city of

Zamora had declared for Portugal was delivered to both our camps. Ferdinand and I had designated Zamora as a major base for resupplying our troops. Ferdinand determined that he must immediately strike his banners for battle, and with trumpets blaring, the kettle-drums echoing throughout the valley, they broke the stillness of the new dawn as they stormed the walls of Toro.

The battles raged for two weeks with both sides suffering severe losses. Our army had been so hastily assembled, so totally lacking in experience with battering artillery, we weren't able to use it to the best advantage -- not even enough to annoy the city! Ferdinand's communications with me were cut off. Food and supplies became scarce.

I had been skirmishing with my troops. Unafraid, I put on my battle armor and rode at the head of the columns designated to act as a "pincer" cutting their lines of supply. The soldiers fought valiantly echoing their battle cries, "Castile! Castile for Dona Ysabella and Don Fernando!"

Soon after the earlier battles from my side had ended, I mounted Pascha and rode back to the last battlefield. The desolate area was strewn with bodies, flags, standards and empty shoes. The wagons were lumbering up, pulled by tired, lazy mules. Some of my soldiers jumped down and began lifting the bodies of the slain men into the wagon for burial.

I rode up and surveyed the destruction. I watched a soldier walk across the field, stop by a body and using his boot, he turned it over. I urged Pascha forward, the soldier walked on. Suddenly I realized the man lying on the ground was alive. I looked around and watched other soldiers grabbing up the supposedly lifeless men, pulling them along and throwing them into the wagons.

I cantered across the battlefield and looked into the faces of those "dead" men, and I heard one of them groan. I jumped down from Pascha and ran to the wagon, blurting out to the soldiers, "These men, some of them are still alive. Quickly, we must help them. Get the bandages and I'll try to stop the bleeding..."

The soldiers looked at me as if I was an idiot. They were afraid to speak to me directly, finally one of them got up enough courage to say, "Bandages? I've never seen a bandage on a battlefield."

Dumbfounded, because I hadn't thought of medical supplies, I countered with, "But we've got to take care of our people."

Another soldier asked, "How?"

Quickly assessing the situation, I realized there was no way to care for the wounded. I had provided no bandages, no doctors, no hospital. Only priests to dignify the dying process by giving the Last Rites. Shocked and numb, I strode back to Pascha. I looked back to survey the battleground, etching into my mind the fate of those men still breathing who may be buried alive.

I uttered a prayer for them and vowed, "Never again, dear God, never again will my soldiers be without hospital tents, medicine, bandages and a crew of men to rush straight into the heat of battle and drag a live body off to the side and administer first aid."

I rode back to Tordesillas wondering about all the other battlefields across Europe. How did those leaders care for their wounded? I decided I would contact the foreign embassies and pose that vital question.

Things had gone from bad to worse in Ferdinand's camp. He called together his Council of War and decided to retreat without further delay. As soon as this misfortunate decision was relayed to the troops, the retreat orders rippled through the camp. The boisterous, stalwart soldiers, unable to accept the reality of defeat, declared among themselves that "Fernando has been betrayed by his nobles!" Gathering together a group of over-loyal Biscayans, taunted by the conviction that a conspiracy against the king had actually taken place, they broke into the church where Ferdinand was meeting with his officers. Before the startled men could inquire about their strange behavior, the Biscayans grabbed Ferdinand, hoisted him to their shoulders, and carried him safely back to his tent.

The voluntary retreat of the undisclipined soldiers was so disorderly, many were wandering off into various directions, abandoning their military posts in search of food and clothing. Some found their way back to Tordesillas. Because our lines of communication had been cut, I had no current dispatches about the state of Ferdinand's battle area. When those soldiers began drifting back to Tordesillas, I promptly began the military exercise of regrouping them, getting them ready to charge back into the fray of battle.

Ferdinand arrived in person to bring me the disquieting news of his decision to retreat.

Toledo had remained at his home at Alcala de Henares receiving dispatches daily about the progress of the battles raging at Toros. When he received word that Ferdinand's soldiers had mutinied against him forcing his retreat, the old warrior gleefully saddled his big, black war horse, donned his flaming red cape and gathered together five hundred lances to travel north and jubilantly link his fortunes to Alfonso's great victory.

The disastrous turn of events filled me with anxiety. Revolutionary tactics which had for so long agitated Castile had an effect on every man's political principles. The allegiance of even the most loyal hung so loosely about us it was difficult to assess how far our support might be shaken by our loss at Toro.

Alfonso calculated his position and decided he was in no position to profit from his success. He had counted heavily upon Villena and Arevalo providing a substantial number of lancers, horses and troops. Convinced that they could not compel their vassals to become involved, he decided to negotiate a favorable truce with Castile and return to Portugal.

The envoy he chose to approach Ferdinand in Tordesillas expressed Alfonso's willingness to withdraw his claims to Castile's Crown in return for the territory of Galicia, the cities of Toro and Zamora, and a considerable sum of money.

Ferdinand and his Council of War discussed the proposition, studied our military options, calculated the odds against Castile's ability to mount any further offenses and proposed to me that I accept the odious truce. I looked around the table studying each face. They were calm, serious, sensible men and I respected their sound judgment and considerable concern for Castile. Firmly and calmly I stated, "Yes, we can agree to the money, but I, Ysabella de Trastamara, will not relinquish one square inch of Castile. Not one, single, square inch." From the tone of my voice, the expression in my green-blue eyes, the shrug of my right shoulder, Ferdinand knew any further arguments were fruitless and relayed my reply to Alfonso's camp.

We had failed at a time when it was vital that we make a good first impression. It came at a crucial time when we needed to make a strong show of strength. Defeated we were, but there was no time to waste on tears. Instead of making excuses we studied our blunders realizing we should not have thrown everything into battle at once. It was a mistake we never made again.

More determined than ever was I to rule over Castile. I smiled when I learned that Arevalo and Villena were having difficulty moving their wayward, well-trained and battle-ready troops against me. They, too, were experiencing mutiny among their soldiers.

Our morale undiminished, minds sharpened and clear, Ferdinand and I began our preparations. What had been done earlier with enthusiasm was now replaced with cool precision. First, we needed money.

In August I convoked the Cortes in Medina del Campo. The cities had been unfailingly loyal to me and had given all they could toward our cause. It was not enough. With the full consent of the clergy, I moved forward with one of the boldest and most remarkable decisions of my reign. I requisitioned half of the silver belonging to the Church -- 30,000,000 maravedies! I, Ysabella de Trastamara, guaranteed to repay the entire sum within three years. I assured the officials of the church that Ferdinand and I had already strengthened our tax collection efforts and from these increased revenues the obligation would be repaid. It was a guarantee that was scrupulously kept.

Once again Alfonso gave us time. He remained quietly biding his time in Toro. I pounced upon his relaxed vigil with all my might. Tireless, constantly on horseback, I rode from one end of my kingdom to the other, making speeches, holding conferences, sitting up all night dictating letters to my secretaries, holding court all morning to sentence a few thieves and murderers to be hanged, riding a hundred leagues or so over cold mountain passes to plead with some undecided noble for five hundred soldiers. No distance was too far. No limits to the crusade were invoked.

If I suffered from physical exhaustion, aches and pains, it was to be expected for there were no alternatives. Now that I had money it was much easier to build our depleted military ranks. Over Ferdinand's loud objections I ordered provisions for medical supplies, hospital tents, doctors, and medical assistants. I was firm in my decision. Castile would be the first European nation to provide medical care for the wounded and dying.

I ordered cannons from Germany and Italy. The army was paid, rearmed and trained. By the end of the year we had a skilled and tightly organized force of fifteen thousand troops.

Time and time again, the thought crossed my mind how close we had come to total defeat. Had Alfonso struck into the southern districts of Castile where so many were friendly to his cause, and if he had coupled his forces with the feisty young Marquis de Cadiz, he might have won our kingdom.

Our tactics had improved and we had learned the bitter consequences resulting from undersupply. Now we decided to disrupt the base of supplies for Alfonso arriving daily from Portugal.

In December Ferdinand and Cardinal Mendoza linked our forces with the Count de Monterey and Count de Lemos who were bringing their troops from Galicia. They marched westward with our new army and recaptured Zamora, so strategically situated between Toro and the Portuguese border. I set up my camp at Tordesillas and took charge of our mobile squadrons trained to intercept reinforcements being transported to Alfonso. As we intercepted more and more wagon trains, my granaries were groaning with food and the ammunition dumps were filled. Alfonso's horses, mules and swords were welcomed. We were gaining ground.

Early in January changes began to take place in Alfonso's camp. We had confined him to Toro and his troops were getting restless. There were certain factions in southern Castile that were loyal to me and they moved their trained troops along the border of Portugal with skirmishes into Portugal's undefended territory. Alfonso had to send some of his troops from the north into the southern arena to defend his southern borders. His troops rebelled. They were unhappy being cooped up in Toro while their southern borders went undefended.

Alonso Carrillo and his private army arrived at the gates of Toro early in February. From Portugal, Alfonso's son, Prince Juan, taking the northerly route around Galacia connected his troops with his father in Toro arriving with nearly twenty thousand soldiers.

Alfonso was triumphant. He immediately dispatched circulars to the Pope, King of France, to his dominions and all of those in Castile who had pledged their support, proclaiming "Portugal's intention to drive Ysabella and Ferdinand out of Castile."

Buoyed by all the reinforcements, Alfonso left Toro under the cover of the night on February 17th and marched westward along the bank of the Duero river. It was near daybreak when his troops arrived outside the ancient city of Zamora. Zamora was situated just north of the river, connected with the broad flat plain beyond by one narrow bridge. The Portuguese positioned their cannons in such a way as to dominate the bridge and Alfonso confidently established his headquarters at the Monastery of San Francisco.

Ferdinand was awakened by the clanging of his captain's bell signaling him they were in peril. He looked out his window in utter disbelief, and then suddenly he was engulfed with the emotion that he was now "bottled up."

Across the river was the display of a jovial celebration with floating banners, flashing swords that glittered in the early morning sun, trumpets sounding the call to battle. Volleys were shot into the air and the festivity of having already won their battle had begun.

Ferdinand quickly gathered his military aides into his quarters and began to plan his first attack to drive Alfonso back. Our eager troops were ready for battle. With trumpets blaring, Ferdinand's well-equipped and trained army struck at the very heart of Alfonso and his jubilant troops. Surprised, Alfonso beat a quick retreat in an attempt to position his soldiers for a raging battle. The battles raged back and forth with Ferdinand advancing and then Alfonso regaining some of his lost ground. Advance, gain, and then fall back. It was becoming a pattern and soon Alfonso became battle scarred and weary. He needed to have a face to face meeting with Ferdinand.

With great care and secrecy a meeting between the two adversaries was arranged. Alfonso suggested they meet at the stroke of midnight in the middle of the river. He thought the center dividing line of the river was a neutral point for negotiations. Ferdinand's crafty mind didn't agree. He stuck to his demands that Alfonso travel across the river and he would meet him on the bank of the river at the stroke of midnight. The date and time were set. Early that evening the north-westerly winds rose and a driving rain began to fall. Alfonso and his two aides got into their small boat and started rowing across the river. The water was so choppy, the wind so fierce, the rain so cold, the waves tossing the boat to and fro, Alfonso panicked. He ordered his aides to return to his headquarters.

The next morning Ferdinand had a quiet visit with one of Alfonso's aides who sheepishly admitted the reason Alfonso had failed to keep his appointment. It was mutually agreed they would try again that night. Ferdinand and Alfonso would meet at one o'clock in the morning on the bank of the Duero river on Zamora's side.

Ferdinand arrived at the appointed hour and as he sat quietly waiting for Alfonso, the town clock, which had mistakenly been set forward two hours, struck the hour of three. Ferdinand thought he had arrived too late and that Alfonso had come and gone. He departed. Meanwhile, Alfonso's little skiff rowed into the now quiet cove and finding no one waiting, returned to his quarters at the monastery. Frustrated at every turn, confused, running low on troops, horses, supplies and ammunition, he decided not to make another attempt at negotiations. He sent a message to Ferdinand asking for a thirty day truce. Ferdinand replied he would "not concede one hour, let alone thirty days."

With no remedy in sight, Alfonso broke camp before dawn on March 1st, quietly steering his soldiers on an eastward course along the river back to Toro.

Rising early in the morning, Ferdinand looked out at the now bare fields across the river. Alfonso had "turned tail and ran!" Ferdinand reasoned that if he could move his troops quick enough, he might catch them before they reached walls of Toro. The raging waters of the river made a hasty chase difficult. Fortunately for us, Alfonso had overlooked ordering the narrow bridge to be burned or destroyed when he raced against the clock to make his withdrawal. Ferdinand's horses, guns and ammunition slowly inched from one side of the river to the other across the narrow bridge. By late afternoon the last of the knights were across the river.

In nervous haste Ferdinand organized his troops. On his left, he placed six battalions under the joint commands of Cardinal Mendoza, Admiral Enriques and the Duke de Alba. Six other battalions with less august leaders made up the right flank. Ferdinand would take command of the center. His uncle, Don Enrique Enriques, was appointed the royal standard bearer supported by all the levies of Galicia, Salamanca, Medino del Campo, Cuidad Rodrigo and Valladolid. Ferdinand mounted his horse, rode to the front and turning, sitting straight and tall in his saddle, reviewed his troops. Everything was ready. He commanded Don Enrique to break out his royal pennon, then each of the nobles unfurled their own, the drums beat and in the quiet of the misty grey evening, the stalwart army filled with gallant confidence and indomitable spirit marched.

The night skies hung low with thick, heavy, rain laden clouds. Ferdinand urged his troops to move quickly to avoid the drenching rain, if possible. All night they traveled, and in the wee hours of the morning they reached a safe haven just ten leagues from Toro. Ferdinand decided to stop here, rest his horses, allow his men to have some food and get some much needed sleep. He wanted them fresh and ready for those perilous days ahead.

Cardinal Mendoza took a scout and cautiously rode out to determine how far Alfonso had moved his troops. Discovering Alfonso had pitched his camp only five leagues away he determined the Portuguese Monarch had decided he would mount his battles from this vantage point. A short time later they returned informing Ferdinand that Alfonso had made his camp about five leagues away.

The next morning Ferdinand and his troops, rested and battle ready, marched over the hills. Riding confidently to the top of the last hill, Ferdinand paused a moment, looked around at his men, and motioned for the onward march down the hill and on to a chosen spot on the plain directly opposite the Portuguese camp. The rain soaked ground caused the loaded wagons to bog down, the mules to stumble as they pulled their burdensome artillery, and the soldiers bravely fought off their chills as they organized their running games to stay warm. Quickly they struck their camp and prepared for immediate confrontations.

An eerie quietness seemed to permeate the entire plain, then suddenly there was a burst of trumpets, Ferdinand signaled and the first battle cry, "Santiago, Santiago!" rang out. The battle to the finish was on!

Ferdinand's right flank, his weakest, was pitted against the Portuguese flank under the command of Prince Juan who had amassed a formidable artillery to lob the lombards into the center of our troops. Under the heavy fighting the Castilians broke first and fled into the hills.

The superb actions of this terrible battle that began on the cold, damp, grey morning was forever etched on the minds of these courageous men. Both

Kings fought with valor and ardor. The old Archbishop of Toledo mounted on his great war horse, his flaming red cape tied around his neck, slashed away with vengeance. Cardinal Mendoza, with his quick mind and agile body, galloped back and forth through the shadows, muddy and bloodstained. Two warriors of the Church, each having exchanged the crosier for the corselet, met on that battlefield vowing to protect their chosen leaders.

Nobles went down, their sure-footed horses stumbled on the bloody, muddy field. Ferdinand's left flank fought with such magnificent fury, the Portuguese began to lose ground.

Alfonso's heroic standard-bearer, Duarte de Almeida was surrounded. First his right arm was nearly hacked off. He transferred the standard to his left arm, and Ferdinand's troops struck their blows deep into the flesh. Valiantly Duarte placed the standard in his teeth, and then his body crumpled on the ground. His standard captured, Alfonso fled.

Ferdinand's reserve troops came storming down from the hills. The Duke de Alba turned his flank and created another disorder. The defeat soon became a rout. Some of the dazed Portuguese attacked each other in the dark. Others rushed off in the darkness running they knew not where. Still others, finding themselves at the Duero river, flung their bodies into the turbulent waters.

It was the Cardinal who stopped the slaughter and pillage. Ferdinand, leaning on his blood spattered sword, watched the curtain come down. He knew that night, "Our Lord had given him all Castile." Three nobles were chosen to ride quickly to Tordesillas to tell of the great victory.

Ferdinand stayed with his troops as they moved throughout the battlefield, taking our soldiers who were wounded to the medical tents, helping others clean up. They worked feverishly until daybreak.

The nobles reached Tordesillas early the next morning. I was sitting at my desk working with del Pulgar. We both looked up when we heard the clatter of the horses hooves and soon rounding the corner were the nobles with our flags unfurled, and I knew we had won!

My first response was to give thanks to God for prayers answered. Just a short distance from my headquarters was the ancient Alcazar Alfonso XII had dedicated to become a monastery. His Throne Room, glittering with diamonds and rubies, became the main chapel and the area his Throne Chair occupied became the altar. It was here I knelt each morning in prayer, and my first thought was to kneel again at King Alfonso's altar, but suddenly it seemed important that all of the people share our historical victory. I sent pages scurrying all over the city summoning the clergy to join with me at the Monastery of San Pablo. Together we would bow our heads in prayerful thanksgiving. The clergy arrived and were assembled at the steps of my headquarters, the Alcazar built on the banks of a lovely winding river. As I walked down the steps, I suddenly stooped down and removed my shoes and stockings. Barefoot, I walked through the streets, the churchmen following behind me. The townspeople were suddenly caught up in victory fever and their shoes and stockings came off. Behind the clergy they walked, chanting, "Castile! Castile! for Dona Ysabella and Don Fernando!"

Ferdinand and his victorious troops rode into the city with their banners unfurled, marching as the great victors they ever were. The trumpets sounded, the drums rolled, and the church bells rang. So proud was I of each and every one.

Ferdinand was carrying the captured armor of Duarte de Almeido and my eyes filled with tears as they told me of this heroic Portuguese's bravery and dedication to his country and King. I handed the armor and flag to del Pulgar and asked him to send it to the Cathedral in Toledo where it would be hung as a trophy and as a poignant remembrance of a desperate act of heroism.

It had been eight long, grueling months since Ferdinand had straggled back along the river road from Toro defeated and outwitted. Today he had returned the victor. And that, I knew, was ever as it should always be.

CHAPTER XXIV
Nobles Subdued

It was indeed an impressive victory. We had gained priceless military experience and our stature in Europe had soared after we crushed the rebellion. Now it was time to move quickly and deal with these rebel noblemen.

Within days after Portugal's capitulation, I moved to convene the Cortes presenting to them the suggested laws which I thought should be invoked. These serious gentlemen adjourned with statutes passed that would clearly forbid powerful noblemen to build new fortresses; train their own armies; challenge each other to a duel; or annex property into their domains which did not belong to them.

Certain noblemen began to hint they would be willing to negotiate their positions, each anxious to secure the best terms possible. Throughout Castile the dissenting nobles realized their control over a kingdom had ended, and now they were openly proclaiming their allegiance to the Crown. Those who had been hostile to the government now vied with each other in their demonstrations of loyal submission. My plan for our futures held no place for long-lasting resentment.

I sent a confidential letter to Pope Sixtus the Fourth requesting he overrule his previous dispensation in which he approved the marriage of the divorced

King of Portugal and my niece. The Pope now noted in his latest bull his "approval of such a marriage had been obtained by a misrepresentation of the facts." When I received word this new bull had been issued I was confident my Throne was secure.

Some nobles in the kingdom of Biscay were still defiant. Ferdinand traveled with a contingency of troops with battering lombards, storming the Biscayan fortresses and burning them to the ground.

I studied my map on the wall noting we had made progress bringing reluctant nobles to serve our Monarchy; however, there were still stubborn, defiant ones who had retreated to their vast estates and word had reached me they were building additional fortresses to protect their domains. Villena and his cousin, the Count de Uruena, lost no time in gathering stones, wood and mortar to erect more forbidden structures. Cardinal Mendoza and I decided to place another faction of our trained army under my command to ride west and destroy the half-completed fortresses and effect the total destruction of their existing ones. In the back of my mind I had always felt Villena had been the prime cause for my young brother's untimely death. In my heart I knew Villena's father had poisoned my brother Alfonso's fish because he was determined to be the Grand Master of the Order of Santiago. That was many years ago, but I still grieved for Alfonso. Now I was riding forth on a mission of destruction. A mission that I hoped would lighten my grief.

From my headquarters at Truxillo I gave orders to my troops, now spread out in every direction, to conquer. Our plan of attack against the nobles and their vassals was devastating. Private mansions and farm houses were pillaged and burned to the ground, cattle and crops were swept away, and highways were blocked bringing all travel to an abrupt stop. Rich lands were reduced to rubble.

I returned to Valladolid confident my decision to rule with a firm hand was a correct one. Word of my excursion into Villena's territory reached the ears of Beltran de la Cueva, the Duke de Albuquerque. His position of power had dimmed when my half-brother was forced to accept the elder Marquis de Villena's terms for a peaceful reconciliation, and for nearly five years he and his Duchess had lived quietly on their estates. True, he had presented himself to me at my coronation, but once again he wanted to reassure me of his support. Del Pulgar's quick wit informed me that "the clothes-horse wanted an audience as quickly as possible." I knew he meant Beltran. Sometimes in moments when we both needed some laughter to break the tensions of our work, Pulgar would relate some of the charades Beltran presented at Enrique's Court.

For more than a year there had been no Grand Master of the Order of Santiago. All the nobles who were fighting for their position and stature among the members now seemed relatively quiet. In the back of my mind I wanted that Grand Mastership to be presented, once again, to the Monarchy. My eleven year old brother had been the last official Monarch to be the Grand Master and I wanted the tradition restored. Word reached me that a date had been set for the election of the new Grand Master in Ucles. I looked at the calendar and saw that I had exactly three days to travel one hundred fifty leagues to intervene. Without a moment's hesitation I mounted my new black stallion, and along with my closest aides, we raced out of Valladolid toward Ucles. There was no time to waste.

It was an exhausting ride holding our horses to a gallop along the bad roads as torrents of rain poured from the darkened skies. The brisk, chilly winds lashing about us failed to deter my mission. We pushed our horses and our own individual strengths to the limit every single one of those one hundred fifty leagues. Late in the evening we rode into Ucles. The blackened clouds unrelentingly continued to pepper the landscape with drenching rain. Our winded horses rounded a cobblestoned street and the ancient monastery loomed into view.

I pulled my horse to a halt, tossed the reins over my stallion's head, and raced toward the huge wooden door. I lifted the latch and pushed. It was reluctant to give way, so I stepped back and with my shoulders braced lunged toward it. It gave way and I nearly lost my footing as I stumbled through the door in my rain soaked clothes.

The members of the Order were just preparing to cast their votes. Their startled expressions evidenced I was the last person they expected to see standing before them. Some were staring at my wet face streaked with wisps of hair, others were looking at my soaking wet clothes dripping puddles of water at my feet. Within a matter of seconds I had my composure and brushing the wisps of hair back from my face, my voice clear, I calmly stated, "I would like you to honor my husband, Ferdinand, and elect him your new Grand Master. Such an important Order of Knights deserves no one less than the King himself at its head."

The nobles quickly cast their votes and before I left their presence, Ferdinand was the new Grand Master of this ancient Order of Castilian Kings.

We rode back to Valladolid at a much easier pace. The sun was shining and warm, and as I cantered along the roadway I formulated in my mind the next step I wanted to take in regard to the two remaining Orders. I would discuss the merits with Ferdinand, who was presently in Aragon attending to some urgent business there. My plan was to elect him the Grand Master of the remaining Orders of Calatrava and Alcantara when those offices became vacant. We would then control the religious strife.

I arrived back in Valladolid feeling confident and in a wonderful frame of mind. Positive changes were taking place. The people were supportive and full of confidence.

Late one afternoon, as I was sitting at my desk, del Pulgar brought me the disquieting news that two young noblemen, Ramiro Nunez de Guzman, Lord of Toral and Frederick Enriques, the son of the Admiral of Castile had gotten into an argument that morning while waiting in my antechamber at the Alcazar in Valladolid. Del Pulgar informed me they had challenged each other to a duel. This was flagrant disobedience of our new law and I had vowed never to permit another duel to take place. I quickly dispatched some aides to notify the Constable to locate Toral because I thought he was probably the weaker of the two. My orders directed the Constable to escort Toral safely out of the city. Don Frederick discovered the plot to foil his plans and he ordered three of his men armed with bludgeons to seize Toral. Toral was overtaken, beaten and tossed into a side street.

A constable discovered the near lifeless body, and aware that their own men had been ordered to escort Toral safely out of the city, he immediately brought word to me.

As usual, I was busy at my desk when the constable arrived well past midnight. The Constable described in detail how he found the bludgeoned body of Toral. I quickly assessed the situation. I would not allow our laws to be flagrantly ignored by noblemen, and it made no difference to me that Enriques was Ferdinand's youthful uncle. I grabbed my wrap and raced for the stables. Sleepy aides came running after me knowing not where I was headed or what crisis had now risen. My horse saddled, I dashed out of the courtyard and raced along the countryside in the blackness of the night. Storm clouds were hovering and suddenly the lightning streaked through the sky and the heavy clap of thunder reminded me that soon I would be drenched. I galloped onward, my aides spurring their horses trying to catch up.

I arrived at the castle of Simancas where Admiral Don Frederick lived. I jumped from my horse and jangled the gate bells loudly with a sense of urgency. A servant let me in and I demanded to be taken to the Admiral. I was shown into a small room to wait for Don Frederick to be awakened. When he entered, I demanded that he turn his son over to me for he was to be brought to justice.

The Admiral shook his head and insisted that Don Frederick was not there. I really didn't believe him and I noted there was a large ring of keys hanging from his waist. I asked him to surrender his keys to me. Quietly, and without a word, he handed them over.

I swept through the castle, inspecting every room, poking into every turret, even the deep, dark dungeon.

There was no Don Frederick to ferret out. Without a word, and just a nod of my head to the Admiral, I handed the keys back to him.

The rain was still pelting down as I left Simanca retracing my way back to Valladolid. The sun was rising as we cantered into the courtyard. My horse was tired, my aides complained of aching bones, and my sniffles signaled I was catching a cold.

Admiral Enriques knew I was very angry and he decided to discuss the situation with some of his friends. They urged him to turn his son over to me before I took punitive actions against the entire family. With no other choice at hand, the Admiral asked his brother, Constable Count de Haro, to escort his son to Valladolid.

The Constable positioned his nephew in a safe house just outside the city and then approached me pointing out that his nephew was only twenty years of age. I listened and decided to admonish the young man to be publicly conducted as a prisoner by a member of my Court through the great plaza of Valladolid and then to the fortress of Arevalo where I had him imprisoned.

Ferdinand returned home from Aragon to receive the good news that he was the new Grand Master of the Order of Santiago, and the bad news his uncle was languishing in jail. Shocked, Ferdinand asked me to send Don Frederick off to Sicily. I issued the command for his release and with a military escort, he was placed aboard a ship setting sail for Sicily. He left clearly understanding that he could not return to Castile without my royal permission.

The Admiral's dilemma, plus the earlier destructive measures I took against the dissenting noblemen caused the principal holdout, Alonso Carrillo, to reconsider his position. After the rout of the Portuguese, he left Toro taking a circuitous route back to Alcala de Henares where he virtually barricaded himself, remaining very quiet watching my actions and reactions. Anxious that his estates remain intact and concerned that I would suddenly exercise my full authority and confiscate his considerable domains, he convinced his nephew, Villena, they should sue for pardon. Villena sent a courier to Valladolid requesting an audience with me.

Villena was crafty, but his abilities would never match his father's talent at intrigue. In my foray into the western and southern territories I had decimated some of Villena's most prized houses. Carrillo had urged him to stay at Alcala de Henares until the storm clouds blew over. In our meeting I allowed Villena to retain his title of Marquis, honoring my father, King Juan II, who had initially bestowed it upon his father. I agreed to Villena's retention of the old, clearly defined lands where there was no question of the legal ownership. I disallowed those lands with questionable title which his father had demanded be his when he reconciled his differences with my brother.

The Archbishop sent his aide to ask for an audience. I needed the Archbishop's talents and experience, and I welcomed the opportunity to renew our friendship. At the appointed hour he arrived, nattily dressed, his flaming crimson cape fastened at his neck, and kneeling, he kissed my hand. It was good to see him again. Childish and churlish he may be, still I looked upon him as a father figure. He had been my benefactor during those turbulent years when there were few I could trust, and grateful always I would be.

I could sense his anxiety as I motioned him to sit nearby. To put him as ease I assured him that I wanted to forget the past and make a fresh start. His vast lands and cities were his. I wasn't certain that he was listening to my words. It was a few seconds before his look of desperation had changed to relief and a smile spread across his face. Now relaxed, I drew him into a conversation touching upon the changes Ferdinand and I had already made and explaining new directions we hoped to lead. I reassured him that my administration would be in need of his vast experience and would call upon him often. Nodding in agreement he sat quietly and made appropriate comments now and then. When it was time for him to leave, I knew we had made our peace.

Liberty and justice for all was my command as I crisscrossed the country to establish fairness and restore property to the rightful owners. The robber-knights were still flexing their power in the north. Ferdinand and I decided to gather a small military force and travel into Galicia which was still a stronghold of tyranny. Before our departure I had seamstresses busy stitching night and day making the style of dress worn by the women there. The necklines of every dress encircled my throat. The sleeves puffed out from the shoulders but fitted tight from the elbow to the wrist. The high waistlines began just below my breasts. My favorite bright colors of red, yellow, purple and royal blue were never worn in Galicia. The women dressed in grey. My new gowns were either grey or a shade of grey-blue. I took no jewels with me because none seemed to look right with those dresses. When I arrived in Galicia, I borrowed pieces of jewelry from the various noblemen's wives, always returning it to them along with my gift of a diamond broach, bracelet or ring.

The most notorious noble in Galicia was Alvaro Yanez de Lugo. De Lugo was brought to trial for capital crimes and convicted. In a desperate attempt to bargain his way to freedom, he offered me 40,000 doblas of gold! I swallowed and stiffled a gasp -- 40,000 doblas of gold was more than the Crown's annual rents. Ferdinand and some of my aides strongly urged me to accept it. Instead, the law of the land took its course. Refusing the bribe I committed de Lugo to a long term in prison.

We had made no progress in getting Portugal to sign a peace treaty. Ferdinand and I were concerned that France might decide to invade our northern borders and were convinced that we should negotiate a peaceful treaty with King Louis XI as a protection for this border. We had been anxiously waiting for word from our French envoy, and while still in the north we received a communique that France had agreed to our proposal.

Quickly assembling our royal contingency, we set out for the northern border to meet the French, solidify our friendship and sign the document. All went well, and we were ready to depart from the northern provinces to return to Segovia. We had not seen our little daughter for many months and we were looking forward to a much needed rest.

While many nobles had stepped forward there were some in the north and three or four very powerful ones in the south remaining independent and threatening. The total establishment of the Crown's authority was to be the major cornerstone for the future. Ferdinand and I decided to take a firm stand against them. He would march north over the Guadarrama mountains and contain the northerners, while my contingency of soldiers would ride south into Estremadura and Andalucia.

Estremadura lay just to the east of Portugal with one of its major border cities being Trujillo. This kingdom had been the center for Villena's power and many still insisted upon recognizing his authority and jurisdiction as absolute. After the Cortes had passed the laws forbidding large fortresses to remain standing, Ferdinand and I sent forth the communiques demanding their demolition. Upon receiving his notice, the hard-headed Alcayde of Trujillo, Pedro de Baeza, threatened revolt.

I departed with my troops and as we crossed over the mountain passes I realized why each of the kingdoms in both Old and New Castile had been successful in retaining their independence from the Crown. The mountainous terrain separated the kingdoms. Traveling along the impossible roads I made a mental note that as quickly as possible we would begin to build new bridges, new roads and new way stations for travelers which would make it easier to access our Castilian outposts.

It was the middle of June, the weather hot and sticky, and in many ways it was a more difficult and tiring ride than traversing the northern area. As we cantered along the deeply rutted roads, I never tired of the landscape. There were groves after groves of well tended olive trees. I knew that the harvests this year would be good for we had been blessed with a lot of rain. The bright June sunshine would bring out the best in the olive trees dotting the entire countryside. We traveled south on course and then turned west. After five full days of long, hard riding, we saw the tall, dark, stony towers of Trujillo off in the distance. I sent the Alcayde a polite but firm note asking him to deliver the Alcazar and the city to me. Baeza snapped back, "I have no intention of turning the Alcazar or the city over. Instead, I will defend it to death, and dare you to advance one step closer."

I was given no choice. I sent back my note saying, "Am I to obey the law that one of my subjects presumes to lay before me and fail to chastise that which he thinks to put up? Shall I not come to my own city? Certainly no good King ever did so -- nor will I!"

Promptly exchanging action for words, I sent a courier racing toward the Master of Calatrava's estates several miles away. Then I positioned my light cannon and even a few lombards directly behind me. The Calatrava troops and three thousand horses arrived the next day. As a precautionary measure I directed the neighboring castles around Trujillo to be surrounded and sealed off.

Sizing up his precarious position Baeza now sent me another message saying that he would hand the Alcazar and the city over only to Marquis de Villena because he considered him to be the legal owner. I was not happy with that communique but decided to contact Villena and ask him to join with me and together we would approach Baeza.

Villena and I gathered the troops of the Calatrava Order behind us and triumphantly marched into the city, direct to the steps of the Alcazar where Baeza, his eyes filled with tears, delivered the city of Trujillo and the keys of the Alcazar into my hands.

Wasting no time we directed our course toward another center of insubordination -- Caceres. Situated only forty leagues from Trujillo, the news of my victory had gone before me. Before two kneeling scribes at the Puerta Nueva, I swore to respect their ancient rights and the laws of their city. Now having fulfilled my obligation to them, I insisted the citizens fulfill theirs to me. Setting my royal standards, I promptly began the imposition of sovereign will. I stripped the intimidating officials from their powerful positions and appointed twelve new councilmen. Those families who had ignored orders to stop molesting their neighbors were brought into line by the simple tactic of reducing their houses to one story and bricking up the arrow-slots and gun emplacements of their roofs. Firm though I was, I moved with tact and caution.

I took time to mend, with my own hands, the town's sadly tattered ancient banner. I strolled among the display of fresh fruit and vegetable stands on market day, and talked with the craftsmen who had set up their stalls for business. For nearly three weeks I subtly commanded their attention.

It was nearly August when I left Caceres and began my journey to the kingdom of Andalucia. With the success of the submission of the two test cities of Trujillo and Caceres, I had demonstrated the Crown's unalterable rule over the land.

Pleased as I was, I had anxious thoughts riding eastward through Estremadura for I was now going to confront two independent, hot-tempered nobles who had fought each other with a passionate flair of military astuteness. Each was defiant of the Crown's authority. Each, I knew, was a formidable foe.

Several years earlier when the civil skirmishes engulfed the nation during Enrique's reign, Enrique de Guzman, the Duke de Medina Sidonia, had sworn his support and allegiance to me. Now I was puzzled, for I knew not where his loyalties might lie. It was a dangerous course I was taking, but I steadfastly knew it was a right course for Castile.

I chose to first confront the Duke de Medina Sedonia in Sevilla. When I reached the Guadalquivir river on July 24th, a tapestried barge, sent by the Duke, was docked and waiting for me and the next day I made my State entry into the capital. Standing at the Macarena, the mighty Duke de Medina Sedonia handed to me the keys of the Alcazar. Onward we paraded through the ancient streets designed by the Moors, its arches hung with bright silk banners. Then the magnificent fabled Arabian Alcazar I had heard so much about now loomed before me.

While the city of Sevilla threw itself into the celebrations, I quietly studied my nagging problem -- it was the Duke. He had provided great pomp and ceremony but delivered none of his formidable fortresses to me.

A few days after my arrival he made an appointment. Arriving promptly at his appointed time, the Duke was soon alluding to me the kingdom of Andalucia's problems were all caused by Cadiz. He emphatically insisted, "The Marquis de Cadiz is not content with continuously stirring up sedition against the Crown, he is also guilty of aligning himself with the Portuguese and 'La Beltraneja.' The shocking state of Andalucia's lawlessness riddled with robberies, rape and murder are all the fault of the Marquis."

I was listening carefully, turning over in my mind every word he uttered. The Duke paused for a moment, and sensing that I was not going to make a comment, he continued saying, "Let me assure your Highness my loyalty to the Crown is implicit. I urge you to promptly take appropriate measures against the Marquis de Cadiz."

I very carefully weighed every word the Duke said and then decided to skirt around it when I responded. "The execution of justice is precisely why I have come to the kingdom of Andalucia. I fully intend to uphold your rights and honor." Then sitting up very straight in my chair, I looked into his eyes and said, "But you will do well to see that none of your troops get out of hand." He nodded his head and I knew he understood exactly what my words meant.

Deciding the situation with the Duke could be negotiable, I now turned my concern toward the feisty Cadiz. The reports I received about him were unfavorable. Rumors abounded that he had backed Alfonso in the war with Portugal. He was Villena's brother-in-law. It was the bitter rivalry between Sidonia and Cadiz which had turned Andalucia into a battlefield that truly concerned me. The outreach of the territory controlled by the Marquis stretched from Xerez to Alcala de Guadaira and beyond, and from their regional strongholds they both emerged to attack each other whenever they chose.

The days went by. The Marquis de Cadiz failed to present himself at my Alcazar in Sevilla. The Duke's friends and advisors constantly reminded me that I should take a dim view of his absence. It would have been quite correct for me to have sent him a summons, but I was hesitant. Why? I didn't know.

The state of the affairs of Castile consumed all my waking hours. Day after day, del Pulgar placed the packets which had arrived from my couriers during the night on my desk. I studied the wreckage I had inherited. How much could be salvaged? The industries had been crippled. Hundreds of towns were still exercising their independence and defying royal authority. The people were hungry. My daily reports were filled with robberies, rapes and murders. All across the land it seemed anarchy prevailed. I needed a strong foundation from which to begin bringing order out of chaos. I was convinced it would be possible through two avenues -- the submission of the nobles and the development of a strong money base for the Crown.

Early one morning I heard the welcoming shouts and greetings to a small contingency bearing the Crown's emblems. Someone had arrived on official business. Jumping down from his horse, I recognized the mannerism and walk of my Treasurer, Guiterre de Cardenas, carrying a thick packet in his hands. I was anxious to speak with him; however, I reminded myself he had been riding all night. I summoned del Pulgar to tell Cardenas I would see him immediately.

Shortly after I had appointed Gutierre the Treasurer, I had asked him to review every document that could be found tracing the lands owned by the Crown during my father and Enrique reigns that had been transferred to the nobles. I also wanted to know how much money was collected by those nobles from these considerable holdings. In the packet that he held in his hands was the compilation of the information I had requested.

Gutierre was obviously tired from his long ride, but his long strides into my working quarters assured me he was anxious to make a report. He handed me the packet saying, "It has been a weary, back-breaking, almost impossible task. The official records have been so poorly kept it was a very difficult assignment." He went on to say, "There were many local townsmen who quietly came forth to give me the missing information, and each name has been carefully recorded. Citizens stepped forward and supplied to me old, old recordings and deeds as well as vital financial information. Out of this I have been able to compile these lengthy findings."

I was so grateful for this packet of documents handed to me, and looking into his tired face I said, "Thank you, Gutierre, I know you are very tired. Please get some rest and as soon as you have had sleep and food, we will talk again. In the meantime, I will carefully study this report."

Gutierre's report was fascinating! I spread out a map of Leon and Castile and began to trace in the lands long ago owned by the Crown and the incomes they had provided. I asked Pulgar to see that I was not disturbed. I wanted no one to know that I had these vital documents in my hands. I traced property boundary outlines on the map noting the income by the nobles proclaiming ownership. Why was I doing this? At the moment I didn't know. I knew I needed to have a clear picture of what had transpired during that historic period. With the last territory sketched into place, along with the notation of its yearly income, and present owner's name noted, I studied that map. The Crown didn't have very much land left from which to collect rents. As my eyes roved over that map, my mind calculated the incomes. As I concentrated upon it, a plan began to take shape. A plan so bold and dramatic -- and equally dangerous! It was a course of direction that I knew I must take. I dispatched a courier to the north to Ferdinand. His couriers had been delivering daily reports that he had been remarkably successful in subduing the cantankerous nobles. I knew he would soon gain total control over that area. In my note to him I asked that he join me as quickly as possible in Sevilla.

My plan was daring, very daring, and I needed the spiritual reassurance that it was God's will. As I knelt in prayer I felt the same warm glow that I had experienced when I decided to ask the church to lend me their money for the Portuguese crisis. That had brought Castile victory. Now this plan could secure the foundation stones I needed for the nation.

Late one night in August a sentry sent word to me the Marquis de Cadiz was at the gate of the Alcazar seeking a midnight audience. The sentry added, "Cadiz has just arrived from Xerez and seems very anxious to speak with your Highness." Gutierre, del Pulgar and I had been studying the current tax collections, determining where certain funds should be allocated, where it appeared our collection efforts were weak, and in general attempting to grasp control over a wobbly economy. I looked up at del Pulgar and Gutierre and said, "Why not?" Gutierre didn't object and as was his habit by now, del Pulgar nodded his head in agreement. I decided we must give this dissident Marquis an impressive welcome. I dispatched an order for three of my ladies-in-waiting to be awakened and told to dress in their finest gowns. I sent another aide to bring the spectacular gold and silver candlesticks and placed them on a table. I dressed in a deep red silk brocade gown, wearing my silver crown, the ruby and pearl necklace Ferdinand had given to me as my wedding gift. I was ready to give this bold, brash, unpredictable noble a royal welcome.

As my page swung the door open the Marquis and his three aides made a dramatic entrance. Cadiz wore a flaming red jacket, yellow shirt and royal blue trousers. His polished black boots shone as bright as a reflecting mirror. His confidence was evident with every move as he knelt to kiss my hand. His curly red hair, blue eyes and fair complexion was a distinct departure from the black hair and olive skin of the other nobles -- and he was young, just about my age. I don't

Trastamara of Castile Family Crest

Crown of Ysabella

Queen Mother with Children in Court

Alcazar of Segovia

Segovia Thrones of Ysabella and Ferdinand

Alcazar of La Moto

Ysabella

Ferdinand

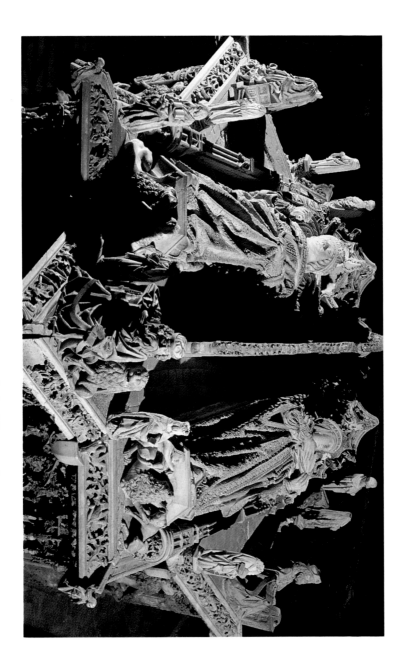

Sepulchres of Juan II and Isabel of Portugal

Ysabella and Ferdinand Entering Granada

Courtyard of Lions - Alhambra

Christobol Colon

Colon Meets Ysabella and Ferdinand

...nk my astonishment was apparent; however, this man kneeling before me was a gentlemen of culture, intellect and a charmer. I waited for him to speak.

Still kneeling before me, in soothing, well modulated tones, he boldly presented his case. "Most powerful Queen, you see me here in your hands. I beg of you, execute the wrath and indignation in which my enemies, with their lies, have put against me. I am here with no safeguard of my own innocence, nor do I come to speak words. I come to act. Since, your Highness, you have reconquered the fortresses of Xerez and Alcala, and if other fortresses of my own patrimony can serve you, I will order them delivered to you, as I deliver my person."

This was not the aloof, distant, and non-cooperative noble I had heard so much about. My inner thoughts raced. I was so pleased with the submission of this formidable personage, I decided not to render him accountable for his former activities of conspiring against the Crown. Thanks to Gutierre's timely report, I knew exactly where his activities had been directed. Out of the corner of my eye I caught the half smile on Gutierre's face and his look of total approval as I calmly proceeded to extract from Cadiz the property and fortresses he had filched from the Crown and the city of Sevilla. There was an incredulous expression of surprise on his face as I recounted his activities, using dates, areas, and the exact sums of money that he had illegally gained. Finally, he nodded in agreement -- but only on one condition -- "That your Highness study the property the Duke de Medina Sidonia has also stolen. When Sidonia returns his, I, Cadiz, will surrender my lands into your hands."

That ploy would give me a considerable opening

wedge to bargain with the Duke and I accepted the opportunity so deftly presented. The Marquis and his aides departed with a flourish. As the door closed behind him, I felt this dashing young hero would some day be a trusted friend.

The next morning I summoned the Duke and informed him of the midnight visit from his rival and the agreement we had made. Unable to match his enemy's bold stroke, Medina sat down to a lengthy meeting. Gutierre sat confidently by my side as step by step I pointed out the land he had stolen, yearly income which had made the Duke ever richer, and when each transaction had taken place. A look of absolute astonishment covered his face. Bowing, he assured me the Alcazar and all of the fortresses would be turned over. Now all of Andalucia and Estremadura were mine.

I arranged for a lavish banquet honoring the Duke and the Marquis, presenting them face to face in a civilized setting. They were polite, cautious and distantly cool to each other. I hoped they would bury their grievances against each other and become friends. As I watched their demeanor, I realized that in all probability they would remain enemies for life, but this reconciliation would bring to an end the rape and pillage of Andalucia.

Ferdinand joined me at Sevilla in September. We strolled through the magnificent gardens with tinkling fountains, met the townspeople, reviewed their City council and replaced those that had hastily been appointed during Enrique's tenure. We were beginning to mold the future shape of the nation.

Far into the night we discussed our plans. When I revealed my next step, Ferdinand looked at me as if I were a little "loco." I never for a moment hesitated to give him a chance to discredit my scheme. He listened quietly. He shook his head "no" dozens of times because it was a move too incredible to believe would work. I was confident and determined it was right for Castile. In the end he reluctantly agreed to support it, and I knew it was with grave misgivings. True, it was a gamble -- a dangerous gamble -- but I was willing to stake "my Crown" that it was going to work.

We decided upon the wisdom of appointing Alonso de Cardenas to keep the "watch" over the Order of Santiago. Ferdinand would remain as the Grand Master, but the Order's affairs would be administered by Cardenas. This workable plan became the cornerstone governing our policy for the future of the two remaining Orders when Ferdinand was elected as their Grand Master. Ultimately it gained for us the masterful control of major segments of church politics and power.

Our plans were now set, we packed up our small Court and departed Sevilla on one of the Duke de Medina Sedonia's luxurious ships. The Admiral, the Constable, the Cardinal and the Duke de Alba had ridden into Sevilla and joined with us as we moved about the southern peninsula.

We sailed up the Guadalquivir river to Sanlucar where Duke de Medina Sidonia entertained us in great splendor. From Sanlucar we traveled to Rota where the Marquis de Cadiz presented me with a pair of gold candlesticks and a glimmer of his lavish lifestyle. The banquet he presided over was as opulent, perhaps more so, than the Duke's. The southerners definitely had a far more luxuriant social lifestyle than the northern nobles. At Xerez we mounted our horses and were homeward bound, traveling at a leisurely pace towards Segovia.

A dispatch was waiting for me upon my arrival

informing me that Portugal's King Alfonso, still licking his wounded pride and battle scars, had traveled to France in an attempt to interest Louis XI in joining with him in a conflict against Castile. Totally defeated, he left in haste when the French revealed to him they had signed a friendly Treaty with us just weeks before his appearance in France. I put the communique aside with a confident feeling that my statesmanship and political instincts had been correct. With a prayer on my lips, I asked that my next bold move would prove fruitful.

The next few days I was preoccupied overseeing the invitations that were being carefully hand printed and inspecting the special pouches with our new royal crest emblazoned on the outside ready for official use. Inside the royal pouch went an invitation to every noble in Castile and Leon. Ferdinand and I were inviting them to a "gathering of the nobles" in Toledo. It wasn't just an invitation, it was a summons and a royal command their presence was required.

Far into the night I worked on the plans for the banquets, the housing of the nobles when they arrived in Toledo and the Court. Ferdinand and I had agreed we would have an impressive lavish Court personified in stateliness with grandeur. This was to be our first royal presentation with all the pomp and splendor of two Monarchs, standing together, in total control and ruling the land.

After our victory at Toro I had made a vow to God I would found a Monastery in His name. I had chosen a site in the gothic city of Toledo, giving it the simple name of "Monastery of San Juan de los Reyes." Traveling to the city earlier, Ferdinand and I had laid the Portuguese armor stripped from Duarte de Almeida before the tomb of my grandfather, Enrique III.

There were reasons why I chose Toledo for my delicate but risky political venture. I wanted to preside over the dedication ceremonies of the breaking of the ground for the Monastery which was to be built on the northern part of the high plateau. The plateau proved to be a well chosen area for a fortress to be built. The entire plateau was a teaming city surrounded by deep valleys dotted with trees, olive groves, and blessed with rich soil, rain and warm sunshine. Toledo was a city with a great history and its impressive Alcazar and surrounding courtyard would contain all of the invited guests.

Nobles began arriving in Toledo with their special escorts, bright banners flying in the breeze, astride their silver bridled high bred horses and accompanied by an array of prominent hidalgos and gifted musicians. I had carefully made my plans. As soon as my lookout man spotted a retinue in the far distant horizon, he ran with word to the stables and the king and Queen's small envoy raced to meet them, with great pomp and circumstance they were escorted through the gates of the city direct to the steps of the Alcazar where they were met by my officials and delivered inside. Ferdinand and I, dressed in our royal robes, greeted them one by one. They left with smiles on their faces, looking forward to promised festivities. As they exchanged greetings with other noblemen who were arriving, they all spoke in amazement of this "gathering of the nobles" for in all their memories, this had never been.

The Monastery dedicated, the banquet behind me, the nobles were now invited to gather the next day in The Cathedral which had been dedicated by Saint Ferdinand centuries ago. At the appointed time the nobles arrived at The Cathedral relaxed and full of happy anticipation.

I had prepared for this day carefully. My white satin gown was simple in style, the royal ermine cloak placed around my shoulders, and the Crown of Saint Ferdinand firmly placed on my head. In my hand I held the royal scepter. Ferdinand's kingly attire was just as carefully chosen. He wore a royal blue jacket and trousers trimmed in gold, and on his head he placed the emerald and sapphire crown King Juan of Aragon had given him at the time of my coronation. In his hand was the sword of justice. At the appointed hour, the royal pages announced our personages and with a roll of the drums, the trumpeter sounding the call, we descended into their midst and walking to the center of The Cathedral we stood before them, their king and Queen. The nobles responded as they rose to their feet proclaiming, "Castile! Castile! for king Don Fernando and the Proprietress of these realms, Queen Dona Ysabella!"

I motioned for them to be seated and after a moment or two of hesitation Ferdinand sat down in the gold chair provided for him. Still standing before them, I spoke. "Ferdinand and I, from our hearts, thank each of you for coming to Toledo and taking part in the healing of our nation's wounds, and rebuilding old friendships that somehow became estranged in the course of hostilities. Now we must all work together for the common good of all." Looking into their faces, I noted they were an attentive group. I went on. "All of our kingdoms, from the north, east, south and west have been embroiled in civil war for fifty years. Now we must put our kingdoms, our cities, our townships and our courts in order. For any nation to have a great future I believe it must be strong and dominant at home and on the international scene as well. The fulfillment of my dream will come when we reconquer Granada!" The nobles sprang to their feet and the great Cathedral chamber echoed with their shouts of approval.

Motioning for them to again be seated, my voice full and confident, I went on saying, "I stand before you, my brave and distinguished noblemen, knowing I must be very frank. If our nation is to become strong and dominant, I must ask everyone to make personal sacrifices. Without your sacrifices, our future will be dim, very dim indeed. I do have a plan -- a plan that will affect every family, every citizen." I looked around the room and noticed a few were shifting in their seats, their arms reaching for their swords, crossing and uncrossing their legs. I carefully measured my next words, as my voice remained firm and notably controlled. "I am today asking every noble to return to the Crown lands that were illegally transferred into your estates during the reigns of my father, King Juan II and my brother, Enrique IV."

The nobles immediate response was total silence. It was so quiet I was certain I could hear Ferdinand breathing. I broke the stillness as I made the quick decision to recount to them some of the noblemen's dishonest deeds. "For fifty years the rape of this nation by the nobles has left it in a state of utter wreckage. Together we must build a solid foundation with the firm administration of our government backed by a sound monetary policy. You, my good nobles, must return to the Crown your ill-gotten gains!" The carefully documented report that Gutierre had prepared was etched into my memory. In his thoroughness, Guiterre had included stories behind the transactions -- some which I thought were ludicrous, ridiculous and utterly shameful. I was watching them, carefully reading the expressions on their faces and understanding the reasons why they now shifted in their seats. They were uneasy -- but they remained silent. I wasn't ready for them to file out of The Cathedral without their acquiescence of my plan. I raised my voice to make myself clearly understood as I continued. "During Enrique's reign there was the unfortunate division among nobles. Some of you deserted him to claim the Throne for my younger brother, Alfonso. Two nobles who supported Alfonso, and sitting before me in my person today, discovered you had been outwitted by another powerful nobleman. You then presented yourselves before King Enrique in Madrid professing your loyalty to him. He believed you! He was so happy to have your prestigious support he placed into your hands several deeds to valuable properties that he knew you each coveted. You took the deeds to those properties, left immediately for your new dominions to get those deeds properly recorded at the Town Halls, and then you returned to my young brother's side." The nobles began to look around the room to see if they could discover which nobles had accomplished such a clever act of deceit. Admiral Fadriques de Hernandez remained quiet, the expression on his face never changing. The Archbishop of Toledo's face flushed bright red to the very roots of his white hair, but he, too, remained docile and quiet. I went on, "During my father's reign many of you hired the most dangerous men to be found -- men who robbed, raped and murdered! With each robbery they committed you became richer. With each murder you annexed that murdered man's property to yours leaving the murdered man's widow and children to become scavengers in the streets of our cities. You continued to support the actions of those savage robbers to the extent that using your private troops you stormed the fortresses which had been built by the Crown to protect citizens of the city. You evicted the law abiding guards from the fortresses and installed your robber-barons. From the strategically important vantage points of the fortresses those robber-barons could observe every person who came into, or went out of the city.

"More than anything else, I'm certain that my father and brother wanted to have peace among the nobles and they bought their peace, by giving away -- piece by piece -- the Crown's land. This was the great price our distinguished nobles placed upon the heads of our Kings for peace. Today, nobles in the far off kingdom of Murcia and Estremadura reign as if they had conquered the kingdom." The stunned nobles remained silent as I continued. Without using names, I related some of the most astonishing acts of which Castile's great nobility were guilty. I did not hesitate to use dates, name the area, and state almost to the exact maravedis of the monetary rewards gained. Each word uttered from my lips was so clearly enunciated, so directly spoken it was evident from the expression on their faces a flicker of guilt flashed across their consciousness. I observed Guiterre de Cardenas sitting to the left, his hands folded across his chest, his face serious, but I was certain he wanted to smile. At the other side of the room, the ever faithful Hernando del Pulgar's pen was racing across the pages of his note pad, historically documenting this occasion.

"The noblemen of Castile and Leon have brought dishonor to their noble inheritance. By your very actions you have disgraced a glorious noble heritage handed down to you from your ancestors. I stand before you and state most emphatically no Monarch should consent to alienate his lands since the loss of revenue necessarily deprives him of the best means of rewarding the attachment of his friends and of making himself feared by his enemies."

I paused for a moment and before I could continue Admiral Enriques suddenly stood up and acknowledged he would turn back his land which produced more than 240,000 maravedies a year. The Duke de Alba stood up to surrender land which earned him 575,000 maravedies a year. The Duke de Medina Sidonia gingerly agreed to return land which would enrich the Crown 180,000 maravedies a year. Then Beltran de la Cueva, the Duke de Albuquerque, taking a few steps toward me and with a dramatic flourish bowed offering his lands which would bring the Crown 1,400,000 maravedies! Soon all the nobles were nodding their heads in agreement.

Next I rescinded three of their oldest aristocratic prerogatives. I forbid them from being attended by a mace-bearer or a body guard; to string their titles at the beginning of a letter and other distinguished marks of authority; or to include a crown in their shields.

This announcement struck like a thunderbolt on their ears. They were totally subdued. Suddenly, it seemed to me they all rose to their feet at once proclaiming, "Castile! Castile! for Don Ferdinand and the Proprietress of these realms Queen Dona Ysabella. Long live the Queen!"

I, Ysabella de Trastamara, had won!

CHAPTER XXV
Marvels of Change
"Tonto Monta"

I was pleased with the success of the Toledo "experience." Ferdinand was still shaking his head in disbelief, but my prayers had been answered and I felt the course we were taking to steer the nation's affairs was correct for the people.

Fernando de Talavero, a brilliant Dominican priest, and I plunged into a marathon of one on one negotiations with the nobles for the readjustment of their land and revenues. Obviously, we were both aware that some would be defiant and others would be reluctant to turn it "all" back to the Crown. We opened our negotiations with cautious optimism and diligent care, and when the last noble had returned to the Crown portions of their ill-gotten gains, the Crown's yearly income had been increased by 30,000,000 maravedies.

At the end of the war with Portugal, my heart ached for the widows and orphans whose husbands and fathers were killed serving their country. I was reviewing with Ferdinand the allocation of this additional income and commented that I would direct our Treasurer, Gutierre de Cardenas, to set aside 20,000,000 maravedies of the first year returns to be distributed to these unfortunate ones. Ferdinand jumped up from his chair, grabbed his sword which had been placed nearby and flashing it with a swift execution of hand movements, he stood before me yelling, "Twenty million maravedies for worthless citizens? You are crazy! What about my armies? I need foot soldiers, lancers, horses, cannons. My father is still under-financed and under-supplied with his continuing battles with France. I need that money for a truly just cause."

Ferdinand and I hadn't had any serious differences since we had signed the concord agreement after my coronation, and I was somewhat startled with his reaction. My mind had been made up and I quietly retorted, "Ferdinand, your father will always need men, arms and ammunition. He will never negotiate a peaceful settlement. These widowed women and fatherless children are the innocent victims of a war that you and I did not start. Now that we have the monetary means to help them, we absolutely must do so."

Ferdinand's inner rage was boiling over and he snarled, "Where in Satan's Hell did you come up with that sordid plan? Who on this earth ever heard of a Monarch giving money to widows and orphans after a war had been won? You will make me a victim of such gossip among my fellow troops and Aragon nobles, I will never be able to return to Aragon!"

I didn't have a comment for that, and pointing his sword at me he blurted, "You -- you must be mad! You must have inherited your mother's insanity. I tell you -- if you give all that money to those worthless citizens your own nobles will rise up and destroy you." With that said, he picked up his riding whip and left my presence.

I sent for Gutierre and after reviewing some other important financial matters, I suggested we discuss the allocation of the 30,000,000 maravedies. In my heart I knew my desire to help those widows and orphans was right, but I thought I should tactfully review my decision with Gutierre, and I simply stated to him, "Gutierre, I want you to allocate 20,000,000 maravedies for the widows and orphans of our war with Portugal." I watched the expression on his face. He looked at me and started to shake his head "No". Then he said, "Give to the orphans and widows, your Highness? Really, I'm not certain that I can remember that this has ever been done in our history. Why should we do this? When I make my lists of areas that need immediate attention which this money could be used for..."

I interrupted saying, "Yes, Gutierre, I know how many directions we must stretch our money, but I must always remember that these widows and orphans are having a very difficult life. By the will of God I am their Monarch. I must look after them to the very best of my ability. Gutierre, I do know how difficult life can become when a father dies. My own father died when I was three years old and we were left penniless. I had a very bleak childhood. My dear mother is mentally ill, and I know in my heart that the shock she experienced with the death of my father and being cast out of her home and packed off to Arevalo is the root cause for her illness today. Gutierre, I know from my own life experience how difficult it is when the father is gone." Gutierre was listening carefully to me, but I thought he wasn't totally convinced, so I added, "You know, my good friend, that when we give each of these widows a certain sum of money they will buy food, shoes, clothing, window shutters, mules, and some may even buy a little fruit and vegetable stand. When they make purchases this money is then distributed to the shop keepers and it helps them to become prosperous. We won't be helping just the widows and orphans we will help many businesses, too."

Gutierre was quiet for a minute or two, thinking over everything I said, and then shaking his head and smiling, "Yes, when you think of all the avenues this 20,000,000 maravedies will be spread all over Castile, it will help the economy in many ways. We'll do it, but I feel that I must again remind you, never in our history has this ever been done!"

I smiled at that and commented, "Never in our history had we placed tents, medical supplies, and doctors on the battlefield. Because we did, there are many fathers still alive taking care of their families. This action we take for the widows and orphans will be another first time in Castile's history. Change we must make to build a better future for all the people."

I was still ever mindful that I must pay back to the church the 30,000,000 maravedies I had borrowed to mount the offensive against Portugal and working with Cardenas, we developed a workable timetable to repay this debt.

The last thought that crossed my mind before I dropped off to sleep, and the first thought when I awakened was, "How could I protect the people from the lawless robbers and thieves that were everywhere?" In my prayers I asked to be given the wisdom and guidance to take constructive, permanent measures for their safety.

We needed to reform the administration of justice. For as long as I could remember anarchy had prevailed. The authority of the Monarchy and its judges had fallen into such ill repute laws were not being enforced. Bandits and thieves still roamed the cities and countryside plundering the property of others. Citizens were not safe in the streets or on the roads. Our churches and holy sanctuaries were being desecrated. Our Monarchs had built fortresses scattered throughout our cities to protect our people. Those fortresses had been seized by the nobles and their mercenaries to become their headquarters. It seemed every man's hand was lifted against his neighbor.

My grandfather, Enrique III, had implemented a police force he called the "Santa Hermandad" -- Holy Brotherhood. That wise and brilliantly conceived institution brought criminals swiftly to justice stabilizing the nation and there was peace for the people during his short reign. Grandfather died at the young age of twenty eight and my father, only ten years old, became the young King. I decided to revive the "Holy Brotherhood" and presented my recommendations for review, debate and passage by the Cortes which I convened in Madrigal at the end of the year.

Wanting to secure and solidify the foundation for the Hermandad's power, Ferdinand, I and the Cortes met at Duenas to develop a plan for a general junta to be made up of deputies from the cities throughout the kingdom. The junta would meet once a year to review the regulation of the nation's affairs. When new regulations were passed, the junta would instruct the provincial junta who were then responsible for overseeing the execution of new laws and regulations.

The criminals, swift and fleet footed, had an uncanny ability to race from a city and disappear somewhere in the countryside after they had committed a crime. The crimes of breaking into a home, rape, and the resistance of justice now came under the jurisdiction of the Hermandad and junta as new laws of the land.

The villagers quickly elected the "watchmen"

who would sound their trumpets as soon as a crime was detected. Those trumpet calls would alert the Hermandad who quickly mounted their horses and the chase was on. The Brotherhood had officers stationed at different points who would take up the hot pursuit so promptly a criminal had no chance to escape.

A court with two justices was established in every town comprised of thirty families. These courts brought thieves to trial for their crimes. The capital offense of murder was brought before a supreme council.

The Cortes established there should be a yearly voluntary contribution of 18,000 maravedies from every one hundred householders. This money would be used to pay the salaries of the Brotherhood, purchase fleet footed horses, equipment and in general, cover the overall expenses of the Brotherhood.

Towns which refused to pay their voluntary contributions were simply excluded from the protection of the Hermandad and for years some of them refused to participate. Others were soon won over by the success of the experiment wherever it was tried.

I thought about the reactions of the nobles to this dramatic departure from "business as usual." I kept my weary horse saddled, planning to travel into every territory from north to south, east to west, and all points in between to admonish, cajole, coax, discuss and announce in bold, frank language the new laws which had been invoked.

In making my preparations for my first foray into those unchartered waters, Ferdinand and I asked Beatriz to once again look after our little Ysabel. It was a heartbreaking decision, but one I felt I had no other choice but to make. In later years, I was to discover neglecting my tiny daughter while I tried to bring order out of the chaos I had inherited was a very dear price to pay.

There was no time to waste. I saddled my horse, mounted and was off, racing against the wind to the northern province to see my good friend the Count de Haro, Constable of Castile. Haro was a nobleman with great authority, personal integrity and the largest landowner in Leon. I presented my cause and Haro immediately adopted the reforms. Under his leadership, other noblemen of lesser note followed. One by one, as I traveled from one nobleman's domain to another presenting the laws, they capitulated. Haro's open support encouraged the Duke de Medina Sidonia and the Marquis de Cadiz in Andalucia to accept the change, as did the Marquis de Villena in Estremadura. Before that historic year had ended, I had crisscrossed my realm, meeting with the nobles and the people. Little by little, segment by segment, kingdom by kingdom, we gained control over the land.

By the end of the year we had effectively organized a standing body of two thousand troops, thoroughly equipped and mounted on the swiftest of horses, ready at a moment's notice to enforce the laws and suppress domestic insurrection. Within just a few years the country's bands of roving banditti and robber chieftains were no more.

Ferdinand had wisely chosen Quintanilla to be the Chief Deputy of the Santa Hermandad. Enthusiastic and tireless, he carried out the reform against the violent objections of some of the nobles. Many nobles were opposed to the Brotherhood by their simple reasoning it had failed when my half-brother had attempted it in 1465. Others decided it was too expensive, and still others saw it as a clever manipulation to forge an alliance between the Crown and the common man.

The fleet footed Santa Hermandad soon became a formidable foe against crime. There were certain nobles who had secretly thought that, once again, the Holy Brotherhood would soon wither and die. Under the able stewardship of Ferdinand and Quintanilla, it soon became very clear to those nobles, who had quietly retained and restrained their mercenaries, something must be done. The Duke de Infantado and other nobles wrote to us requesting we abolish the Hermandad. They cited that keeping such a police force was too expensive for the people to bear. They suggested a Council of Nobles be formed, responsible for the "general direction" of the affairs of state. The Council's advice would be given to Ferdinand and me and after having been given such advice, we would be so governed in all matters of importance -- just as was done during Enrique IV's reign.

Ferdinand and I were mortified. I drafted a haughty reply informing them, "The Hermandad is an institution most salutary to the nation and is approved as such. It is our province to determine who are best entitled to preferment, and to make merit the standard of it. You may follow the Court, or retire to your estates, as you think best; but so long as Heaven permits us to retain the rank with which we have been entrusted, we shall take care not to imitate the example of Enrique IV in becoming a tool in the hands of our nobility."

The high-minded Lords were so startled with this rebuke they each made their way to Valladolid to make their peace with us.

There was another faction objecting strenuously to the new reforms of change. It was the Jewish community. Many of them had publicly renounced Judaism and had taken the required Catholic instruction and were publicly worshiping in our Catholic cathedrals and churches. These converted Jewish citizens were soon to be called the "conversos."

The Hermandad soon became an effective branch of the government bringing justice into focus, a distinct contrast from all the turmoil of prior years. The Hermandad commanded a network of Brothers who effectively devised ways to capture criminals. Ferdinand worked tirelessly with every segment of government, crisscrossing the land helping to implement the change and meting out the strong sentences.

I was overly anxious about every detail of the reforms being carried out "to the letter" and personally involved myself in superintending the execution. Through it all, it seemed that my presence conveyed a certain sense of respect for my integrity and well-being to the people, all of which helped to bring about the reforms.

Overseeing the administration of justice in Segovia was my confidant and husband of my dearest friend Beatriz, Andres de Cabrera. Cabrera was such a firm and persuasive administrator that some of the principal citizens became so unhappy they decided to cause an insurrection by conspiring against him. They inflamed a select group of people who in turn incited the tempers of a great many others. Soon they were gathering in angry groups in the streets of the city to march against the Alcayde. Taking possession of the outside quarters of the Alcayde's residence, they soon had their blocade barriers in place.

Beatriz, disguised as a peasant, stole out through a side gate at the back entrance and circling around on a plodding mule escaped the mob. She rode through the city toward a trusted friend's home where she exchanged the mule for a swift horse and galloped toward Tordesillas where I was discharging justice. As soon as she related the crisis to me, my horse was saddled and along with Cardinal Mendoza, the Count de Benavente and a few others of my Court, we were off to Segovia. Reaching the outskirts of the city we were met by a group of friendly citizens who stopped us. Looking directly at me, they suggested in very bold words I should leave the Count de Benavente and Beatriz behind for they would not be responsible for the consequences if anything should happen to them.

I drew a deep breath, straightened myself in the saddle, and in a very haughty voice stated, "I am the Queen of Castile; the city of Segovia is mine by the right of inheritance. I do not receive conditions made by rebellious subjects." With that said we made our way into the city and entered the grounds of the Palace through an undetected gate.

Safely inside, we quickly dismounted. My little daughter was within and I was anxious to make certain she was safe from harm. We rushed up the steps and as the doors of the Palace safely closed behind us, I beheld Andres holding my little daughter in his arms as well as frightened servants who had gathered at the entrance praying for the end of the crisis. I grabbed Ysabel into my arms, for she sensed the tenseness of the situation. Everyone was waiting for something to happen. I looked into their faces and realized that I was the only person to calm the storm clouds gathering at the gate. I asked everyone to be calm and to remain inside. Then I turned and motioned for an aide to open the doors of the Palace for me and commanded him to stay safely inside with the rest of the household.

The angry crowd which had grown larger outside the Palace gates was beginning to get rowdier and louder, making threats, calling out "Death to the Alcayde! Attack the Palace!" Inside the courtyard were a few anxious, visibly frightened gate keepers. They had barricaded the entrance gates from inside and were preparing to add reinforcements. I motioned for them to pull down the barricades and open the gates. Their reaction was to stare at me in stunned silence. I commanded them, "In the name of the Crown, I, Ysabella de Trastamara, command those gates be opened."

The barriers were removed and as the gates slowly swung open the angry crowd with stones and large clubs in their hands, screaming at the top of their lungs, surged through the gates. Suddenly they realized there was only the lone figure of a woman standing in the middle of the courtyard waiting. They stopped and became quiet.

In a clear, firm voice that rang out over the crowded courtyard, I said to them, "I am your Queen. Tell me, what is the problem? Is there a grievance which I need to know about? If so, I'll do everything in my power to correct it. Believe me when I say that everything that is of interest to you must interest me also. Your concern for your city is my concern, too."

The angry crowd's reaction to my first direct confrontation and response was so unexpected, I faced a speechless audience. I looked directly at a big, surly, angry man standing in front of me. He was breathing heavily and held an oversized club in his work-worn hands. Walking up to him, I asked, "You speak for your people. Tell me, what is wrong?"

The angry man blurted, "The Alcayde, it's

Alcayde Andres de Cabrera. He's illegally arresting and sentencing innocent people. He's confiscating our possessions. We want him removed from office."

In a quiet, firm voice, I replied. "He is deposed already, and you have my authority to turn out any of his officers within his home. I shall entrust this directly to be carried out by one of my own servants that I can totally rely on."

The shocked citizens' automatic response to that unexpected promise was to lift their clubs and stones over their heads and joyously proclaim, "Long live the Queen!" Then trooping out of the courtyard, they marched through the now quiet city, the stillness broken by the echoes of their shouts, "Long live the Queen!"

After turning the edge on this angry outburst I went back into the Palace and calmed their fears. The Cardinal, Count de Benavente and a few aides accompanied me as we rode through the streets of Segovia to the stately royal residence, the Alcazar, situated on the northern hill of the city, surrounded by the black pine trees, high walls and watchtowers. Outside those gates another angry crowd had gathered. In a clear, controlled voice, I greeted them saying, "I understand your concerns and I am doing something about it. I promise you, if you have a grievance it will be looked into. I ask you to select three or four representatives to meet with me tomorrow and we will review the problems. I promise to examine and dispatch justice." With this unexpected pledge given from my lips, the mob scattered in four directions.

I asked the Cardinal, the Count and a few aides to get to the bottom of the outburst. By the next day they had traced the origin of unrest back to a jealous Bishop and a few of his associates in Segovia. Cabrera was reinstated. The crisis had ended.

Ferdinand and I made a rapid reorganization of the Consejo Real -- our Royal Council. We eliminated the weak nobles and replaced them with brilliant middle-class lawyers, theologians and technocrats. My predecessor, "Enrique, the Impotent," as he was often referred to, had also tried his hand at democratizing this high office, but his was a dismal failure because of his inverted snobbery. He made appointments to the uneducated commoners. He merely substituted one group of imbeciles with another. Ferdinand and I moved cautiously. We made the decision to appoint men with ability culled from a pool of intellects whether it be a Duke or a commoner.

By the end of 1477 we were comfortably basking in the success of the nation's progress which our changes were bringing about, and happily looking forward to the birth of our second child.

The bright warm sunshine and tropical vegetation of Andalucia seemed a perfect setting to spend the next few months. I was enamored with the profusion of bright flowers, the trees that bloomed, the smell of the night blooming jasmine, the songs of the nightingale birds and white pigeons were everywhere. We moved our Court to Sevilla to wait for the birth of our son.

Sevilla was a city swarming with dangerous criminals. The threat of anarchy seemed eminent and I knew I must take immediate action. It was time to reinstate another ancestral tradition, the "Sala de Justica," where I would personally hold court in the salon of the Alcazar and preside over the administration of justice.

The machinery was simple and direct. Access to the Queen was immediate and universal. Any citizen could come. Every Friday I seated myself on the chair of state placed on an elevated platform covered with gold cloth. I insisted that always in view was to be the "Insignia of Justica." The Council would arrange itself on the benches, to the right and left below me. The mace-bearers ushered the plaintiffs to the steps of the throne, where I listened carefully and impartially. The rich and the poor, the noble and the common man were all permitted to bring their causes and complaints before me. Sometimes I made a decision immediately, other times when I felt the matter needed to be investigated, I would appoint someone from the Council seated below me asking facts to be checked. Each aide was instructed to present their findings back to me within three days so that the people were not obliged to waste time and money.

Within two months an astonishing number of accumulated civil and criminal cases were settled. Alienated property was restored. Doubtful inheritances were cleared up. Those guilty of rape, robbery and murder were ferreted out and brought to retribution. Many were executed. Many were exiled.

There were so many offenders being brought before me receiving such swiftness of deliberation, the citizens began to take note. Sevilla, used to the law of the jungle and dagger in the night, was thunderstruck by this awesome display of legality. Some were grateful, others were terrified.

The worthy burghers of Sevilla were alarmed. They began counting the departing families and discovered nearly four thousand had already fled. Forming a committee headed by Bishop Cadiz, they implored me to remember that there was scarcely a single family living in Sevilla that had not committed some crime or other. If I continued on my quest for justice either the entire city would be imprisoned or everyone would flee. I confided to del Pulgar that enough had been accomplished and probably those remaining and not brought to trial would mend their ways. I willingly tempered justice and mercy, granting amnesty for all past offenses on the condition that a general restitution of property unlawfully seized was restored to the rightful owners.

Those six months had passed so quickly. Ferdinand and I were still planning more changes, but first we waited for the birth of our second child. All of Castile waited. We needed a son. The eyes of the country were fixed on the Alcazar when I gave birth to my only son on June 30, 1478. The nation went wild with celebration, and even in far off Sicily the jubilant crowds burst into festivities.

In the early morning of August 9th, the Court rode in state to the Cathedral for the baptism of our tiny son, Juan III, named after his two grandfathers. The Papal Nuncio, the Venitian Ambassador and the Constable Count de Haro, were his godfathers at the christening, and the beautiful Duchess de Medina Sidonia was his godmother. Ferdinand was dressed in expensive gold brocade bordered in silver, and I chose a yellow and gold gown sparkling with small jewels sewn into the lace. I spent a few sleepless nights stitching my little son's baptismal gown. I had made my daughter's baptismal dress, and from time to time my needle and thread was busy stitching into the wee hours of the morning making Ferdinand's shirt, too. Athletic Ferdinand's sleeves of his shirts ripped easily. There were times, when in my practicality, I would replace the torn sleeve with some matched fabric and he would proudly wear the shirt as if it were new.

Our new little son was blonde, blue-eyed and fair skinned. I was certain God had blessed us with an angel. It seemed so right for me to think of our little Juan as a special blessing that I often referred to him as "my angel." Ysabel still resembled my mother, and my special name for her was "my little mother."

Ferdinand and I were not totally in agreement on every issue. We each had our differing opinions, but we kept those opinions from erupting in public. Outwardly, we were one in accord with the other. His was a difficult and trying role, and there were times when he was totally miserable dealing with nobles. At the time of my coronation the Castilian nobles were determined there would be no interference from Ferdinand. Ever mindful of nobles and others casting him into "second place" I always presented papers for his signature first. Taking the paper as it was handed to me by del Pulgar, I would hand it to my husband saying, "My Lord, the king," and Ferdinand would attach his signature with the proper flourish. I knew in my heart he resented my total authority, especially when he was trying to get some noble to cooperate. They were ever so correct, polite, distant to him, and in the end would defer the matter to "the Queen." I would mount my black stallion and chase over the countryside to see the noble and take care of that unfinished business.

I chose the ladies of my Court with consummate care. It seemed that no matter how careful I was, they still indulged in that ancient, bothersome custom of gossiping. There was a time when gossip reached my ears that Ferdinand's roving eye had caught the fancy of a young lady-in-waiting in my Court. I asked del Pulgar to have it carefully and discreetly investigated, and he reported Ferdinand, indeed, was having an affair with the young lady and, in fact, she was quite pregnant. What should I do? I prayed over that dilemma, and decided to send the young woman to a remote kingdom. Later I received word that a little girl was born. I made a mental note to send the child to a convent as soon as she was old enough. A peace treaty with Portugal still had not been signed. I had an aunt in Portugal, my mother's sister, whom I had never met. Through her private couriers, Aunt Beatriz sent a note to me offering to be a mediator of peace between our two countries. My immediate response was "That's the solution!" I responded with a very positive note, assuring Aunt Beatriz that above all else, I wanted peace between our nations.

We each agreed to travel quietly, without fanfare, and meet at the border town of Alcantara. Here, two reasonable women with no jealousy, no distrust or power struggles between us sat down. In our marathon negotiations which were to last eight days, we were determined to express good faith and a sincere desire to establish cordial relations. Finally the Treaty of Peace was ready and I handed my aunt her copy. My royal envoys and I escorted her to Portugal's border where we embraced and I bid her God speed on her journey and mission for peace.

I had kept a little bit of pressure on my aunt, for after all, we had won the war. The document Aunt Beatriz returned to Portugal with was definitely written in my favor. The "Articles of Demands" was so disagreeable King Alfonso was furious. Aunt Beatriz continued exerting pressure and wore the Court and Alfonso's aides down. Six months later Alfonso "relinquished the title and attendant bearings he had assumed as King of Castile; resigned his claims to marry

'La Beltraneja;' and within six months would place the fated princess in a convent."

Receiving the news that Alfonso had at last accepted the Treaty and signed it, brought the episode to a triumphant conclusion. I had prayed God would continue to guide me in His wisdom and had applied it with vigorous direction, seconded by Ferdinand's alert vigilance. Now I was confidently and firmly in absolute possession of the Throne.

I made a vow to build a little chapel in the Cathedral of Sevilla in remembrance of the birth of my son and our peace pact with Portugal.

It was early in January, 1479, when word was brought to Ferdinand that his father had died. We left immediately for Zaragosa to attend the State funeral and the elaborate coronation ceremonies -- the crowning moment for my beloved husband when he became the King of Aragon. From that day forward we signed our papers with our full titles, "Don Ferdinand and Dona Ysabel, by the grace of God, King and Queen de Castile, de Leon, de Aragon, de Sicily, de Toledo, Valencia, Algeciras and Gibraltar, Count and Countess de Barcelona, Lords de Biscay, Duke and Duchess de Athens, Count and Countess de Roussillon and Sardinia."

Castile and Aragon were at peace. Our people were productive and happy. Together we had moved mountains, and now the rest of my dream began to take shape as we cast our eyes longingly to the south. The Moors were "occupying our ancient land of Granada." Regaining Granada for Castile had been the prize I wanted for my country since I was a little girl. I wanted to recapture it for the onward march of the Cross of our Lord, the Christ. It would take time, money, dedication and perseverance. I wanted my people to walk on the golden sands at Malaga and bask in the beauty of Alhamar's fabled Alhambra.

The subtle reminders and rumbles of Ferdinand's infidelity continued, and I decided that an emblem which would convey our love, strength of purpose, dedication and commitment to each other would be strengthened by a positive picture. I appointed an artist to design our "personal arms" and asking him to place the Latin words "Tonto Monta" -- meaning "one is equal with the other" at the top of the emblem. Then I would have a likeness of Ferdinand holding a yoke with my initials emblazoned inside the yoke, and my likeness would hold a sheaf of arrows where Ferdinand's initials were placed. The artist became a permanent member of my Court. I took him with me everywhere I went. He was kept very busy placing those "personal arms" over doorways in the various Alcazars I lived in, on pieces of furniture and in books. Wherever the Court went, we left our 'insignia' stamped everywhere.

CHAPTER XXVI
"Ordenanzas Reales"

My restless energy and grand designs for Castile's bright future spurred me ever onward. Ferdinand and I were pleased with all that had been accomplished. The Crown's authority over commoners and nobles alike was solidly affirmed. Justice for all had been imposed. From kingdom to kingdom my concern for the safety of the people was evident everywhere. Still my quest to erase the scars of injustice and wrongs suffered by them and ease their burdens burned within my breast. In the wee hours of the early mornings, when the world was still, my mind raced with ideas as I worked over State papers, sifting through the problems, area by area. There were literally hundreds of flaws that jumped out of those pages conveying a message that our old ways of governing needed to be modernized.

I had a dedicated group of well paid royal couriers who were assigned specific routes traveling to various towns and cities delivering to them the latest news from the Crown, and in turn, packets from the townspeople and the city authorities were all carefully prepared and brought to me by the same couriers. Throughout the land they cantered, galloped and raced keeping everyone abreast with news and more important -- "change!" As the packets from the courier pouches arrived, del Pulgar would scan the submittals and assign them to various governmental departments which we had devised. I'll admit I had made it a point of wanting to know about everything that was happening in the land, but the barrage of packets arriving daily discouraged me from reading them all, one by one. Those matters directly confronting the Crown's governing postures were placed before me in neat piles on a large table in my working quarters.

Traveling from kingdom to kingdom during the early years of my reign, I realized a major reason why each kingdom continued to remain so uniquely, even fiercely, independent of each other, intent upon retaining their laws, customs, and habits. It was because of the natural terrain of the land. The hills and mountains provided the barriers for each area to remain literally an enclosed kingdom. I saw the need for roads to be built to carry the farmer's products to new markets. The decaying bridges were unsafe and in need of repair, and we needed to build many more. The aqueduct bringing water to the city of Segovia which the Romans had built when they ruled the land had been destroyed by the Moors hundreds of years ago, and no Monarch had ever reconstructed it. I knew that was an important project for me to begin as quickly as possible. As the taxes and our rents increased, I appointed the appropriate committees to recommend which roads, bridges, and water aqueducts needed the earliest attention; and as those were completed, we began to build or repair more roads, bridges, safe tunnels and highway posts for the travelers to rest in at night. Access to each kingdom was made easier, helping to knit the people and our nation together.

My list of reforms was growing and I sensed it was time to think about revising the laws and literally overhauling the government. My aides were busy shaking their heads when I would bring the subject up, and smiling they would comment, "Well, yes, your Highness, it probably should be done -- and that would be yet another 'first' for Castile during your reign." Toledo was a vibrant thriving city located in the center of Castile, and I decided it was here that I would bring my Court and begin to direct the changes I had in mind. The accessing roads had been rebuilt and commerce was lively. The work on the Monastery San Juan de los Reyes had begun in earnest and I wanted to oversee all the details of its interior and exterior designs.

We arrived in Toledo in late September of 1479 happily looking forward to the birth of our third child. Our second daughter, Juana, was born on November 6th, 1479 in the palace of the Count de Cifuentes in Toledo. It was Juana who was to eventually inherit my Crown and ultimately become part of Spain's bitterest hours.

We began the new year, 1480, assembling the most formidable array of brilliant, dedicated men in the history of the Cortes. The foundation for a prosperous and peaceful nation evolved and was to become known throughout Europe as perhaps the most famous of the entire Middle Ages. The cornerstones for the splendor and prosperity of the final decade of my rule could be attributed to this brilliant group of men, the Cortes of Toledo, meeting that spring and summer.

We divided the Cortes into five Royal Councils which included thirty-four civilian representatives of the Cortes. The Royal Councils met often with Ferdinand and me. I undertook the total supervision of this remarkable work that was to go forward, placing my own influence, ideas, thoughts, suggestions in every area of that governing body. We met on a daily basis at the palace of Marquis de Villena debating, discussing, approving and codifying the social and economic reforms.

The capstones were being put on two of my most cherished dreams -- the centralization of power in the Crown and the social and economic rehabilitation of the realm. In later years, Galindez was to write, "The legislation of that brilliant Cortes of Toledo was so well weighed and executed that it seemed the divine work for the correction and resolution of past disorders." And the ever faithful secretary-historian del Pulgar wrote in his pad, "Done by the hand of God beyond all comprehension of mankind."

In six years more had been accomplished for the welfare of Castile than all its other rulers had been able to do in centuries.

Ferdinand and I signed the orders for the specific administrative changes which began to pour out in steady torrents. There would now be weekly inspections of the jails. The poor were to have legal counsel provided and paid for by the government. As I signed that decree I wondered, "Will this be another 'first' for Castile?" It was! This was a most remarkable decision for that time. My Friday court sessions which were continuing in Toledo convinced me the poor were entitled to proper legal representation. I saw the need for the government to be responsive to their needs and it was my stubborn insistence that convinced the Royal Councils to pass this law.

Judges were forbidden to accept bribes and were commanded to conduct their cases with speed and diligence. Very qualified men were selected to travel to the remote areas to oversee these new regulations and report back to the Crown of any infractions of the new rulings.

In order to tighten our central authority, the president of the Junta which governed the Santa Hermandad was made a royal appointment. The supervision of the local political structures of the towns was appropriately affected by the power of the Crown's Consejo Reales in the name of their representatives.

The economic ills of the country received my same thorough, far-sighted attention. The healthful monetary reforms instigated early in my reign when I issued Castile's new coins gave strength to the commercial credit of the banks and sustained the borrowing ability of the businessman. I sent out a barrage of specific orders which covered both domestic and foreign trade. The customs duties, the stamp tax and the famous sales tax were all regularized. Import duties on foreign books were abolished.

The law was changed giving people the freedom to move from one area to another. Cattle and merchandise were allowed to pass between Castile and Aragon without tariff. The tradesmen were indemnified and the farmer was totally free from armed robbery. The nobles were firmly under control and with the work on the nation's laws begun, I contemplated the next giant step for Castile.

Over the centuries the laws of Castile had become a tangle of contradictory provincial codes, statues and ordinances, inconsistent and impractical. The Visigoths had issued their famous "Fuero Juzgo" and Alfonso the Wise secured his reign with the issuance of the "Siete Partidas." Weak rulers following these wise men passed laws which suited their own greed. Through the ridiculous accumulation of the crazy-quilt maze, my keen intellect cut like a knife. I decided to establish a commission given the responsibility of codifying the laws for national application. My political instincts told me that when the nation began to function in a cohesive fashion, every phase of carrying out our responsibilities to the people would be systematic and correct for the good of all.

I chose one of Castile's most eminent jurisconsults, Alfonso Diaz de Montalvo, as the head of this body of men who would undertake the sorting out and regulation of the entire tangled mess. The final version of this staggering three year task was placed in my hands in 1483. The famous "Ordenanzas Reales" provided the solid lasting basis for Spanish jurisprudence.

The beginning of that decade was a historic prosperous new era for my country. It ushered in the changing tempo of economics establishing the foundation of wealth bringing it into the full blaze of resplendence during the closing years of my reign. The blaze of glory which broke over the Peninsula all began in the year of our Lord, 1480.

CHAPTER XXVII
Citizen's Discontent in Sevilla
The Inquisistion - 1478

Time was a wonderful healing balm. I studied our progress made during those extra-ordinary six years and reflected upon the care of the nation God had placed in my hands. I wanted to bring from my heart, my mind and my person the very best that was in me in order that this great responsibility might be executed with loving and responsible care. I approached my high office with dignity and sincerity. I believed in being direct and never hesitated to promptly take swift action. The great personal interest which I took in every aspect of Castilian life came from a heart that was filled with love for my people. Out of it all, I earned their respect and love.

Ferdinand inspired only respect. He was an Aragonese and by nature a more cautious and uncommitted person than I was. He had the commendable quality of being successful and this brought its own rewards in various degrees of loyalty. He was a man in a man's world. He had the strength to command obedience which I, alone, might have found impossible to enforce.

Together we united a country which my predecessors would never have believed possible. The Crown at last was in complete command. The three estates of Castile -- the nobility, the clergy and the municipalities were firmly subjected to royal authority. After fifty years of anarchy, in only six eventful years, Castile was a united kingdom.

The people still mistrusted one another. I could understand this, for after all, fifty years of lawlessness in every segment of the society could not help but sow seeds for discontent with wounds continuing to fester and blister. I had still another dream. I wanted a united people. A land of happy, prosperous and productive people working and worshiping together. There were many factions which seemed to remain isolated and outside the mainstream of Castile's heartbeat. I felt the answer was to be found in Christianity's creed of brotherhood.

I had made some progress in gaining more dominant control over the church when I personally intervened in making appointments. For years it had been the common practice for the Pope in far off Rome to make his own appointments with foreign clerics who had never before set foot in Castile. These foreign clerics had been assigned high-ranking posts by the Pope. After I ascended to the Throne, those church office vacancies were filled with scholarly Castilian ecclesiastics whose integrity I deemed worthy of a high appointment.

In Sevilla a large segment of that city was populated with Jews, a familiar race in Castile, immersing themselves into the fabric of the nation for hundreds of years. For business purposes, many found it expedient to outwardly become Catholics. Those Jews who were converted to Catholicism were known as conversos, but in the privacy of their homes they continued to practice their ancient rites of Judaism.

In 1478 Alfonso de Ojeda, Prior of the Dominican

Monastery of St. Paul in Sevilla, along with Diego de Merlo, an assistant clerk of Sevilla, brought to me a petition which required of me to create a *"Board of Inquisitos"*. I studied that petition feeling apprehension and uneasiness. The creation of a *"Board of Inquisitos"* would mandate one to determine whether or not a person was a heathen, or one who practiced the ancient rites of Judaism in their home, or even professed to follow Islamic beliefs. To insist that every person in Castile become a Catholic and worship in the same churches and cathedrals throughout the entire kingdom was not a new idea. Earlier Castilian Monarchs had tried and were unsuccessful. It was reported that early in the 1200's King Ferdinand heaped fagots on blazing flames with his own hands. Up to this time I had no inclination that the Jewish segment of our society was so unpopular and the very thought of violence and duress to be brought against them was repugnant. I made a counter proposal to Ojeda and de Merlo suggesting that it might be wiser to use persuasion rather than force.

My mind was in a turmoil. My memory raced back into the history of the Catholic inquisitions and I tried to remember when, how and why it had all begun. My study revealed the Popes had claimed the spiritual allegiance of all Christendom. They regarded heresy as treason against themselves. It was their conviction heresy was an unpardonable offence! Punishment for heresy was exclusively committed to the hands of the Dominican friars by the Pope, and in 1283, under the pontificate of Gregory the Ninth, codes for the regulation of *Ancient Inquisito* proceedings were issued which demanded impenetrable secrecy in all of its proceedings; it allowed insidious modes of accusation to be voiced; offenders were subjected to confiscation of their property, painful torture and suffering as well as other penalties. Emerich, a 14th century Aragon Inquisitor drew up a manual with guidelines for the instruction of Judges of the Holy Office. Those guidelines prescribed ambiguous ways to interrogate those unwary and innocent victims accused of being a heretic. Throughout all of Europe the Catholic Inquisition was invoked against heretics.

I reviewed the seriousness of the situation with Cardinal Mendoza and then asked him to prepare a new and more clearly defined catechism to instruct the wayward Jewish conversos. I ordered the parish priests to sermonize daily upon the dangers of rejection of the accepted beliefs of the Catholic doctrine.

Tomas de Torquemada, a Dominican Monk and native of Old Castile, now the Prior of Santa Cruz in Segovia, had been my personal spiritual advisor and confessor since I was eighteen years old and over the years I had grown to respect his incisive brilliance. His mind could cut through the problems and find solutions with just a few minutes of thoughtful contemplations. We had spent many, many hours together reviewing the perils of the nation and establishing workable ideas which would benefit the land. I had a deep respect and great admiration for this son of God who served Him well. Torquemada's advice was, for the most part, very good. I relied upon his observations and comments. I used it often.

After the incident in Sevilla, I reviewed the problem with Torquemada. I expressed my deep concern saying, "Father, it is my greatest dream for a united people. Somehow I get this feeling that this part of my dream will never come true."

Fray Torquemada just smiled and shook his head. He had been watching one miracle after another take place throughout the country. He remained unusually quiet and in contemplative thought. I went on with my thoughts saying, "I can't really define the problem of disunity. It's an undercurrent that doesn't surface. I keep thinking if it doesn't surface, then it isn't there. But somehow deep within, the problem is that the races do not work together. I think if I found a common denominator to resolve this impasse, I might have a solution."

Finally Torquemada broke his silence saying, "I have felt that problem, too. I feel the pulse of the people so strongly and there is something brewing which is festering like a raw sore. It is an undercurrent which could eventually blow ill winds into the future of Castile."

He paused for that to sink in. I nodded and said, "But how can I change a situation that I really don't know exists? I need to find a solution."

Torquemada nodded, saying, "Yes, I think there is only one solution. It's God. It's a nation united with God. One God, one religion, one people worshiping Him in unison."

I didn't reply to that. I was rolling Torquemada's words over and over in my mind. One God, one nation, one religion -- could it work? Could that be the solution? I was so quiet, Torquemada began to expound a little more.

Waving his hands in the air, punctuating his remarks with his now familiar hand language, I heard him saying, "The Moors -- now they really are barbarians. They believe in chopping off a man's hand if he is caught stealing. And look at the number of wives permitted! Four wives for each husband. Look at the territory the Ottoman's control. Those Muslims totally control the Balkans today. The Grand Turk's navies plunder and pluck the eastern Mediterranean as if everyone else had no power left. Otrano has just fallen, and the rest of Europe might be terrified, but somehow they are unable to build a proper defense. There is danger from without, but within there is a greater danger ceaselessly at work -- the enemies of Christ have never stopped!"

My mind raced back into the pages of the history books I had studied and I recalled that eleven thousand Jews had been massacred in Barcelona on the Feast of Nuesry Sonory de la Lieves in 1391. Almost all of the entire Jewish population had been decimated. I shuddered at that happening during my own modern times.

Torquemada then began to expound upon Judaism, the faith of the ancient Hebrews. "It's riddled with ancient beliefs. They won't eat pork. Our pig farmers could raise so many more pigs. They're cautious about cooking with milk. Look at the poor cows so anxious to bring forth healthy milk. Our farmers could be so much more prosperous."

I was listening but remained silent. Torquemada looked at me with an inquisitive expression as if to say, "Aren't you listening?"

I caught the look and said, "But how are we to change centuries old patterns of customs and worship? It's an impossible task."

Torquemada went into a long dissertation about how Christianity began, how the pagans were just as resistant to change as the Moors and the Jews of Castile. Now, looking back in history, Christianity had continued its steady progressive march. How was this possible? Because of the dedication of the Catholic priests who took over the spiritualization of the pagans. Torquemada paused to take a breath and commented, "Now I do believe those areas with which you have already addressed in the reforms and appointments have strengthened the church. It was all very necessary, and as the Queen, you have sole authority over the nation." I always knew that whenever he reminded me that I had this 'sole authority' he was getting ready to inject upon me one of his own specific ideas.

Torquemada then chided me somewhat by saying, "You are possibly too over-zealous in wanting your personal hand to guide every department of the government. This could become dangerous, too overpowering for the people. They need room to breathe. Not to be stifled by a Queen who never sleeps because she's too busy overseeing every segment of life in Castile!"

With that caustic remark, my right eyebrow went up, my green-blue eyes flashed, and the good Father knew he now had captured my full attention. With that accomplished he plunged on saying, "It is not the responsibility of the Queen to meddle in the spiritual affairs of the priests. The priests have been educated, trained and now have a wealth of experience in directing the course of the nation in spiritual matters." Then he looked directly at me and asked, "Can't you allow the priests to have the free reign to bring your subjects into the church?"

I was still a little numb from his previous comment, and now this question. How should I answer that?

Torquemada's hands went back into the air and again punctuating his words with his hands he said, "A fine line needs to be drawn between the church and the state."

Well, that was an interesting observation. A fine line needs to be drawn between the church and the state. What would that mean? I wondered. Torquemada was again expounding upon the history and success of the church's authority over the Christianization of those of "unbelief." How? It's success was attributed to "the Inquisition." It had been so successful it had virtually stamped out paganism.

As the conversation ended, Torquemada extracted a promise from me that from that day forward I would not interfere with the affairs of the church as it undertook its role and responsibility to bring the people together under the umbrella of one God, one religion, one nation.

As I rose to leave, Torquemada asked me once again, "Promise me that you will not interfere as I undertake this work." I looked at him, raised my right hand and said, "As God is my witness, I do hereby give you complete and total authority to direct the affairs of the church in stamping out paganism and heresy in Castile. And I, Ysabella de Trastamara, promise not to interfere nor intervene under any circumstances. This I pledge to you now, and forever."

The historical meeting ended. It was the last face to face exchange between me and my confessor.

I reviewed Torquemada's conversation with many of the clergy in whom I regularly confided, as well as with Ferdinand. He saw nothing wrong with being a little firm with the Jewish segment or with those who sloughed off their religious training. We decided to ask Pope Sixtus the Fourth for permission to introduce into Castile an Inquisition which we hoped would stamp out heresy and bring religious orthodoxy into prominence.

The Pope issued a bull on November 1, 1478 granting permission for us to proceed; however, I really had second thoughts about that promise I had made to Torquemada. I was uneasy about it and I didn't know why. In my quiet maneuvering, I bought two years of time before my carefully laid plans began to come unraveled.

The ever observant, and fanatical Tomas de Torquemada, cautiously stepped lightly at the beginning of his quest. His fanatical temperament was played out in a very low key manner. He quietly went about his business of discovering groups of conversos practicing their forbidden religion in secret.

The Christians were jubilant. They cheered with glee at the opportunity presented to vent their dislike of the Jewish race. These Christians were certain it was their patriotic duty to discover every false Christian who practiced his former religion. My original intent when I asked Cardinal Mendoza to revise the catechism was that by means of penances given by the priests to the wayward Jews that after the conversos reviewed the correct spiritual teachings they would come back to the Church. This would solve the social and racial unrest. Eventually it was to serve as a stage for increased racial persecution.

The introduction of an Inquisition was the first step in the Crown's solution to Castile's religious problems. Only those who had been baptized under the Catholic banner and not practicing Catholicism now would come under the edict's jurisdiction. I emphasized that this must be clearly understood, because the definition made by the Catholic hierarchy stated only the baptized could be guilty of heresy. In no way could it interfere with the religion practiced by orthodox Jews and Moslems. The Christians decided this was a satisfactory state of affairs -- for the time being.

Those Jews and Moslems who had not accepted Christianity suddenly became an inferior social minority, easily recognized and officially discriminated against. They represented no direct threat to Christian superiority for they moved in their own closed social and business circles causing very few problems.

A committee of prelates under Alfonso de Ojeda, the Dominican Prior of Sevilla and vigorously supported by Niccolo Franco, the Papal Nuncio of Sevilla, again presented a petition to us requesting the creation of a *"Board of Inquisitos"*. On September 18, 1480, Ferdinand and I signed the royal certificate authorizing the appointment of the Inquisitors of Sevilla and nominating two Dominican Monks as Inquisitors along with two other ecclesiastics.

And so began the historical record of pain, torture and great suffering which history would chronicle as one of the blackest eras in the history of mankind.

PART III

Granada Conflict

CHAPTER XXVIII
Incident at Zahara
Granada Conflict Begins

Changes had been taking place in the leadership of the Moslems in Granada. Aben Ismail who had been their ruler during my father and most of Enrique's reign died in 1466. Succeeding his father was Muley Abul Hacen who was of a very different temperament. This fiery character spurred him into making unprovoked forays into Andalusia obviously displaying a degree of animosity against the Christians to the north.

In 1476 Ferdinand and I sent Hacen a note through diplomatic channels to renew the Treaty for peaceful border keeping and their payment to us of their annual tribute, the commitment the Moors had continued to honor since Alhamar reigned. Hacen sent back a short, curt note stating, "The mines of Granada coined no longer gold, but steel." I read that note through and through, trying to make a determination as to what his real thoughts and subsequent actions might be. Ferdinand and I were still working to unite Castile, and my only response was to secure our border posts along the Granada frontier.

On the stormy night of December 26th, in 1481, Hacen and his troops scaled the walls of Zahara, a small, poorly fortified town bordering Andalusia. The town was situated high on a cliff, barely accessible from the

Granada side. Abdul and his men scaled the heights of the treacherous cliffs, clambered over the walls, killing every guard, soldier and most of the men. Then they gathered up the women and children and carried them back to become slaves in Granada.

Ferdinand and I were mortified when news of the disaster reached us. Ferdinand was especially upset because it was his grandfather, King Ferdinand, who had fought those successful battles recovering Zahara from the Moors. Immediate directives from my quarters were given to strengthen our entire southern borders.

Ferdinand, ever the crafty militia man, soon had a plan to retaliate with a surprise, pincer-like manoeuver. In the Roussillon war with France, Aragon had a brilliant soldier, Captain Juan de Ortega, who had trained a group of men to scale mountains and walls. Ferdinand promptly sent for de Ortega and his trained contingency of scalers and directed them to report to Diego de Merlo, assistant of Sevilla.

The fortress of Alhama, located deep in the heart of the Moors' territory and not far from the capital city of Granada was selected as the target. The city was built high on the crest of a rocky cliff with a river at its base. Alhama was famous for its baths which the Emirs of Granada often frequented. It was a designated depot for the collection of taxes and a thriving textile center.

Alhama was sheltered by the outstretched wings of the capital city of Granada a short twenty leagues away, and was not easily reached. It was surrounded by the precipitous chain of Sierra Mountains which closed off a northern military approachment.

Diego de Merlo chose Don Rodrigo Ponce de Leon, the Marquis de Cadiz, to take charge of the militia. Ponce de Leon was the illegitimate son of the Count de

Arcos, the head of the House of Ponce de Leon, who died in 1469, designating Rodrigo as the heir apparent and head of the House. Don Rodrigo began proving his military skills during his teenage years and at the young age of seventeen successfully lead troops into battle against the Moors. He married the daughter of Pacheco Giron, the elder Marquis de Villena, who had used his considerable influence with Enrique IV to obtain for Don Rodrigo the title of Marquis.

Don Rodrigo quickly assembled his men, and along with Captain Juan de Ortega's expert scalers, set out to capture Alhama. They traveled a route along the Antequera, across the wild sierras of Alzerifa. It was the middle of February and the weather made the mountain passes difficult to manoeuver. In order not to be discovered, they traveled at night and slept in hidden valleys during the day.

After a rapid and painful march they reached a deep valley about a half a league away from Alhama. Here the Marquis gathered his troops and for the first time revealed to them their military objective. Shortly before dawn on the 28th of February, a small party under the command of Captain de Ortega, scaled the walls of the citadel. The chilling winds and a light drizzle provided a perfect cover for their early morning encounter. After ascending the rocky heights, the ladders were silently placed against the walls of the citadel and the troops succeeded in gaining the battlements unobserved. A sentinel was found sleeping at his post enabling Ortega to stealthfully move forward to the sleeping guards nearby.

The alerted Moors rushed to open their city's gates and found Cadiz waiting with his five thousand troops triumphantly poised with their banners flying, ready to enter the courtyard of the fortress with their drums rolling and trumpets blaring.

The dazed city quickly regrouped. Full of confidence Cadiz and his troops moved into the center of Alhama. The frightened Moors gathered into the narrow streets to place barricades, and from their rooftops commanded considerable respect with arquebuses and crossbows. Cadiz was forced to retreat to the citadel.

A council of war was called. Some advised Cadiz to dismantle the fortress and then abandon it as it was an impossible site to hold and defend because it was too deep into the Moors' territory. Cadiz's fiery spirit rejected that idea, and instead decided to demolish part of the fortifications which faced the town and then, at all hazards, he would force a passage into the city.

The Moors responded with well-directed volleys of shots and arrows. The women and children dashed to the rooftops and poured boiling water, oil and hot pitch, as well as tossing down missiles of every description. But their makeshift weapons fell harmlessly upon the Castilians whose habiliments covered them from head to toe. Still the Moors retained a stout resistance continuing to impede the progress of Cadiz with barricades and disputing every inch of ground with the desperation of men who were fighting for life, fortune, and liberty. At the end of the day Castilian valor proved triumphant!

When word of the Castilian victory reached the ears of the inhabitants of Granada, they rushed to their Mosques crying, "Allah has left us!" When he arrived back in Granada, Muley was "hissed," and soon discovered his son, Abu, proclaimed the Emir. Hacen was abolished to Malaga.

The news of the Marquis' success reached Ferdinand and me three hundred leagues away at Medina del Campo while we were attending church service. Ferdinand was elated and immediately began planning his own foray into the Moors' territory. It was very clear to us if we were to hold Alhama there must be a fresh reserve of troops and supplies rushed south to support and hold the fortress. Ferdinand's preparations to leave were hastily completed and by the end of the day all was ready.

He accompanied me in a solemn procession of the Court and Clergy to the Cathedral of St. James where the Te Deum was chanted and a humble thanksgiving offered to the Lord of Hosts for the success with which He had crowned our arms. Just as the sun was setting, Ferdinand, escorted by nobles and cavaliers, set forth with his troops on their journey south. I would follow later at a more leisurely pace, for I was pregnant with our fourth child.

By early March, Abdul Hacen had regrouped his soldiers and marched from Malaga back to the walls of Alhama with three thousand five hundred soldiers. They attacked the outside of the town, but Cadiz and his men fought so defensively Hacen retreated losing nearly two thousand of his bravest troops.

Cadiz dispatched couriers who took the disquieting news to the Duke de Medina Sidonia, the most powerful nobleman in Andalucia. Sidonia mounted his war horse and taking a contingency of well-trained men, traveled first to the home of Cadiz to lend assistance to the Marchioness to make certain all was well in her husband's absence. Knowing that she was safe, he then combined his forces with those of the Marquis de Villena and the Count de Cabra, riding at the head of this powerful army of quickly assembled military might.

Ferdinand and his troops arrived at the little town of Adamuz about five leagues from Cordoba where he was informed of Medina Sidonia's troop movements. Ferdinand sent word for them to halt and wait for him to catch up for he was going to take personal command.

Medina Sidonia, feeling the urgency of need to reach Alhama, sent his regrets and pushed onward.

Hacen's scouts informed him of the Duke's powerful reinforcements and he broke his camp on March 29th retreating back to Malaga.

Cadiz and Sidonia, for the first time in their bitter, life-long feuds, stood face to face and embraced each other in the presence of their united armies pledging themselves to a mutual oblivion of all their past grievances.

I had known in 1476 the storm clouds would be gathering when Hacen refused to pay his annual tribute. At the end of April, I joined Ferdinand in Cordoba. I had spent the previous six weeks making endless lists and placing orders for supplies. I moved through the process of summoning the Crown vassals, and the principal nobility of the north requesting them to hold themselves in readiness to join the royal standard in Andalusia.

Arriving in Cordoba, I received the unwelcome news that Hacen had again reassembled his forces and was marching back to Alhama. It would be difficult to successfully hold Alhama not only because it was so deep into the Moor's territory, but it would become a costly defense trying to move troops and supplies over the treacherous terrain to hold the city. It was decided that Ferdinand would march south to Alhama taking with him a very large number of soldiers and war supplies. Ferdinand arrived in the territory on May 14th. When Hacen observed our disciplined troops, lances and foot soldiers, he broke camp and returned to Malaga.

Ferdinand strengthened the garrison with new recruits, left three months' provisions and placed it under the able command of Portocarrero, Lord of Palms. Returning to Cordoba he laid waste to all the valleys of grain lying in his wake.

My midnight vigils had begun. Far into the night I dictated to my secretaries dispatching couriers throughout Castile and Leon, as far as the borders of Biscay and Guipuzcoa, prescribing the subsidy of provisions and the quota of troops each district respectively would furnish along with an adequate supply of ammunition and artillery.

Ferdinand was anxious to protect Alhama by capturing the border town of Loja fifteen leagues north of Alhama. The Marquis de Cadiz was steadfast in opposing the plan saying we were not prepared for such a formidable battle.

Heavy with my pregnancy, I sat at the table with the war councils and listened. On June 29th, 1482, in Cordoba, I gave birth to my third daughter, Maria. And 35 hours later, Maria's still-life twin sister was delivered.

On July 1st Ferdinand took matters into his own hands and marched undermanned and undersupplied into the fateful trap at Loja.

CHAPTER XXIX
The Granada Conflict Begins in Earnest

And so began ten years of war which was to occupy all my waking hours, consume my energies, face the defeats and draw deep from within to gather courage with renewed determination, ever onward to victory. It was a decade filled with hardships and a testing of our endurance. It was an intense, laborious, backbreaking job requiring me to hone my skills and keep the watchful vigilance.

In the late 15th century the capital city of Granada had nearly two hundred thousand people. The entire kingdom which stretched two hundred leagues long and sixty five leagues at its widest point was inhabited by nearly three million vengeful and cruel Moors. Treacherous mountain ranges protected this kingdom's areas on the north, east, and west, and to the south the Mediterranean sea had thriving major ports in Malaga and Almeria. The mineral wealth seemed inexhaustible, and its rich soils combined with frequent rains and warm sunshine produced an abundance of grapes, sugarcane, olives and fruit. Their textile and metalwork industries were famous throughout all of Europe and the Middle East. The ultimate prize -- the rosy walls of a thousand towers crowned with the gorgeous palaces of the Alhambra and the Alcaiciben had been the unrealized dream of Christianity for two centuries.

Foreign dispatches kept me constantly informed of the shifting political sands among the quarrelsome Moors of Granada. Since 1468 Muley Abul Hacen had been Emir. The aging, unyielding ruler was bitter and quarrelsome towards his northern Christian neighbors, spoiling for a fight. His fourth wife was a young Greek captive so beautiful the Moors named her Zoraya, Star of the Morning. Muley Abul's senile obsession for his young bride created a rift between him and his first wife, the Sultana Zotya. Zotya was a remarkable, strong willed woman, dominant in her family and determined that her eldest son, Abu Abdallah, become the next Emir. She began to lay a plot against her husband. The Emir discovered her intrigues and imprisoned her in the fortress of the Alhambra, but the Sultana promptly escaped out the upper windows by tying together scarves.

Insurrection soon spread and a civil war among the Moors erupted. The Sultana triumphed and Muley Abul Hacen was expelled from Granada, fleeing to Malaga. He had devoted followers in the kingdoms of Baza, Guadix and Almeria who swore their allegiance to him. Granada proclaimed the weak, vacillating and unpopular oldest son of the Sultan, Abu Abdallah, as their new Emir.

Muley Abul Hacen's brother, El Zagal, exerted his influence toward his own power and dominance. It was this three-cornered struggle for power which Ferdinand and I shrewdly and subtly exploited throughout the entire course of the war. The division among these rulers was a great boost to our cause.

The Moors' religious zest gave them a peculiar advantage over Christians. The Muslim believers were taught there were large rewards waiting for them in heaven for those warriors killed in battle and their soldiers fought with a fierceness unmatched by their Christian counterparts. They had proved themselves so self-sufficient over the last eight hundred years they failed to keep in step with the changes in the modern world. Their military strategies were hampered by their out-moded weapons of war, rocks and poisoned arrows which hindered their military strategies.

Toward the end of October we moved our Court from Cordoba to the central area of Castile in Madrid where I laid down the foundations for the forthcoming battles in which we were to become embroiled.

Early in 1483 at Pinto, I convened a General Congress of the Deputies of the Santa Hermandad to reform certain abuses which were going unchecked. The Hermandad offered to supply eight thousand men and sixteen thousand mules and horses to move essential supplies to Alhama. Maintenance of the Royal Guard and the vast national police of the Hermandad, along with the vigilant military troops kept our national treasury drained.

The Pope granted 100,000 ducats to be raised from ecclesiastical revenues by the churches of Castile and Aragon. Our credit, justified by the punctuality which the maravedies borrowed to win the war against Portugal were repaid, enabled us to borrow heavily from several wealthy individuals. Ferdinand and I could now order cannons, munitions, tents, wagons, horses, mules, troops, food and clothing. With this accomplished, we moved the Court back to Cordoba to oversee the assembling of the vast supplies beginning to pour into the southern Andalucia territory.

My little daughter Maria had brown hair and blue eyes. Ysabel's features still resembled my mother and I constantly referred to her as "my little mother."

And our son -- how proud Ferdinand and I were of this blonde, blue-eyed "little angel." Juan was rather quiet and reserved but very bright. My problem child was my second daughter, Juana, who resembled Ferdinand's mother. Her black hair, flashing brown eyes, deep olive complexion were in distinct contrast to the red haired Ysabel and blonde Juan. Juana was stubborn, defiant, and unmanageable. I never understood her, and throughout my life, we never grew to know one another. She didn't want any affection, but adored her father almost becoming his second shadow. And Ferdinand spoiled her. His excuse was he had not been permitted to know his two daughters fathered out of wedlock. It was his subtle reminder to me that he resented my intrusion into his romantic escapades by sending my two ladies-in-waiting who had become pregnant by him to the remote kingdoms.

I plunged into the administration and organization of the gigantic tasks of assembling an army, providing the supplies, ammunition, and hospital facilities. It was a backbreaking job which consumed all of my waking hours.

I had no time to wonder about what progress Torquemada was making with the conversos. He had begun his investigation into heresy with caution. He knew me. He understood my innermost desire for fairness and justice. He had extracted from me a "Holy Promise" and he wondered whether I would honor it.

The Inquisition was begun in 1480 in Sevilla. An edict was ordered to be published requesting all citizens to give a report to the authorities about anyone suspected of heresy. These accusations could be made anonymously and it was not long before hundreds and hundreds of accusations began to surface.

On August 2, 1483 Pope Sixtus the Fourth appointed Tomas de Torquemada Inquisitor-General of Castile and Aragon, and on October 17th the Pope gave Torquemada the full powers to frame a new constitution for the Holy Office. This was the beginning of the terrifying tribunal.

Torquemada must have overwhelmed the two administrators and the two Inquisitors I had appointed. There were so many reported victims that this small tribunal was forced to move to a fortress outside the city, the only building in the area large enough to hold all the prisoners.

Torquemada followed the policy set out for the *Ancient Inquisitos* and anonymous accusations became the most insidious and unjust aspect of the Inquisition's machinery. Men, women and children languished for months in prison, awaiting trial, without ever knowing of what they were accused or who had made the accusations. Torquemada defended the "anonymous accusations" callously saying it protected the poor man who denounced the wealthy and powerful without fear of reprisals.

Citizens wanting to report a converso had no problem finding pretexts. Any behavior connected with the Jewish way of life was considered evidence of heresy. Over the years the conversos had found it comparatively easy to renounce all outward evidences of their deep Jewish roots, but found it impossible to forget an entire "way of life" within the confines of their own homes, continuing to practice their religion on Friday evenings and Saturdays. Their watchful, underpaid and often beaten servants reported anonymously on their activities.

Del Pulgar was inwardly mortified at the development of the events of the Inquisition. He received reports sent from Sevilla, Segovia, Valladolid, Burgos and the northern province of Leon, all reporting on the Inquisition. Carefully he labeled each report by placing a clean piece of paper on the top and from a red-inked inkwell, he dipped his quill and boldly wrote "Inquisition." Then he placed these packets at the side of my working desk. Without making any comment, daily he placed the packets. There was no noticeable outward expression on my part, for it seemed as though the packets were invisible to me, and yet as the piles of reports began to grow, it became impossible for me to continually ignore them.

It was late at night, and as usual, I had been working at my desk reviewing reports, making lists for the war efforts and talking to God. All matters of urgency concerning the accumulation of medicines, arms, clothing, food for the troops seemed to be finished. I was tired, but I picked up a shirt that I had been making for Ferdinand. I tried to concentrate on the stitches, making them exact and even. The needle wasn't following my mental concentration. I ripped out the seam and started over again. Still, the stitches were uneven. Heaving a sigh, I placed the shirt back in my personal attache case and looked over at the pile of Inquisition reports.

I opened the first report, glanced through it and placed it to the side. I opened the next one, then the next and the next. Each report seemed to convey a disturbing agitation. My mind raced back to that fateful afternoon when I made my "Holy Promise" to my confessor, Tomas Torquemada, a solemn oath I had sworn to uphold. I picked up the half-read reports and tossed them into the fire. Then I grabbed the rest and cleared off every last one of them by tossing them into the flames. As I tossed the last packet into the fire I made a cross whispering, "God forgive me." Then gathering up my courage and strength from within, I took a deep breath and resolved, "I cannot intervene."

CHAPTER XXX
Military Defeat and Battle Preparations

After the victory at Alhama, Ferdinand, intent upon continuing to hold the fortress, made a fateful military miscalculation. Several miles to the north of Alhama at the border of Andalucia and Granada was the Moors' fortress city of Loja, built on the steep, rugged terrain and hillsides above the banks of the Xenial river which meandered through a valley of luxurious vineyards and olive groves. Over the years the Moors had fortified Loja bound by the Xenial river forming a natural moat at its southern border, fordable only at one point by a very narrow bridge, which the city could easily command and defend. Haley Mucen's defeat at Alhama increased his own vigilance and he strengthened his garrison at Loja with three thousand choice troops placing them under the skillful command of Ali Atar.

Loja was Ferdinand's worst military mistake. I had sent the couriers to every town and city in Castile and Leon asking for money, supplies and troops, giving them each a quota to fill. The seriousness of our plight didn't spur the townspeople and citizens to provide the supplies and the armed troops and we were woefully undermanned and undersupplied.

At that particular time, I was burdened with my difficult pregnancy and did not review every detail.

Within days after the birth of our daughter, Maria, Ferdinand had mounted his horse leading our army south toward Loja.

On July 1st, two days after the birth of our little Maria, I received the sad news that Alonso Carrillo, the rebellious Archbishop of Toledo, who had contributed more than anyone to raise me to the Throne, and who, by his same rebellious nature, nearly hurled me from it, had died. The Archbishop of Toledo had closed the last years of his life in disgrace at Alcala de Henares. I moved promptly to appoint Don Pedro Gonzales de Mendoza, Cardinal of Spain, to become the new Archbishop of Toledo.

The steep hillsides, the deep ravines, and the hot sticky weather made Ferdinand's progress painfully slow. Ali Atar's alert scouts allowed Ferdinand to progress until he was well inside his territory, and then with violent fury they fell upon our troops. The young Grand Master de Calatrava, Rodrigo Tillez Giron, was killed, and the Duke de Medina Celi, the Constable and Count de Tendilla were seriously wounded. Ferdinand was trapped by the Moors and barely escaped from being captured when he was rescued by the daring exploits of the Marquis de Cadiz. Ferdinand returned to Cordoba trailing his banners in defeat.

The defeat was disquieting. The war was escalating and we could not afford to lose. In March of 1483, the Andalusian leaders, under the command of Alonso Cardenas and the Marquis de Cadiz, attempted to take the Axarquia, a rich region of valleys lying immediately north of Malaga. The vigilant Moors again allowed the proud commanders to become deeply entrenched in the dangerous terrain and finally when they were hopelessly entrenched in the deep ravines, the Moors fell upon them with a murderous ambush. For twenty five hours they valiantly endured the chaotic terror before they fought their way out. Their horses, unable to scale the rocky walls, fell back into bloody heaps. Everything collapsed in the inferno.

The Count de Cifuentes was captured, three of the Marquis brothers and two of his nephews were killed. For days the survivors wandered the countryside attempting to make their way back across the treacherous terrain into the safety net of a calm and peaceful Castile. Axarquia, in war's wary way, soon brought to Castile our just reward.

Abu Abdallah, the young Emir and oldest son of Sultana Zoyta, was probably the only person in Granada who did not swell with pride over the rout of the Christians at Axarquia. Abu had a secret uneasiness about all the laurels now being heaped upon the old Emir, his father, and his ambitious uncle, El Zagal. He wanted to dazzle his relatives by winning battles and he decided upon an excursion into Castile. Quickly raising nine thousand men and seven hundred horses, and strengthened by the presence of his father-in-law, Ali Atar, the defender of Loja, he sallied forth through the gate of Elvira. Boldly he advanced and word soon reached the ears of Don Diego Fernandez de Cordoba, Alcayde de los Donzeles, and Captain of the Royal Pages who commanded the town of Lucena. He quickly forwarded a report to his uncle, the Count de Cabra, who was posted in his own town of Baena, alerting him of the invader's march.

Lucena was lightly armed and not heavily fortified against an attack. There was a light fog and the Moor commanders mistook the banner of the Count de Cabra for that of the cities of Baeza and Ubeda. Thinking that "all of Castile" was upon them, they broke rank running in every direction. Their calvary was annihilated and Ali Atar lost his life.

The young Emir, mounted on his sleek white charger, saw fifty of his men fall around him. He pushed his heavily burdened horse into the rushing waters of the stream. The horse lost its footing tossing Abdallah off. Scrambling to the banks of the river, he hid among the reeds and bushes where Martin Hurtado, a foot soldier, discovered him and took him prisoner.

The capture of Abu was an unexpected stroke of good fortune for Ferdinand and me. We received the news of the Emir's capture while in Vitoria located in the Basque kingdom. Quickly we sent dispatches to the Count de Cabra who was holding him in custody, urging him to treat his prisoner with caution and care.

Ferdinand hurried south to Cordoba. Abu's mother, the Sultana, was frantically offering a huge sum of money as ransom along with the release of some Christian captives. Ferdinand and the Royal Council debated the fate of our royal captive. The Council was divided in their opinions. Some contended the Emir was too valuable a prize to be sent home, while others insisted Abu could continue to divide the Moor leadership if he was home. Ferdinand deferred the decision to me and after careful deliberation, I decided to follow the tradition established by King Ferdinand when he allowed Alhamar to return to Granada. I directed the Royal Council to prepare a Treaty to be signed by Abu and then permit him to return to Granada.

Ferdinand drew up a two-year Treaty of Peace acknowledging Abu as the Moor leader of those certain territories in Granada which were divided after the fall of Alhama. In addition, Abu would release four hundred captive Christians, pay 12,000 doblas of gold annually to Castile, and permit free passage and supplies of our troops into Granada to pursue the war with Hacen and El Zagal. In addition, Abu would deliver his own son to Castile for safekeeping as our insurance he would honor the Treaty. Ferdinand added the final clause which clearly stated the Treaty would not be officially recognized until Abu Abdallah had returned as the victor to his capital city of Granada.

Abdallah sneaked back across his borders and gathering up fresh troops from the Abencerrajes, a savage civil war broke out, finally ending when Muley Abul Hacen agreed to Abu Abdallah's governing Granada. Muley Abul Hacen would rule over the southern territory of Almeria.

As the reports filtered back to us of the civil war among the Moors, Ferdinand and I took advantage of their preoccupation with their own problems and began to formulate our battle plans to regain Granada for Castile.

CHAPTER XXXI
Winning the Battles

Recapturing the Castilian territory held by the Moors was an endeavor far beyond my total comprehension at the time we became involved. It was always my dream to regain that ancient land and christianize Granada. Pushing the war forward at that particular time was not an easy decision for me to make. Ferdinand's early training and nature was militarily oriented. Leading troops into battle and winning was his dream, and he was anxious to regain the chivalrous honor of his ancestors. The decision was made to plunge ahead and commit troops, horses and artillery. I thrust my energies into planning and overseeing every detail of elaborate preparations.

I studied the maps of the territory held by the Moors and for the first time in my life I clearly understood why the Kings who had ruled before me were unsuccessful. There were impassable mountain ranges all over the southern territory. I sat down with the Marquis de Cadiz and plied him with questions. For days we studied the maps and discussed the impossibilities of penetrating the Moors' defenses. Fortresses which the Moors built high on the cliffs overlooking their fertile valleys could not be easily reached. We would have to build roads for horses, foot soldiers and mule trains pulling supplies and artillery. New bridges would have to be built before our troops could fight the battles and win.

While Ferdinand and the nobles slept, I was busy making out long, long lists of everything that I could possibly perceive we needed. I sent out the call for thousands of volunteers, food, clothing, axes, shovels and cement to build the roads and construct safe bridges enabling us to invade and conquer.

It would take time, energy and a lot of money. Meeting with the Council of War I unveiled my plans and it was decided we would spend the next several months planning and marshalling our resources. In order to keep the Moors off guard, we would keep up the skirmishes along their borders. After winning the border skirmish, the road and bridge builders would be sent ahead to lay more roads and bridges and we could penetrate their interiors. For the next two years the nobles played at their games of war and won.

The pomp with which our military movements were conducted gave the impression of a Court Pageant rather than the stern array of war. There were two principles which were emphasized to recruit the troops and gain the support of the people -- religion and patriotism. Both were well calculated to inflame the imaginations of the young Spanish cavaliers and they poured into the field, eager to display themselves for their Queen. I made a habit of riding through the ranks mounted on my war horse clad completely in my mail as I inspected my troops standing in rigid attention and as the colorful banners dipped, I proudly passed by.

The wealthy barons exhibited all the magnificence of princes. They decorated their pavilions with banners of every color and description and emblazoned the armorial bearings of their ancient houses which produced a great show of splendor. They dined on their gold plates, and dressed in exquisite brocades and satins. Ferdinand and I would appear in their midst surrounded by a throng of pages and if we made our appearance at night, we would be preceded by hundreds carrying torches which shed a radiant light all around.

The nobles contended with each other for the post which posed the greatest danger. The Duke de Infantado, the head of the powerful House of Mendoza, presented the most ostentatious show of magnificence with his entire train.

While the nobles displayed their wealth and military prowess, Ferdinand undertook the major task of training the soldiers that I had recruited. The call went out and volunteers arrived from every part of our lands. Word spread throughout Europe that the Spanish Christians were marching south against the dreaded Infidels and the volunteers arrived from Germany, Italy, France and England. From Switzerland came a band of Swiss mercenaries, trained to fight on foot without armor, only the buckle and shield for protection.

At the outbreak of the war, most of the war levies were paid by the Andalusian cities who had long been accustomed to warring against the Moors. They provided well appointed chivalry and military Orders. The organized militia of the Santa Hermandad supplied thousands of men for service, and along with a splendid throng of cavaliers and hidalgos from all over Castile, the ranks of the great nobles were swelled.

My constant correspondence with the Pope resulted in his granting bulls of the crusade which offered large indulgences to those who assisted in driving the

Infidel from the Peninsula. My mind worked overtime thinking of everything.

Out of my personal funds the "Hospital de la Reina" was equipped with medicines, beds, bandages, tents and doctors. It was the first fully equipped military field hospital in history. I ordered enough tents to equip and care for twelve hundred wounded soldiers. I was very proud of this, for no other kingdom in history had ever before commanded better medical attention. I understood the value of psychological warfare. I ordered bells of every size and description. The Koran forbid the ringing of bells and when the Moors heard our bells begin to ring in their land, they scampered into hiding.

I was determined that our artillery would be the most formidable ever assembled. I brought engineers and gunsmiths from Italy and Germany, gunpowder from Portugal, Sicily and Flanders. The star of the new artillery was the famous twelve foot long lombards capable of hurling balls of iron and marble weighing 165 pounds. This would provide the proper defensive backup for our foot soldiers and calvary. As I studied the project, I realized what a monumental task it was going to be to place my plans into motion. Our small factories that would manufacture the war materials were located in the central and northern kingdoms. I would have to purchase thousands and thousands of plodding mules to pull the loaded wagons hauling the lombards, cannons, balls and munition powder. How long would it take to move the artillery from north to south and then into Granada? How many mules and wagons should I buy? Everywhere I asked the questions, and everyone shook their heads, "They didn't know."

I came across a name in one of my little note-books. When Ferdinand and I had traveled north to Madrid after the loss at Loja, someone had told me about Don Francisco Ramirez, a hidalgo who lived in Madrid. Don Ramirez seemed to be a man of great experience with an extensive knowledge of military science. Something told me I needed to send for him. Why? I didn't know.

On the appointed day, Don Francisco Ramirez arrived at my Court in Cordoba. As we talked images flashed through my mind of small manufacturing plants being built right in the midst of our military camps. As the assembling of the new manufactured cannon balls and munitions for firing was completed, they could be immediately loaded into the cannons and lombards and lobbed into the enemy's towns and cities. I hesitated to broach the subject of such an impossibility. Gathering my courage, I finally asked him if we could do it. A broad smile lighted up his face, his eyes began to twinkle, and he shouted with glee, "Of course, that's the answer!" He would design and build the small plants which would manufacture the artillery. We would transport the raw materials to each military encampment, set up the equipment with his trained men manning their positions, and they would provide the "on the spot" firing power. I placed Don Rameriz directly in charge of this monumental endeavor.

I was making progress. Now to think about food. We would need pack-trains moving food, clothing, blankets, tents and fresh medical supplies. I managed to obtain sixty thousand mules and supplied twenty thousand bushels of barley and flour to be mounded in heaps at the various military encampments.

Commissaries needed to be established. These

were divided into departments. Supplies arrived daily from every European port, Castile, Leon and Aragon. An orderly plan was devised for the housing of all equipment, grains, tents, clothing, harnesses, mules, and when a nobleman's supplies ran low, he sent me a list for resupply. From the commissaries they were replenished, the wagons loaded, the mules fed and watered and ready for their long tedious journey back to the battle lines.

I moved my Court along those frontiers. Posts were established for couriers to ride daily, pick up dispatches from the battle areas and return with them to my quarters. Things were moving slowly, but well. There were six thousand members of the special corps of sappers who were cutting new roads, leveling mountains and building bridges. Night and day they hacked away at the trees and brush in the wilderness, filling up gullies, crevices and valleys with rocks, timber, cork-trees and cement.

The fortresses built by the Moors perched on the crests of the mountains made it seem totally inaccessible for any invasion. When their astonished gaze focused upon the heavy trains of artillery emerging from the mountain passes where no foot had ever before ventured, they muttered, "Allah has left us!" The high walls which surrounded their cities were not strong enough to withstand the long assaults of our formidable engines.

The Moors had relied totally upon their cross-bows and arquebus. They had adopted the African custom of poisoning their arrows by soaking a piece of cloth in the juice of aconite, or wolfsbane, which grew rife in the Sierra Nevada mountains near Granada. Then wrapping the soaked cloth around the razor-sharp metal arrow point, they shot with deadly aim at the

Christians. A wound, however slight, meant certain death.

We also needed foragers. Troops who would move along on each side of our military to burn the enemy's fields of grain, destroy their orchards and vineyards and lay waste to their land. We gathered together nearly thirty thousand foragers who proceeded to systematically destroy the fertile valleys of Granada.

The fiery tempered nobles were often at odds with Ferdinand, refusing to follow his orders. They looked to me as their Sovereign. I wrote frequent letters to them at their camps complimenting them on their achievements. I lavished honors upon the deserving ones which cost me little, but earned them great prestige. To the Marquis de Cadiz, who was by far the most pre-eminent Captain in the ten year Granada conflict, I gave the city of Zahara and the accompanying title of Marquis de Zahara. All the regal pomp of royal pageantry was paraded before him as I honored my friend and military genius, Don Rodrigo Ponce de Leon, the Marquis de Cadiz and now adding the honored titles of Marquis de Zahara and Duke de Cadiz.

When the Count de Cabra rode north to Vitoria to bring us the news he had captured Abu Abdallah, I marshalled all the clergy and cavaliers of the city marching out to receive him. He entered Vitoria in solemn procession with the Grand Cardinal of Spain, the Archbishop of Toledo, riding on his right. As the procession advanced to the hall for his audience in the Royal Alcazar, Ferdinand and I walked down the steps to personally greet him. Then, escorting him to our dining table, we declared, "The conqueror of a King should sit with Kings!"

The young Alcayde de los Donzeles who had

alerted everyone about advances on Lucena was provided with another royal reception. The nobles of the Court were dressed in their finest clothes, the drums beat and the trumpets blared heralding the approach of this young noble grandly escorted by our great nobles. I personally undertook the correspondence between Castile and the Pope, constantly informing him about our triumphant progress. He, in turn, sent his benediction always accompanied by more bulls for our crusade authorizing ecclesiastical taxes to be given to the Crown.

Pope Sixtus IV presented a massive silver cross to us. The cross was placed in Ferdinand's tent and carried throughout all of his campaigns. As new towns and cities were captured, the standard of the silver cross would be mounted on the summit of the principal fortress, then the soldiers would drop to their knees silently worshipping the Almighty while the priests chanted the glorious Te Deum. The banner of Santiago would be unfolded and all invoked His blessed name. The Crown's royal banner emblazoned with our royal arms was hoisted and the army shouted with one voice, "Castile, Castile!" After the solemn rite, a bishop would lead the way to the principal mosque to perform the rites of purification.

Churchmen of the highest rank were always in attendance on our expeditions. They mingled in the councils of the camp and at times boldly buckled a harness over their rochet and hood to lead squadrons into battle.

Wherever I had stationed myself, I celebrated every success by gathering together my entire household, the nobility, foreign ambassadors and municipal functionaries, and together we paraded in a solemn procession through the streets towards the cathedral to give our grateful thanks.

When Ferdinand returned from his campaigns, he would be met at the gates of the city and escorted in solemn pomp beneath a rich canopy of state to the cathedral church where he would prostrate himself in grateful adoration of the Lord of Hosts.

The burden of the war was primarily borne by Andalucia but there were thousands of volunteers from Galicia, Biscay, Asturias, and Aragon and even from Sicily arriving to help our cause. Ferdinand and I offered amnesty to thousands who had fled Castile under the cloud of their illegal activities. We promised not to prosecute them providing they served in the war against the Moors.

Our steady progress and penetration was painstakingly slow. Every cliff was crowned with a fortress defended by desperate men willing to bury themselves in its ruins. The constant barrage from our artillery caused tower and town to fall. The principal towns of Cartama, Coin, Setenil, Marbella and Llora were the strong outposts which fell. Now these exterior defenses of the city of Granada had fallen to us.

In the spring of 1485, Ferdinand put into motion his well laid plans to march on Ronda, a major city located in the westernmost province of Malaga and considered to be impregnable because it stood on a rocky cliff totally protected by the narrow barrier of a wide gorge, Tajo de Ronda. Accompanied by the Marquis, the Constable, the Masters of Santiago and Alcantara, along with an entire roster of Spanish nobles and thousands of troops, Ferdinand marched with his columns. No longer a brash neophyte, Ferdinand craftily planned his military approach by first marching toward Loja. The Moors' calvary watched the troop movement and rushed all of their soldiers to Loja to defend that city. Ferdinand quickly swung back and marched with high speed to surround Ronda. The siege of Ronda established the techniques to gain control of other cities that were to follow later. Ferdinand placed his cannons with exact precision. He studied the terrain with his captains and in particular with the Marquis Duke de Cadiz who knew the territory of Ronda very well. He carefully struck his camp on every side of the city which was not protected by the Tajo. Hundreds of colorful silk tents went up dotting the hillsides with a burst of bright color. The Marquis discovered the spring at the bottom of the gorge which furnished all the water to the city of Ronda. Then he daringly descended to the bottom of the gorge and cut off the entire water supply to the soon paralyzed city. Ferdinand proceeded to systematically destroy Ronda.

The city surrendered on May 14, 1485. The formalities of the raising of the silver cross, chanting of the Te Deum Laudumas, raising the banner of Santiago and then the royal pennons now completed, Ferdinand marched to the dark, damp dungeons and threw open the gates to free the Christian captives.

The fall of Ronda shook the entire western province of Granada. Ferdinand returned to Cordoba in a grand, triumphant march with his nobles, bringing with him the Christian captives. The prelates and Ambassadors of Venice, Naples and Portugal rode out to greet him and escorted him under the rich canopy of state to the gates of the Alcazar where my children and I, along with the beautifully dressed ladies of my Court were in the courtyard waiting to greet him.

With tears running down my face, I gazed at

more than four hundred unfortunate Christians, several of whom were cavaliers of rank who had been taken captive in our fatal expedition of the Axarquia. I looked at those wan and wasted figures with their disheveled hair, beards reaching below their chest; their arms and legs shackled with heavy chains. One by one I stepped forward to greet them, then I removed their chains. After the celebration of public thanksgiving for their return, they were given a hero's welcome as our troops escorted them to their homes. I ordered the chains to be sent to San Juan de los Reyes in Toledo, the monastery I was building.

Ferdinand was spoiling to capture Loja and we began preparing for the assault on this formidable city in 1486.

Muley Hacen, blind and ravaged by gout, died. Abu broke his Treaty with us and joined with Hamet El Zagri and his terrible African Gomeres to defend Loja.

Our artillery firmly in place, Ferdinand began the bombardment of the city on all sides, methodically demolishing the walls, towers and buildings. On May 29th, Abu, wounded and leaning on Gonzalo de Cordoba, was brought before Ferdinand. Ferdinand looked at the frightened, pitiful, weak and vacillating man, and decided to let him go free, permitting him to return to Granada to sow more seeds of dissension among his war torn land.

Ten days later I made my way to Loja to review my troops. The Marquis Duke de Cadiz gave us a sumptuous banquet in his tapestried pavilion. Ferdinand and I greeted our gracious host as we bowed formally three times. The next day I donned my mail, mounted my chestnut horse, the drums began to roll and the battle flags dipped before me as I reviewed the brave, valiant, victorious troops.

Their shouts of "Viva la Riena" echoed and resounded throughout the valleys of our victorious Spain. With a prayer on my lips, I looked toward the heavens and gave thanks to the Lord of Hosts for all that was, and now is, Spain.

PART IV

Cristobol Colon

CHAPTER XXXII
Cristobol Colon

It was September, 1484, when Hernando del Pulgar placed an intriguing packet on my desk. Hernando and I had a wonderful working relationship. He had certain places on my desk where he would place reports of noteworthiness. This "packet" was placed directly in the middle of my desk.

I had overslept that morning for I was again pregnant. My doctor had cautioned me about over-exertion and I was to absolutely cut down on my normal energetic non-stop activities.

I picked up the dispatch and noted it was from Fray Juan Perez, a priest who had once been my confessor and now assigned to La Rabida, a Jeronymite monastery situated high on a cliff near the seaport village of Huelva. Fray Perez had a wonderful mind, and I admired his foresight and visions which many times proved to be prophetic. In his dispatch to me he explained that a tall stranger, Cristobol Colon, born in Genoa, Italy had arrived at the gates of his monastery in July asking if he could leave his five year old son there. Perez went on with the stranger's "story." He wrote this tall stranger with red hair and blue eyes had a great vision -- an impossible dream -- that if a ship were to sail due west, they would discover two things. First, the world was a round sphere and not flat as all scientists had been claiming, and second, by sailing west, they would discover a new waterway to the East Indies to open a new route to the lucrative silk and spice trades. He was very intrigued with this impressive stranger. Perez informed me that he had given Colon a letter of introduction to Antonio de Marchena, custodian of the Franciscan sub-province of Sevilla. Marchena was a spirited, intelligent cleric, highly regarded among his fellowmen. Perez went on to state that he had also presented Colon with a map he had drawn tracing a route for him to follow to reach Sevilla.

Fray Antonio was a man of imagination and great ideas. He embraced this stranger as a brother, listening to Colon's wild plans. I soon received a "packet" from Marchena who very frankly stated he "thought Colon had something and he wished to be Colon's advocate." He informed me that due to the war with Granada and the heavy financial commitment to it, he had presented Colon to his very close friend the most magnificent Don Enrique de Guzman, Duke de Medina Sidonia, Grandee of Spain and one of the wealthiest subjects of our Crown. He attached to his letter an outline for the adventure, requesting ships, men and money which he had presented to Sidonia.

I read that letter from Fray Antonio through and through. I pondered upon the possibilities of discovering a new route to the eastern spice lands. I thought of the excitement it would create among our European neighbors, and especially the impact it would have on France. There were many ideas forming in my mind. I placed the dispatch carefully among my important papers and asked del Pulgar to notify Marchena and the Duke that I was very interested in following this stranger's activities and asked that reports be sent to me on a regular basis.

Not too many days had passed when we were informed that the Duke de Medina Sidonia had gotten into a brawl with the Marquis Duke de Cadiz. I thought these two illustrious gentlemen had buried all their old hates, jealousies and frustrations at Alhama when Sidonia and his troops arrived in time to rescue Cadiz and contain the Moors, but this was not to be. I asked for an investigation into the matter and when we received the report we found the incident was started by the Duke de Medina Sidonia, Ferdinand and I promptly ordered Sidonia to depart from Sevilla and reside for a time in Valladolid. That ended the possibilities of Colon's dream to quickly obtain ships, men and money for his discovery of the new route to the Indies.

Another dispatch was placed in the very center of my desk arriving a short time later informing me Colon had now been introduced to Don Luis de la Cerda, Count de Medina Celi, a large landholder at Puerto Santa Maria, owner of a large merchant fleet. Medina was totally captivated with the idea, absolutely fascinated with the prospect of discovering a new route to the spice trade. He thought to himself, "Never mind whether the world is flat or round, it is the idea of discovering a new route to the Far East that holds my interest." He decided to underwrite the expedition with three or four well equipped caravels, for Colon has asked for no more. Then Celi decided it would be quite appropriate to "ask for royal permission" to enter into this grand enterprise. His reasoning for that was if he "had our royal blessings" when he arrived back from the expedition with a new route discovered, he might receive untold honors from the Crown.

He dutifully prepared his application and it was promptly placed in the center of my desk by Pulgar, ready for my immediate review and attention. I read the application through and through. Then I asked Ferdinand what he thought about it. Ferdinand read it and said, "Everyone is 'loco!' Colon is 'loco,' Celi is 'loco,' and you are 'loco' if you embark upon such a crazy venture." With that I knew Ferdinand had spoken his thoughts but this didn't change my mind. Whenever some unusual idea was presented to me, I would get a hot flush of energy which would flow from the top of my head spreading throughout my body. When I received the application from Celi, this "hot flush" was my signal this was something from God. I decided that I should meet this tall, red-headed stranger.

We had moved our Court to Alcala de Henares, waiting for the birth of our baby. On December 5, 1485, I gave birth to my daughter, Catalina. When the doctor placed our little daughter in my arms, I knew this was the last child I would bear. It was true, both Ferdinand and I had great hopes that the baby would be a boy, but this healthy, happy little girl was to become one of my greatest joys and inspiration.

Juana continued to be a major concern. She didn't like to study. She was rude to her teachers. She was bossy, defiant and independent. As far as discipline was concerned, she wanted none of it. She had a very bright mind. She could add and subtract like a little wizard. She had a definite flair for languages and had little trouble learning to speak Italian, French and German. Ferdinand continued to protect her from all my attempts to more clearly define her royal studies and develop discipline.

Ysabel had completed her studies and was a very lovely young lady in my Court. She was fifteen years old and very mature in her deportment, manner and address. She was still shy, and I felt she would always be uncomfortable around strangers, not adapting easily to change. I thought this quite interesting for all of her life, as my household domiciles changed, I packed up the children and took them with me. I had realized that one of our greatest mistakes with Ysabel was leaving her when she was so little with my dear friend, Beatriz Bobadilla de Cabrera, now the Marchioness de Moya. When I realized my daughter was emotionally attached to Beatriz, I vowed those many years ago that all of my future children would remain by my side. Wherever it was in my realm that I needed to be, my children would travel with me. Our parental influence would always be there for our children.

I chose their tutors with great care. I invited brilliant Italian educators, the erudite Geraldinos, Antonio and Alejandro, and later Lucio Marieno arrived to teach our royal children. Our son's chief tutor, Beatriz de Galido, arrived from Italy to teach Latin. Ferdinand and I planned our son's education very carefully. We decided at the age of twelve he would have a small group of boys his own age to "act as his Conejo Reales" and then a second group of boys a few years older who, too, would become "his royal advisers." This, we felt, would give him experience in learning to listen to advisers as well as teaching him to make decisions.

My father had been one of Castile's leading Latin scholars. His brilliant mind was constantly in search of the enhancement of his knowledge of this ancient language. I had never studied Latin when I was in school. My ladies-in-waiting and others at Court had this abominable habit of gossiping. I decided that rather than these ladies waste their time gossiping, they should study Latin and I would join them in those classes and learn to speak it, too.

I continued to receive the progress reports on the Monastery that was being built just outside Burgos where I had decided I would place the tombs of my father, mother and brother. The architect, Gil de Siloe, sent his bi-weekly reports on the progress, detailing the expenses, and reporting on the completion of the Monastery. There were so many areas for the Treasury's money to be disbursed, I daily asked God to provide the funds for the La Cartuja de Miraflores. It was destined to be a Carthusian Monastery and I was looking forward to its completion. Before leaving Alcana de Henares, I decided to ask an expert wood carver living in Valladolid, Martin Sanchez and Gil de Siloe, who was also an accomplished sculptor, to meet with me. They arrived for our celebrated meeting and I spoke first, expressing exactly what I wanted. For the most part, they shook their heads in agreement. In one section was to be the hand carved Choir of the Brother's chairs, and near the front, off to the left side, would be the Choir of the Father's chairs to be carved by Martin Sanchez. Then the discussion came up about where to build the chapel for the tombs, and I stated, "No, no chapel is to be built. We will place the tombs of my father and mother directly in front of the altar of the Chapel, and then to the left, in a small alcove will be placed the tomb of my brother, Alfonso." The most incredulous look registered on their faces. After a measured silence, Siloe boldly stated, "Tombs placed directly in front of the altar? Your Highness, this is not done. No, this would not be correct." Martin Sanchez shook his head in agreement with him. Without expressing to them my reasons for the tombs to be so prominently placed, I looked at each of them and then in a matter of fact manner stated, "The tombs will be placed in front of the altar." With that statement I concluded the meeting.

They filed out of the room, one by one, still somewhat shaken by the thought of the tombs being placed so prominently in the Monastery. I knew why I wanted those tombs placed directly in front of the altar. My father's reign was destined to gather dust in the annals of our nation's history, and the misfortunes of life had struck bitter blows to my dear mother and young brother who had no opportunity to bring fullness to their lives. I did not want our nation for forget that King Juan II and his wife, Ysabel of Portugal had been a King and Queen of Castile. If the tombs were prominently placed directly in front of the altar, all who came to La Cartuja de Miraflores would remember.

In late April, 1486, we moved our Court back to the front line of our war skirmishes with the Moors, and again situated our Court at Cordoba.

I suggested to Medina Celi that he escort this Christobol Colon to Cordoba for an audience with Ferdinand and me. Ferdinand wanted no part of this "loco" man's foolish ideas and was abrupt and opinionated about it. Nevertheless, on the appointed day for Colon's audience, Ferdinand was there beside me -- I think more out of curiosity than for "affairs of state." Ferdinand at times was a very outspoken person, and he spoke out against even holding a meeting with this imposter, this misguided "loco" foreigner from Genoa.

I had heard Colon described, and as he entered I saw this six foot tall, red haired, blue eyed stranger with a very fair complexion bowing before me. Aragon and

Castile men were short, somewhat stocky and had straight black hair. When I looked at Colon, my mind raced back to the midnight meeting when I first met the Marquis de Cadiz. Cadiz had become one of my dearest friends, the greatest and most daring commander in our Granada campaigns. Without Cadiz, my husband, on more than one occasion, could have been captured and killed by the Moors. I wondered if the red headed gentlemen standing before me had the magical forces around his that so set Cadiz apart from all of our other military commanders.

I allowed Ferdinand to ask all the correct questions while I listened to the answers. I was struck by this man's apparent inner strength. I watched his body movements, the way he threw his cloak to the side as he knelt before us, and his direct gaze into Ferdinand's eyes. This man was totally in command of his person, his language, and even his very outlandish ideas. This was not an ordinary man standing before us. I listened to his voice as he answered Ferdinand's questions. It was well modulated and he was a man who obviously chose his words carefully, speaking with intelligence, directly to the point, seemingly very knowledgeable in maritime affairs. I concentrated upon every word for I knew these words would play back in my mind if I were to give the matter further consideration.

As the interview ended, I graciously thanked him for coming and informed him I did not mean to give him further encouragement. There were certain very important questions that would have to be resolved. I assured him I would personally need to review with my own maritime experts whether a westward journey to the Indies was practical, and if we could afford to underwrite such a scheme when we were in the middle of a difficult military conflict. I told Cristobol that I would give the matter considerable thought, review it with Medina Celi, and consider allowing all of the expenses of such an expedition to be underwritten by him. In the end all this must be reviewed with others before any real decisions could be made.

Colon bowed and departed. Ferdinand was silent. I instructed del Pulgar to introduce Colon to my dear friend and confidant, Don Pedro Gonzales de Mendoza, Archbishop of Toledo, Grand Cardinal of Spain and First Minister of the Crown of Castile. I further instructed that I wished Colon to be Mendoza's guest until the questions concerning his proposed voyage were answered. Ferdinand finally broke his silence as he looked at me and said, "Not only is the foreigner 'loco,' after listening to those instructions you are 'loco,' too."

Cristobol Colon was escorted by my personal envoys to Toledo to meet and discuss the proposed new sea route with Mendoza. My aides assured Colon he should wait for a favorable response from the Queen.

Ferdinand and I were totally engrossed in military affairs, training the army, ordering supplies and raising the money to continue the war. It was no time to be thinking of the "loco scheme" of the red haired stranger.

My instincts focused around people and their motives. I observed a clear and distinct attitude displayed by the wives and daughters of the powerful nobility. Haughty, distant, jealous of their positions of power, and constantly protecting their social ranks. They had enjoyed the heady experiences of being treated almost a "Queen" or a "Princess" when their husbands gained their power through their feudal wars. When the presence of a Crowned head appeared in their midst they withdrew behind their masks, aloof, distant and non-communicative. As I traveled through my kingdoms crisscrossing the land, I was often a guest in a noble's castle. Dressing for dinner, I would ask Maria, my faithful maid, to go to my hostess and ask if I might borrow a broach, bracelet or necklace. The hostess would be so touched the Queen would be wearing her jewelry, she would send it along with Maria. Later when I returned the jewels to the hostess, I always added a new jewel as a gift and a gracious note expressing my appreciation. This caused countless doors to open before me by the nobles and their haughty, aloof wives.

I had inherited from my father the love of art and great literature. I was intent in my desire to begin a magnificent royal art collection. The dispatches received from Florence and Venice extolled the new artists who were painting priceless works of art, and the chisels in the hands of those master sculptors were redefining that craft. I began corresponding with agents in Florence and Venice and soon commissioned some paintings to be painted by those recognized Masters.

To the sounds of great music my ear was ever attuned. The best singers, musicians and dancers were encouraged to make their way to our Court, for our Court was destined to become the most glittering on the European continent.

Late one evening, Pulgar placed the last of a packet of letters for me to sign ready for the couriers the next morning. I looked up at his obviously tired eyes and fatigued body, and said to him, "Hernando, I know it is well past everyone's bedtime, but please, do you think we could get one more thing accomplished?"

Hernando nodded in agreement and I dictated a letter to my confessor, Fray Fernando de Talavera, Prior del Prado (a Jeronymite monastery near Valladolid), asking him to organize a Commission to examine Colon's project.

Early in the summer of 1486 de Talavera's group met for the first time in Cordoba and then adjourned to Salamanca. Salamanca was a university of residential colleges. One college, St. Stephen, was presided over by the Dominican Father Diego de Deza, later to become the Bishop of Palencia and Archbishop of Sevilla. De Talavera invited other wise and learned men, as well as sea mariners, to serve on this Commission. They all agreed the tall red head's concept of a round earth couldn't possibly be correct. Colon found de Talavera the warmest and most useful of all the advocates; however, he could convince no one that the idea was sane and practical. Colon repeatedly asked them to observe a horse and wagon traveling in the opposite direction and note at what distance it was before it moved out of sight. He tried to convince them the reason it no longer was in sight was because of the curvature of the earth. It was the same with ships casting out to sea. Still, his arguments made no sense to the illustrious Salamancan group. I appointed a separate group to make a study of the possibilities and probabilities. This body of scientists met and deliberated for several months. They were absolutely certain they had asked every question possible of every learned man in Castile.

We spent our winter in Valladolid attending to the administrative affairs of both countries. I took time from my tasks to sit for some portraits and visit the studios of Gil de Siloe and Martin Sanchez. Martin's work was moving forward. The Choir chairs were going to be perfect. It was the alabaster carvings of the tombs for my mother and father that Siloe was sculpturing that I was so keenly interested in. I told de Siloe I wanted him to chisel little figures all around the perimeter of the tombs of the King and Queen. I wanted those tiny carved figures to tell the story of their lives to everyone who came. I wanted those small carved figures to convey such a memorable story no one would ever forget.

While in Valladolid, de Talavara sent me a note advising me the Commission was ready to make their report and we proceeded with arrangements for a proper time and place. I sent a note to Cristobol Colon inviting him at attend.

On the appointed day, de Talavera's Commission filed into the large room furnished simply with a very large table surrounded by an adequate number of chairs to seat everyone. Ferdinand and I were seated at the end of the long table and the remaining vacant chairs were occupied by the members of the Commission. Colon was seated at the side of the room. Ferdinand was sullen and silent. He didn't want any part of this "loco" idea. I asked Fray de Talavara, the head of the Commission, to report his discussions and findings.

De Talavera expounded upon the known theory, and then he deftly gave an accounting of the proposed cost of the venture. After elaborating on several technical points, he closed with the last major point of the Commission's heated discussions. It had been reasoned that, "The voyage between Europe and Asia would take three years. Even if it were possible to sail to the other side of the earth, it would be impossible to sail back to this side because no ship can sail uphill!" The Commission concluded their remarks with, "His promises and

offers are impossible, vain and worthy of rejection."
I swallowed and looked down. Ferdinand stifled
a laugh. Colon started to stand up to address the group
but I waved my hand slightly and he knew this was his
signal to remain silent. I thanked the gentlemen and dismissed them. I
then asked Colon to remain seated. In well chosen
words I conveyed to him, "Somehow I still feel your idea
needs more thought and exploration. I don't want to
give up just yet. Are you comfortable at the Cardinal's
home? Is your six year old son happy and well?" Colon
assured me his hosts had been most gracious, he was
very comfortable, and his son was very happy remaining at La Rabida.

It was nearing Christmas and I instructed my
Treasurer to place Colon on my royal payroll, paying
him several thousand maravedies over the next few
months.

As those months lengthened into years Colon
became frustrated. Word reached my ears that his
nerves were wearing thin, that he was outspoken commenting, "It would be so much simpler if the Queen
would permit me to accept Medina Celi's offer." Since
that had not been given, Colon's faith in his convictions
sustained him as the long vigil began -- waiting,
patiently waiting -- to begin his epic journey discovering a new, shorter route to the Indies.

CHAPTER XXXIII
Malaga Victory

Granada was again torn apart by internal feuds. Muley Hacen's two sons, Abu and Ysuf, forced El Zagal to flee from Malaga to Guadix. Before his hasty departure, El Zagal appointed the dauntless and fierce El Zagri to defend Malaga.

Every year I had ordered more ships and now they were plying the waters along the coastlines off the Mediterranean shores of southern Granada. Our flamboyant sea captains effectively set up blockades cutting off the supplies being shipped to the Moors from Asia and North Africa. Ferdinand and his Council of War met to select the battle areas for our spring offensive against Granada. There were three major territories where we would eventually pitch our army tents, military artillery and troops. Malaga at the western border, Granada situated in the central plateau, and Baza near their eastern frontier. Malaga, lying directly south of our major supply bases of Sevilla and Cordoba, was the logical target. First we would march against Velez Malaga, a small city located directly to the east of the port city of Malaga.

On April 7, 1487, Ferdinand mounted his chestnut war horse and with banners unfurled, rode at the head of twenty thousand cavalry and forty thousand foot soldiers, with an uncounted number of mules with small bells tied around their necks, pulling the artillery of cannons, lombards, munitions and gun powder. Velez Malaga's defenses were severely hampered by our successful naval blockades making it possible for our large cavalry and foot soldiers to overwhelm the nearly defenseless Moors. On April 27th the territory of Velez Malaga once again officially belonged to Spain.

Ferdinand immediately proceeded west leading his victorious troops towards Malaga. Arriving at the outskirts of the city, he struck camp and sent an envoy with a message for El Zegri to surrender. El Zegri shot back with, "I was commanded to defend this city of Malaga, not to surrender it." With that terse remark, the envoy returned to Ferdinand's camp. El Zegri had a reputation of being a fierce warrior who inspired his men to fight to the finish. Ferdinand's keen military perception moved him to prepare for a long and lengthy siege of the city before it would surrender.

The battle for Malaga soon broke in a furious reign of terror from both foes. Ferdinand studied the territory calculating where the artillery should be placed for the most effective bombardment of the city. Never in history had such powerful forces of destruction been assembled by any nation's military might. Our camp was teeming with armorers and smiths, carpenters and engineers who were busy late into the night constructing new and strange machines under the watchful eye of Don Francisco Ramirez.

The correspondence from my pen continued to flow to every kingdom in my realm, keeping the cities and towns informed of our progress. My words seemed to ignite the fires of patriotism to burn even more fiercely. The cavaliers and hidalgos flocked into Malaga to help our cause. The army number swelled and at times there was a count of sixty thousand foot soldiers, and at other times nearly ninety thousand soldiers had volunteered to serve. All the while I remained behind the scenes marshalling, equipping, working far into the nights over my endless correspondence developing the order of the shipments of supplies, overseeing mule trains leaving on schedule effectively pushing along our routes to deliver food, clothing, medicines and gun powder.

Besides the high ecclesiastics who attended our Court, the camp was well supplied with priests, friars and chaplains of the great nobility who daily performed the religious ceremonies for our troops.

In the middle of July, I left Cordoba to move closer to the battle front. I set out with my oldest daughter, Ysabel, the Archbishop of Toledo, other church dignitaries and a courtly train of ladies and cavaliers. As we were approaching the outskirts of Malaga, the Marquis Duke de Cadiz and the acting Grand Master of Santiago, Alfonso de Cardenas, rode out to greet me and my little army escorting us to Ferdinand's well protected camp. I looked around at the faces lined with smiles and voices that were filled with enthusiasm and hope. I knew the morale of the troops was high for this was a good omen.

A day or two after my arrival, the Duke de Medina Sidonia, who had furnished his quota of troops at the opening of the campaign, now arrived with reinforcements, along with a hundred galleys filled with supplies, and another loan of 20,000 doblas.

Our naval blockade was so effective the supplies the Moors had been counting on never arrived. Their food supplies and ammunition began to rapidly diminish.

For four months Ferdinand had relentlessly kept up a perpetual bombardment of the city, firing formidable engines of destruction from the hillsides destroying the walls, towers and buildings. Night and day the noise of the war machines echoed throughout the city. Word reached us that Hamet El Zegri's soldiers were running out of food, the citizens reduced to eating animals, disease was rampant and people lay dying in the streets.

Pulling his last line of battle troops together, Zegri retreated behind the walls of the great fortress Gribalfro and decided to negotiate the best terms that he could. A deputation of principal citizens soon arrived at Ferdinand's headquarters offering to surrender the city providing Ferdinand would honor the same terms and conditions he had presented when he arrived at the walls of the city four months earlier. Ferdinand refused.

The Commander of Leon rode through the gates of Malaga at the head of his well appointed chivalry taking possession of the lower fortress, stationed his troops along the fortification, and unfurled the Christian banners of Spain from the towers of the city.

On August 18th, Ferdinand and I made our State entrance attended by our Court, clergy, and military. Our procession moved in a stately manner through the deserted, hushed city. We moved forward to the steps of the Cathedral of St. Mary where we dismounted and attended the Mass and heard the glorious Te Deum chanted. We prostrated ourselves before the Lord of Hosts, giving thanks for His divine presence and help to reclaim these domains which had once belonged to our ancestors.

The ceremony completed, we traveled to the great courtyard of the fortress where the people of the city had been ordered to assemble. The captive Moors stared in grim silence as Ferdinand and I made our entrance. Our appointed magistrate stepped forward, and in a deep booming voice which rang throughout the courtyard, he pronounced the sentence of slavery for every one of them. Then the magistrate continued, "One-third of the slaves would be exchanged for prisoners languishing in prisons in North Africa, one-third were to become the property of the State which would help pay the expenses of the war, and one-third were to be disposed of as 'presents' the Sovereign's whims."

It was true, our actions seemed overly harsh; however, we decided to make this victory an example of harshness because from a strategic standpoint, we thought it to be sound. We hoped, and I prayed with all my heart, that such an "act of terrifying severity" would bring the Moors to total surrender and end the suffering in both our lands. The Islamic law of "fight until every last Muslim is dead" continued to hold sway over the Moors, and my undaunted courage and midnight vigilance fired the flames of the onward march toward victory.

CHAPTER XXXIV
Moclin Surrenders

My prayers were not answered. El Zagel and Abu ignored the severity of the sentence imposed on their people at Malaga. Disappointed, but full of confidence, I began another round of organizing for our next selected target -- Moclin. Ferdinand, our nobles, troops and by now the ever present artillery, began their march. We had moved our Court to Baena. I proceeded to reorganize supplies, secure more troops and would then follow within a few days.

The wily old Bishop of Jaen who heard about our plans to take Moclin hurried to Baena to present to me a formidable plan. The Bishop pointed out that his area had been harassed by the Moors for years. They occupied two fortresses, the Cambiul and the Albaha, each situated high up on the steep rocky cliffs on each side of the Rio Frio river. These two great fortresses commanded all the roads and from their lofty heights they held sway over the entire countryside spreading terror with their constant forays raping, robbing and even murder. The Bishop asked, "Why not pause on the way to Moclin and take these two fortresses?"

With an instinctive sense of knowing we needed to eliminate the Moors from their lofty perch, I decided to move my children, the Court and entire household to the Alcazar of Jaen which stood like a sentinel commanding another mountain road. Then I sent for Don Francisco Ramirez and we sat down to study the maps of the impassable area surrounding these two impregnable fortresses. We formulated a wild idea, but I knew it would work.

The Moors commanding the two giant fortresses watched the approach of my royal army and observed that I had taken command of the Alcazar at Jaen. They concluded that our next attempt would be to force our way in battle to take their well protected citadels scoffing at the idea that we would be so stupid as to make an attempt to pitch a battle there. It was absolutely impossible for us to drag our dreaded artillery over the rugged paths, around the craggy cliffs, and up the steep inclines. Don Francisco and I had agreed, too, that it was impossible to access the well protected fortresses using normal passageways. We had devised our grand plan, one which stunned the enemy and won for us the two lofty citadels. We would build a new road.

My usual thorough organization and ability to spur my people into action resulted in thousands of volunteers arriving in Jaen with pickaxes, crowbars, shovels and every other necessary implement to dig a tunnel through the mountain, move the troops and artillery through that newly provided passageway, with an exit on the craggy plateau just outside the gates of both citadels.

The volunteers went to work with spades loosening the dirt with pickaxes and crowbars to break up the rocks. Far into the night, up again before dawn, they progressed with the new road and tunneled through the mountain. The Bishop of Jaen marked the route and superintended the workmen. Some time later, Don Ramirez and the Bishop announced they had completed the tunnel and were ready to pull the ordnance into place. The next morning the Moors looked out their towers and saw their surroundings dotted with cannons and troops loading them with gun powder ready to blast our way into the very midst of their impregnable fortresses. Within a matter of hours, the two fortresses had surrendered and we had gained an important checkpoint on our march to Moclin.

I received a dispatch from Ferdinand containing the good news that Moclin had surrendered. I left immediately for Ferdinand's camp pitched just outside the conquered city. Arriving on the banks of the Yegus river, I was met by an advance corps under the command of the Marquis Duke de Cadiz, and at a distance of a league and a half from Moclin, the Duke de Infantado was waiting with his principal nobility and all their vassals dressed in splendid colors.

I halted my Court and train, wishing to refresh ourselves and change into elaborate dresses before proceeding on to the formal State entry and ceremonies at Moclin. I dressed carefully, choosing a velvet skirt, and a red mantilla to cover my hair. My hair had always been thin and fine, but as the years passed by it became thinner and thinner. I decided to wear little caps covering my head which concealed the thinning hair. I had a fashionable black velvet hat that was heavily embroidered with gold thread and I secured it on my head, over the mantilla. As I emerged from my pavilion, one of my aides was throwing a bright red saddle blanket over the chestnut mule I would ride. Next he placed the harness with a bridle of silver and gold, and then he cinched the side-saddle which was elaborately embossed with gold and silver. My daughter, Ysabel, would be riding beside me, and her mule was also elaborately saddled, with a bridle decorated in gold and silver.

My ladies-in-waiting were now beginning to assemble, each dressed in an exquisite gown, their brown mules saddled and haltered in satin and silver. Mounting our mules, we were ready for the grand procession.

Ferdinand approached from the opposite direction riding at the head of his nobles. He was dressed in a crimson doublet, yellow satin breeches, and over his shoulders he had thrown a cassock of rich brocade and a sportvest of the same material which concealed his cuirass. At his side he had buckled a Moorish scimitar.

The splendid train of chivalry which followed behind him included the daring, dashing English Lord Scales who had a retinue of five pages appropriately dressed in their costly liveries. Lord Scales was sheathed in complete mail over which he had thrown a French cloak of dark silk brocade. A buckler was attached by golden clasps to his arm, and on his head he wore a French hat with plumes. The horse he rode was covered with an elaborate blanket which swept to the ground made of blue silk, lined with violet and sprinkled with gold stars. Lord Scales managed his fiery steed with a masterful display of horsemanship bringing shouts of approval from the crowds.

Waiting just outside the city of Moclin on the left of the road the militia of Sevilla, glittering in their bright, fashionable dress, were assembled. As I approached the banner of their city unfurled before me waving in the soft breeze, I motioned for the banner of that illustrious city to be passed to my right. Then as I continued to advance, the successive battalions gave me their salutes as they lowered their standards. Their joyous cries echoed throughout the valleys announcing with tumultuous acclamations their Queen had arrived at the gates of the Moor's conquered city.

Ferdinand drew up before me, first bowing and then affectionately giving me a kiss. Then he moved towards our daughter and gave her his parental blessing and then kissed her on the cheek. We were now ready to meet the conquered Moors. We advanced forward through the gates of the city observing the Captain of the defeated Moors moving toward us. We bowed three times in formal reverence to each other, then we invited the defeated leader to ride by our side as we rode in formal state into the fallen jewel in Granada's crown.

CHAPTER XXXV
The Miracle of Baza

We had begun to forge our ring around the capital of Granada. The next question was, "Where do we launch our next attack?" There were three major cities in the east, Baza, Guadix and Almeria. Almeria was on the Mediterranean, protected on the north by the natural terrain of the rugged Alpujarra mountains. It was hopelessly impossible, totally beyond reach. El Zagel continued to hold iron control over Guadix. When the time was right, we would attack Baza.

In the autumn of 1487, Ferdinand and I traveled with our children to Aragon to obtain the recognition of the Cortes of Aragon of our ten year old son, Infante Juan III, as the heir apparent to the Crown, and for Ferdinand to oversee other pressing governmental matters. Aragon had been slowly adopting and implementing, with great reservations, the successful governmental reforms which were working well in Castile. At Ferdinand's prodding, they had organized an institution similar to our Santa Hermandad to catch marauding thieves. The Hermandad was extremely unpopular with Aragon's great feudal nobility whose power, or rather abuse of power, was considerably curbed by this popular military force. Under Ferdinand's guidance the Cortes voted to extend the Santa Hermandad another five years.

After handling other pressing matters, and obtaining an appropriation from the Cortes of Aragon for the war against the Moors, we left for Valencia, traveled on to Murcia and home to Valladolid.

All during the winter of 1488 we were occupied with the affairs of the interior government of Castile, holding our Court in the capital city of Valladolid. I continued to oversee the building and surrounding complexes of the La Cartuja de Miraflores just outside Burgos. The tiny alabaster figures sculpted by the architect and Master sculptor, Gil de Siloe, were taking shape and beginning to weave together the stories of their lives. I was totally fascinated with this artist's progress. Every tiny little figure chiseled out of the original large alabaster piece was perfect. They were going to be spectacular tombs. My younger brother's tomb would be a likeness of him carved out of alabaster depicting him kneeling in prayer. These three tombs would be a fitting tribute to my family, of that I was certain.

An embassy from Maximilian, son of the Emperor Frederick the Fourth of Germany arrived asking for an audience. They wanted our official support of their claims against France for the restitution of Frederick's late wife's, Mary of Burgundy, inheritance -- the Duchy of Burgundy. They, in turn, promised to support us in our unresolved dispute of Roussillion and Cerdagne.

Maximilian and Mary of Burgundy had a son, Philip, the Archduke of Burgundy and of Hapsburg, and a daughter, Margaret, each about the same ages as our two children, Infante Juan and Infanta Juana. Discovering that France had another bitter enemy at its eastern border, Ferdinand's crafty mind began thinking along the lines of uniting the Spanish and Hapsburg dynasties in marriage. I argued the time was not now to negotiate marriage contracts for our nine and ten year old children. Granada was to occupy every precious moment of my time.

We planned our attack against Baza. If we expanded our troops and artillery in the eastern territory we could eliminate the powerful El Zagel. After Baza, we would march south to gain control of the wealthy seaport of Almeria, and then back to Guadix which held rich mineral deposits. We had learned through diplomatic sources El Zagal had gathered the most ferocious troops in their entire empire to fortify Baza and Guadix.

In the spring of 1489 we moved to Jaen where I established my Court. Ferdinand placed himself at the head of fifteen thousand horses and nearly one hundred thousand soldiers, and in keeping with our other military campaigns, riding behind him was the chivalrous array of nobility and knighthood with their stately and well appointed retinues now accustomed to following the royal standard in this Holy Crusade.

Ferdinand's troops quickly won the strong outpost of Cuxar just two leagues from Baza. To the west of Cuxar was a thick forest of trees and bushes. Within this grove of trees the Moors had built heavily fortified hidden fortresses. There was no way we could penetrate the city of Baza without first gaining control of the grove. The Marquis Duke de Cadiz had arrived from the west striking his camp on the opposite side of the grove, unable to link up with Ferdinand. There was no alternative but to hack down every bush and tree. Ferdinand's troops cut and chopped from the east and the Marquis and his troops hacked away from the opposite side of the grove. As they cleared the way, they built roads to pull the artillery along to blast the hidden fortifications. It was tedious, slow progress, taking more than seven weeks. Hand to hand battles in the grove raged throughout the summer before the Moslem chief, Reduan Zafasraga, retreated.

Summer was ending and Ferdinand's Council of War reviewed our precarious position. It would be impossible and unwise to mount a siege against Baza because it was situated just twenty leagues from Guadix. The Moors could launch their vicious counter attacks from that city and demolish our camp. Winter was sure to bring harsh rains, bitter cold winds and snow exposing our troops to famine and disease.

Under these gloomy aspirations, the Council of War met. The Marquis Duke de Cadiz urged Ferdinand to break camp and postpone the demolition of Baza. Gutierre de Cardenas, Commander of Leon, advised him to hold on. With two conflicting opinions, Ferdinand sent a dispatch to me asking for my decision.

I read through Ferdinand's bleak dispatch and quickly realized that all my mighty preparations were about to vanish into thin air. With a prayer on my lips, I dipped my quill into the inkwell and asking God to guide my hand, I replied to my husband's unsettling dilemma. In my note to him I wrote, "Ferdinand, do not distrust the providence of God which has seen us through so many perils. May I remind you that the Moor's fortunes have never been at such a low ebb as at the present time. If your soldiers will be true to their duty, they can rely upon me for the faithful discharge of mine in furnishing them with all the requisite supplies."

The uplifting tone of my letter had an instantaneous effect, silencing those who were grumbling and building up the confidence of others. Gutierre Cardenas was handed the supervision of using all the trees and bushes which had been felled during the summer months to build a border of the camp, fortified with palisades constructed out of the timber. They hastily erected strong towers of mud and clay. For two months ten thousand men with an inexhaustible energy labored under the direction of the Commander of Leon. For some strange reason, Cidi Yahya, the commanding officer at Baza, was silent. No attack was launched against their formidable enemy encamped so near to their protected city. Ferdinand took command of a group of soldiers who promptly erected two thousand huts with walls of earth and clay, and roofs of timber. From their towers the soldiers of Baza stared in amazement as these huts were erected within a matter of days. The huts lined the streets and squares and soon a teaming small city had emerged. In the meantime, I was busy fulfilling my commitment as the mule trains traveled the now familiar roads back and forth from Jaen to Baza. I sent communiques to Aragon, Valencia, Catalonia and Sicily inviting the merchants to visit the camp and sell their goods.

During the summer and early fall the weather had been warm and cooled occasionally by light rain showers. Late autumn was advancing and Ferdinand and his commanding officers knew surviving the winter would tax everyone's endurance.

Suddenly a furious drenching rain flooded the streams in the mountains causing them to overflow their banks, rushing down the mountainside carrying rocks, mud and trees ripped from the sandy soil. Our camp which had been built in the low fields at the base of the mountain was directly in line of the rushing waters. In the dead of night, the raging waters swirled through the fragile mud and clay huts, sweeping them away before the rush of the rocks and felled trees. The road built from Jaen to Baza over which our troops and supplies had moved so freely was totally washed out, the bridges had collapsed leaving rocks and wood obstructing the streams of water still rushing toward the plains surrounding Baza.

All communications with Jaen had been cut off and our daily convoys attempting to deliver more supplies soon became mired down in the mud. Ferdinand's camp was now faced with deep anxieties and possible annihilation.

It was a very grave situation which I faced. I needed to immediately rush aid to Ferdinand and our troops. Without hesitation, I urgently appealed for troops, food, and volunteers to rebuild the roads, restructure the bridges and clear away the fallen trees obstructing the roads. Don Francisco Rameriz mapped out another route for a road that could be easily built. Within a remarkably short time we had rebuilt the main roads to Baza and added another route. From these passages leading to Baza soon appeared the now legendary fourteen thousand mule train with tinkling bells tied around the necks of the mules pulling the wagons piled with freshly ground grains, blankets, medicines and other supplies. The sounds of Christianity were now ringing throughout the eastern sector of the Moors' land.

My next concern was to assemble new levies for troops to relieve and reinforce the Baza camp. With an amazing swiftness men from every corner of the kingdom answered my summons. Meeting these enormous unexpected expenditures drained my treasury and now taxed my imagination to replenish the empty accounts. I made my pleas to individuals and the churches, and received a reluctant response. They came to my aid, but I knew it was with great misgivings. Still, I was in need of more money. I had only one resource and that was the Crown jewels. I had borrowed money using them as collateral during the Portugal conflict, and I did not hesitate to enter into negotiations once again with the merchants in Barcelona and Valencia placing them as collateral for their loans. Much to my personal regret, the merchants of Valencia insisted upon the ruby necklace which Ferdinand had given to me as my wedding gift to be included as part of the Crown jewels. When the messenger returned asking for the ruby necklace, I broke the seal of its hiding place in the wood cross, took it out, and heaving a sigh, placed it in the waiting messenger's outstretched hands. I promised myself the loan on the Crown jewels of Spain would be repaid quickly and the property of the Crown returned to its "keeper."

The siege continued vigorously but Baza made no sign of submission. We had demolished their garrisons one by one, their supply of ammunition was nearly gone and still the town survived. On the other hand, Ferdinand's camp was overrun with sickness and morale was dangerously low.

Receiving these grim reports, I decided to travel to Baza. I knew that my presence would uplift the spirit of the camp and we would win. I had a fresh supply of troops, grains, gun powder and more mules had been purchased. My entire Court insisted upon accompanying me. Just a few days before leaving Jaen, I decided to search for more tinkling bells. I located hundreds of bells of every size and before we departed, they were hung from the horse collars, bridles and wagons of our brigade. We were a merry group filled with laughter and joy as we departed from Jaen. We traveled along our roads and ascended the high Sierra passes where we encountered the howling, bitter cold November winds, the driving sleet, rain and snow as we lumbered over the roads, crossed the bridges, moved through the valleys, and around the mountains making slow, but steady progress.

On November 7th our caravan emerged from the mountain passes with our bright banners unfurled and waving in the wind, and our musicians playing melodious light hearted tunes. The Spanish cavaliers trooped from their camp to receive their beloved Queen, giving me a joyous, overwhelming welcome.

All was quiet in the city of Baza. The change that came over the camp at my arrival permeated the entire area. At the moment I appeared, the cruel skirmishes which had been occurring daily ended. There was not one single report of artillery or clashing of arms. The clashing sounds of swords were stilled. The mood for reconciliation and peace seemed at hand.

The next day I donned my mail, mounted my chestnut horse, and reviewed the army stretched out in order of battle along the rolling hills of Baza. Next Ferdinand, Mendoza and I, cantered all around the city of Baza, protected and insulated from their poison darts and arrows by our well trained Spanish cavaliers.

Arriving back at the camp, we instructed Gutierre de Cardenas to open a conference to arrange an armistice with Cidi Yahya. Yahya thoughtfully reviewed the terms of our truce and stated to Cardenas he must discuss it with El Zagel at Guadix and receive his instructions. Cidi returned the next day with Zagal's acknowledgment of defeat.

On December 4, 1489, riding at the head of our

legions, Ferdinand and I made our triumphant entry into Baza watching from a distance the now familiar spectacle of the standard of the silver cross raised at the top of the city's ancient fortress. Appearing before us was a nervous Cidi Yahya, standing militarily erect, bracing himself, ready for the harsh sentence we would mete out to his people. Ferdinand and I had decided to use a surprise tactic. We presented him with presents and acts of courtesy which so dazzled him he immediately declared he wanted to be "in service" to us.

Cidi left immediately to once again discuss the terms of peace with El Zagel. He spoke frankly as he bravely confronted the old warrior, advising his leader Granada could no longer defend itself. He pointed out to El Zagel the Spanish naval armada was steadily growing, and the Christian troops and artillery were replaced faster than the Moors could destroy it. El Zagel listened without blinking an eyelid. After a long silence, he took a deep breath and nodded in agreement.

On December 7th, our Spanish troops marched out of the gates of Baza. Riding at the center was Ferdinand with me and my Court at the rear. We were marching south to receive the keys to the city of Almeria from El Zagal. We inched our way through the many narrow passes, over the mountains whose peaks were never warmed by the sun, and fierce winds blew. Many of our men and horses, numbed by the intense cold, exhausted and sick, lost their lives.

Just outside Almeria we were met by El Zagal who had ridden forth to escort our great body of nobles to the palace to hand to me the keys to that city.

And so it was that Almeria, nestled on the seashore of the Mediterranean, became another shining jewel in our Spanish Crown.

CHAPTER XXXVI
Ysabel Marries the Prince of Portugal

Baza, Guadix and Almeria had surrendered. We had won the eastern sector of Granada. Now only the capital city of Granada remained to be conquered.

Returning to Jaen, we calculated the heavy losses we had sustained during the siege of Baza. The cost of rebuilding the roads and bridges, providing for the additional troops, supplies and artillery was staggering. It had been a mighty effort.

Our war with Granada had continued for eight long, weary years. The events of the Baza campaign exemplified in many ways everything which seemed to divinely become first possibilities, then realities. For instance, there was the courage, constancy and discipline of our Spanish soldiers. I had a renewed inner strength which came to my rescue during the disastrous flood crises. My words of encouragement to the leaders who faced our enemy gave them new hope. It was a miracle that the supplies manifested so quickly, the roads rebuilt within such a short span of time, the medical supplies arrived and volunteers to care for the sick and wounded answered my urgent pleas. The immense sum of money was raised quickly to carry on with the war. As I moved among my counsel, soldiers and nobles, I shared their fatigue and danger as I displayed my own brand of courage and fortitude.

As soon as the campaign for Baza, Guadix and Almeria ended, we sent an embassy to call upon Emir Abu Abdallah in Granada, requesting him to surrender his city honoring the Treaty he signed when he was our prisoner at Loja and we had allowed him to return to Granada a free man.

Emir Abdallah excused himself from obeying our summons stating, "I am no longer my own master, and although I have the strongest desire to keep my engagement, I am prevented by the inhabitants of the city." Abdallah then sent his troops into El Zagal's conquered cities of Guadix, Baza and Almeria challenging the Moors to revolt against Castile.

Ferdinand acted quickly to retaliate. In the spring of 1490 he marched onto the cultivated plains surrounding Granada burning crops, destroying cattle, sheep, and mules, rolling up the tide of devastation to the very walls of the city.

Our son, Juan, only twelve years old, joined his father in this campaign. Following the Castilian nobles' ancient custom of training our children from their tender years to attack the Moors, our son was ready to be knighted. The Ceremony of Knighthood was performed on the banks of the grand canal directly under the battlements of the beleaguered city of Granada. Our son's sponsors were the Dukes de Cadiz and Medina Sedonia. After the ceremony was completed, our new knight performed the honors of chivalry on his young companions-in-arms who had accompanied him to the field of battle.

We decided to move our Court to Sevilla, directing the affairs of our governments of Castile and Aragon from that southern city and maintain our vigil along our southern borders.

It was at this time we were honored by the Ambassador from Lisbon arriving in Sevilla to propose a treaty of marriage between our nineteen year old daughter, Ysabel, and Prince Alonso, heir to the Portuguese throne. Ysabel, so gentle and sweet in disposition, had endeared herself to many subjects in Castile. We were very proud of her and knew this would be a very good marriage for our oldest child.

The *"ceremony of affiancing"* was held at Sevilla in April, with Don Fernando de Silveria representing the Prince of Portugal. Following this ceremony we celebrated with a succession of wonderful fetes and tourneys. Suddenly the Guadaliquivir river was ablaze with the Spanish galleons of the nobles moored at the docks, decked with billowing gold silk cloth, protected from the Andalucian sun by bright colored awnings, and richly embroidered with the armorial bearings of the ancient houses of Castile. This impressive spectacle embraced the entire rank and beauty of our Court. My pretty daughter was the center of attention attended by seventy noble ladies and a hundred pages from our royal household. Young and old cavaliers thronged to the tournaments eager to win laurels as they participated in the tourneys before this brilliant assemblage of Castilian nobility. Ferdinand broke several lances as he was challenged by the nobles. He was among the most distinguished of the combatants demonstrating his dexterity and horsemanship. Everyone welcomed the laughter and jovial atmosphere after our weary years of discipline and war.

A few months later, Ysabel departed with her magnificent wardrobe and retinue for Portugal, escorted by the Grand Cardinal of Spain, the acting Grand Master of Santiago, and a throng of nobles who attended her wedding to the future king of Portugal.

All during the winter of 1490 and early 1491 we had been preparing for the future conflict with Granada. In the month of April, Ferdinand took command of the army marching toward the Moor's capital determined to camp before its walls and never leave until Abu finally surrendered. The Marquis Duke de Cadiz, Marquis de Villena and the Counts de Tendilla, Cabra and Urena, along with Alonso de Aguilar traveled with him eager to share in the closing triumphant battle.

On April 26th, the army camped at the small village of Ojos de Huescar situated in a valley about fifteen leagues from Granada. Granada was a formidable city to capture because of its location and it was well defended. It was hemmed in on the east by the wild barrier of the Sierra Nevada, whose snow-clad mountain summits dispersed the cool breezes over the city in the early spring. Our Christian soldiers struck their military camp on the rolling slopes just west of the ancient capital city. The inhabitants of Granada were indignant at the sight of those Christian soldiers who dared to camp under the shadow of their own battlements. They sent small bands of military galloping to the edge of the valley touting our soldiers to draw their swords.

I again packed my entire household goods, and along with my children and ladies of my Court, left the Alcala de Reales and arrived near Ferdinand's pitched camp. The festivity which reigned throughout the camp after my arrival did not divert my attention from the stern business of war. I plunged into superintending the military preparations and personally inspected every section of the encampment. Dressed in complete armor, mounted on my chestnut horse, I cantered toward the battlefield to visit their quarters and review my troops, chatting with many, commending some and sympathizing with others.

I wanted to visually see the city of Granada. There was a little house in the village of Zubia just a short distance from Granada which I selected, thinking it offered the best view of the forbidden city. Ferdinand and I stood at one of the windows in this little house and looked out at the majestic Alhambra situated high on the hilltops of that fabled city. My eyes roved the landscape before me, and I wondered out loud, "Ferdinand, how much longer will it be?" Ferdinand took a deep breath, and as he slowly let it out, he finally shook his head saying, "I don't know, Ysabella, I cannot even hazard a guess."

I looked back for a final glance at the great stately and majestic Alhambra and a fleeting thought flashed through my mind assuring me that, "It will be soon, very soon."

CHAPTER XXXVII
Santa Fe!

Pressed as I was for time to arrange all of the details for my daughter's wedding and prepare for the next Granada battleground, my mind continued to swing back and forth, like the pendulum of a clock, dwelling on the possibilities Cristobol Colon posed in his unique and totally incomprehensible scheme. I couldn't shake the feeling that "loco" as it sounded, it might be possible. Then, too, many of the nobles in my Court had been moved by Colon's convincing arguments which were heightened by his eloquence and grandeur when he presented his views. These nobles cordially embraced his scheme and extended to him their intimate personal relationships. Among the nobles was the Grand Cardinal Mendoza, a giant among the intellectuals and very well acquainted with the affairs of the nation which raised him above many other clerics who had narrow views. There was also Deza, the Archbishop of Sevilla, Ferdinand's confessor who had a considerable influence over Ferdinand. He, too, had responded to the eloquence of Colon's pleas. The authority of such an august body of men continued to sway my thoughts. Apparently Colon was a guest of Medina Celi, for I noted that he was among Celi's retinue during the fetes and tourneys at my daughter's wedding celebrations. During one of my conversations with Celi, he casually mentioned that Colon's patience was wearing very thin, and that he was most eager to have some decisions made in regard to his plan to explore the new route to India.

A few days later del Pulgar informed me that a persistent Colon was asking for another interview. I knew that Colon had sent some communiques to me which were not opened, not because I was not interested, but I had no time to waste in pondering his project. I had directed the unread notes to be filed with my other papers I had labeled, "earth is round scheme."

Within minutes Pulgar had returned with a sheaf of papers in his hand with a sort of "half-smile" on his face. He placed them before me and busied himself arranging other papers on my desk. I started to read the most recent letter from Colon. I looked up at Pulgar and said, "He wants to become the Governor of the new land. That's interesting."

Pulgar smiled and motioned for me to read on. My eyebrows lifted a little as I read the next point out loud to my First Secretary. "He wants a royalty of 10% of all the gold, silver and jewels that Castile will receive from his successful adventure."

Pulgar's head nodded up and down, again motioning me to read further. I glanced at the next point and put the paper down. Shaking my head in disbelief, I said, "Colon wants to be named the Viceroy of all the new territories. Well. ."

Pulgar said, "Just one more point, your Highness." I picked the paper up and read it through. I wasn't certain I had read it correctly so I read it again. Yes, he was very clear on his last point, he wished to be named an Admiral in our Navy!

I looked at Pulgar and said, "As soon as the Court is moved to Cordoba, send him a message and tell him that I will speak with him again."

Several weeks later Pulgar sent his communique to Colon advising him that I would see him. I showed the demands to Ferdinand, and after he read them, he looked up at me with the "I told you so" look, and then shaking his head, said, "I don't like this fellow. I don't trust men with red hair and blue eyes. He is a foreigner. Probably a spy for a foreign country. Throw the imposter out." I listened to my husband's ranting and in the end paid no attention to him.

Colon arrived for his audience with us. Ferdinand was moody and non-communicative. I watched Colon's body movements again. His clear, direct gaze told me he was totally unafraid of anyone, anywhere. I listened to his well chosen words. I asked him if he had made any new scientific discovery in his search to prove the earth was round, and if there was further evidence to substantiate his plans to reach the Indies by a new route.

Colon shared the conversations he had with our sea captains, and he interpreted the information they had given him into such a way that for his expedition it could all be possible.

I picked up the sheaf of papers and read his first point. I looked into those bold, blue yes, and said, "That's one of your conditions?" Without hesitation, he said, "Yes." I moved to the second point and then to the third demand. Colon was steadfast in his determination not to waver on his written demands for payment and honors to be bestowed upon him should he succeed.

I looked at the last point and said, "And it is an Admiral of the Navy that we must also bestow upon you?" With a strong emphasis, he replied, "Yes!"

I looked at this confident man standing before me and said, "Sir, your ideas are noble, thought provoking and possibly correct. Our Castilian law permits only a person of noble birth to be appointed an Admiral in our Navy. This is the law of our realm. You cannot be appointed an Admiral for you are not a Castilian of noble birth."

I had expected him to retreat on that point. Instead he shifted his body posture, pulled his shoulder's back, readjusted his cloak, looked directly into my eyes, and then at Ferdinand, who, I noted had a smirk on his face, and addressing both of us said, "Your Highnesses, I am very much aware of your realm's laws. I respect them, for in such an admirable way have you rebuilt a realm shaken to the very depths of depravation, tyranny and bankruptcy molding it into a productive, prosperous land. Yes, your Graces, I know your country by heart. I know your people. I understand your dream. I want to be a part of that great dream. I want your Majesties to be accorded the highest honors the world has yet to witness. I want that for you. I will be named an Admiral in your Royal Navy!" He bowed low, turned swiftly on his heel and quickly departed.

Ferdinand looked at me and said, "You see, he is 'loco.' No sane man of such low birth, uneducated and impoverished, would ever stand before two Monarchs and insist upon becoming an Admiral!"

Colon's words echoed and re-echoed in my ears. Nothing made a lot of sense, but still, I couldn't shake the feeling that I could bend and allow him a portion of his demands.

Late that afternoon I drafted a note to be delivered to Colon agreeing to accept the first three points in his demands. On the last point I stated, "I cannot break the laws of Castile. An Admiral in the Royal Navy you cannot be."

I sent one of my personal couriers off to deliver the note to Colon. Cristobol was at his home when the note was delivered to him. He motioned for my aide to sit in a chair and wait. Quickly he scanned the note, then he took out his quill and found a scrap of paper to respond. "Thank you, your Majesty, for your offer. I am indeed grateful for the first three points to have been concluded in such a forthright and acceptable manner. I insist, an Admiral in your Navy I must be."

I placed his note among the others he had written and decided to think about Colon's adventures later.

It was in the middle of July, a hot and muggy summer. I was staying in a lovely pavilion at our military camp just a few leagues from the city of Granada. One of my attendants carelessly placed a lamp too near a silk drapery and it caught on fire. The flames swiftly spread to all the tents of the camp which were built of light combustible materials. The leaping flames of the burning camp cast an eerie shadow placing everyone in grave danger!

My children and I escaped out a side entrance as the smoke and flames nearly suffocated us. I heard the trumpets sounding the call to arms for it could be a night attack had been staged by the enemy. Ferdinand hastily snatched up his sword and boldly put himself at the head of his troops. Ever vigilant, the Marquis Duke of Cadiz assembled his troops to station themselves on a plateau facing Granada ready to repel a surprise attack from the Moors.

The next morning Ferdinand and I walked through the burned rubble. It was an emotional, troubling problem that we faced. I looked at the charred pieces of burned wood, and then up at my husband. "We'll have to rebuild, but there is no money. We've pledged every maravedis we can spare to win all of Castile." Ferdinand was silent. I heaved a sigh. "Our people have been taxed to their limits, we cannot ask them for more." I continued to survey the scene, wrinkling my nose as I smelled the burned cinders. Suddenly an idea popped into my mind, and I knew it could work. My problem was solved.

A council was immediately convened to review the fire disaster and to discuss ways to prevent a future catastrophe. We made plans to rebuild comfortable winter quarters for the army and decided to build the town with substantial, permanent buildings. Everyone began to ask among themselves, "Where is the money to rebuild?" I let them all speak up, nodding at one suggestion and then another, but they didn't devise a scheme which would raise money.

I looked around the table at this intelligent assemblage who were swearing we could accomplish miracles. I said to them, "Let's rebuild. Let us build a new town, and we will begin with laying out the main streets in the shape of a cross. We'll appeal to the people to give from their hearts, spontaneously, for this grand and noble town that we are about to build. Together, as a nation, we will all cooperate and rebuild. I will call upon the priests and townspeople throughout the land and present the drawings for our new town. I'll promise them we will build houses that are made of mortar and stone, not sticks and cloth."

I watched the frowns on their brows fade out to be replaced with smiles and nodding heads. Someone spoke up asking for my suggestion to be adopted, and without any hesitation they voted. I was ready to spring into action.

This master plan called for comfortable winter

quarters for our army, but the design of the buildings would be conventional so that when the war ended, those quarters would become comfortable homes for people living in the new village.

It had been years since I had mounted my horse and galloped over the countryside to make my personal pleas. I knew instinctively if my plan was to become a reality, once again I must ride from south to north, from east to west, visiting the cities, towns and hamlets to make my appeal direct to all the people.

Everything was readied for my departure. My last act was to kneel at the makeshift altar asking God to bless my mission. Kneeling in prayer, I saw a vision of the new town with large slabs of beautiful marble placed along the avenidas bearing inscriptions from all those Castilian cities and towns that responded to my call. I rose from prayer, renewed in my confidence that this vision, when presented to the provincial cities and towns, would capture imaginations and they would enthusiastically respond. My horse was saddled. My aides were mounted and waiting. In a flurry of drum-beats, the sound of the trumpets and the royal banners snapping in the wind, we were off galloping down the dusty road.

The first city to be presented the plan was Sevilla. Next would be Cordoba, then on to Toledo, Madrid, Segovia, Valladolid, Burgos, Salamanca, and all the other cities, towns and principalities in between. I would travel to every kingdom. There would be no favoritism shown to any of them. I would stop at each and speak with the people. My enthusiasm for this new town was strengthened when I told the people that their own city, in making their contributions for the "soon to be new town" would be honored as they selected a slab of marble, and chiseled their inscription of dedication on it. The marble would later be placed along the avenues of our new town.

I spoke of the great sacrifices our people had already made, of the soldiers who had given their lives for our country, of the hospital on our battlefields caring for the wounded, sick and dying. I asked them to contribute stones, bricks, mortar, cement, nails, roofing supplies, beams, doors, everything to build new structures. I asked for builders and architects to take a month from their own activities and travel south to lay out the town, design the buildings and direct the soldiers who soon would be laboring from early morning until late at night to complete our bold venture.

The response was far beyond my wildest hopes. The people cheered. They rushed forward with money, raw materials, and manpower. I would work late into the night getting dispatches ready for couriers to take to other cities, giving the people a progress report and an approximate time when I would be arriving in their area.

The mule trains, with bells tied to their wagons and hung around the necks of the mules, soon appeared on the roads from the north, east, and west lumbering along pulling wagons loaded with raw materials donated from every part of the country. Within just a matter of weeks after I had begun my ride, as I approached a city, I saw mule trains already moving out before I had even made my plea. Never had I been so proud of my people. It was an exciting, but very tiring trip. I soon realized that my body didn't respond to long days in the saddle as it did when I was young.

I completed my swing through the cities and smaller towns, and now I raced back to the military camp near Granada to see what needed to be done in the way of organizing the mountains of materials and supplies arriving daily at the camp.

Ferdinand's soldiers had become carpenters and skilled artisans, hammering, molding, designing, working feverishly to rebuild. The broad avenues had been laid out, the shape of the cross was centered, with stately portals built at each of the four outer corners of the cross. I watched all this feverish activity, proudly basking in the euphoria that Ferdinand and I, together, had captured the hearts, imagination and spirit of our nation.

Each city was vying to be first for their monument to be placed and, of course, much jockeying for the most prestigious place for their monument was debated. Each city wanted to be "first" in getting its recognition in place. Each was hoping theirs would be the largest and most impressive.

I walked along the streets paved with cobblestones and inspected every detail. As I moved along I selected the sites for the inscribed marble stones. That would resolve the contest now underway.

Within three months the new town was finished. The Moors sent their scouts out to observe all this feverish activity going on, reporting back to Abu that we were building a "city" of stones, brick and mortar. We had erected large buildings so swiftly the Moors went wailing to their mosques, "Allah has left us." They were alarmed! Almost overnight a "city" was rising from ashes. It was time for them to think about their future.

Finally the day arrived when we would formally dedicate the town. It needed a name. The workers clamored for it to be named Ysabella. In unison they shouted, "Ysabella, Ysabella, Ysabella!" I was standing on a light platform that had been erected especially for the dedication ceremonies, and as I listened to those voices shouting and echoing throughout the valley, I was proud. Yes, indeed I was. I looked over the crowd and for a moment reflected upon the clouds in the blue sky tinged with soft hues of pink, gold and green. It seemed to me this valley had been blessed by the Lord of Hosts. I looked down at that sea of humanity who had made daily sacrifices and diligently worked so hard, and I said to them, "Wouldn't it be better to give it the significant name of Santa Fe -- the *"Holy Faith."* For just a few moments there was total silence. They were speechless. I waited for another moment and then heads began bobbing up and down, their hats were thrown into the air, and soon the shouts of "Santa Fe, Santa Fe!" rang throughout the valley.

"Holy Faith." I went to sleep that night thanking God for all that had been accomplished. Little was I to know that the building of the town was, in actuality, the last battle we had to fight for the final jewel in our Spanish Crown.

CHAPTER XXXVIII
The Alhambra

The rebuilding of the town struck at the heart of the Moors. A new "city" had suddenly appeared in their midst filling them with fear and alarm for they beheld an enemy who dared to set foot on their soil and resolve never more to leave. They were suffering from the rigorous naval blockade we had mounted and their communications with Africa was brought to a complete standstill.

We heard rumors of pockets of insubordination and discontent in the city. Abdallah and his counselors became convinced they could not defend their capital.

In October, the vizer, Abul Cazim Abelmalic, opened negotiations for the surrender of Granada. We appointed our secretary, Fernando de Zafra and Gonsalvo de Cordoba to negotiate the terms of the surrender. Gonsalvo spoke the Moors' language fluently, totally familiar with the people, their customs and their religious ceremonies. The peace conferences were stealthily conducted in the utmost secrecy in the middle of the night. Some meetings were held within the walls of Granada and at other times in the little hamlet of Churriana at short distance away. After many sleepless nights, on November 25, 1491, the terms of the surrender were settled.

The conditions for surrender were similar to those granted at Baza. The populace would still possess their mosques and were free to exercise their religion with all its peculiarities and ceremonies -- with one exception. I insisted they would no longer be permitted to have four wives -- only one! They were to be judged by their own laws, under their own cadis or magistrates, subject to the general control of the Castilian Governor. Castile would recognize their ancient usages, manners, language and dress. They could retain their property and had the right to dispose of it as they wished. They could move with total freedom to any city. For the next three years, Castile would provide ships to transport everyone who wanted to relocate in Africa.

Emir Abdallah was given a small territory to reign over in the mountainous area of the Alpujarras near Almeria. He would acknowledge himself as our vassal required to pay a yearly tribute to the Castilian Crown. All their artillery and fortifications would be delivered to Castile. The date of January 2, 1492 was set for Abdallah to formally surrender his city. Our careful preparations went forward for this last dramatic act to ring down the curtain on eight hundred years of foreign domination.

Our triumphant celebrations were clouded when a special envoy, riding night and day from Lisbon, arrived bringing the news that Prince Alonso, our new son-in-law, had fallen from his horse in an accident and was dead. Our oldest daughter was a widow! For nine days the nation mourned the death of our beloved son-in-law and grieved for dear Ysabel, alone and so far, far away.

On January 2nd, every sector of Santa Fe was bustling with activities. First, the Grand Cardinal

Mendoza mounted his horse, followed by his household and our veteran troops. Slowly they picked their way through the winding streets of Granada making their way toward the Hill of Martyrs.

Ferdinand, surrounded by his own courtiers with all their stately retinues, glittering in gorgeous panoply and proudly displaying their armorial bearings of their ancient Aragon houses, was stationed near an Arabian mosque.

My train had stopped at the Village of Armilla. We watched the procession of our Grand Cardinal as his column begin to advance up the Hill of Martyrs. My gaze moved to the top of that hill to see Emir Abdallah and fifty knights traveling from the other side begin their descent down the hill riding toward Ferdinand now waiting on the banks of the Xenil. Abu approaching Ferdinand, prepared to dismount, kneel and formally salute his conqueror but before he could do so, Ferdinand quickly cantered forward and embraced him to demonstrate his sympathy and regard.

Abdallah handed the keys of the Alhambra to his conqueror, saying, "They are thine, oh King, since Allah so decrees it. Use thy success with clemency and moderation."

Ferdinand and Abu moved toward me. Abu dismounted and knelt before me, then he rose and remounted his horse to ride off joining his waiting family.

Ferdinand and I watched the Cardinal now entering the gate of Los Molinos. It was an emotional moment for both of us as we watched the large silver cross, so courageously borne by Ferdinand throughout the entire crusade, raised to sparkle in the bright morning sun. The standards of Castile and Santiago were now waving triumphantly from the red towers of the Alhambra. The Royal Chapel's Choir of voices seemed to be ringing throughout the city with the solemn anthem of the Te Deum. Our army filed into the courtyard, dropping to their knees in prayer and adoration. The grandees surrounding Ferdinand advanced toward me, knelt and saluted as they acknowledged me the "Sovereign of Granada."

Our procession went forth through the winding streets of the shuttered city. Ferdinand, the children and I riding in the center and emblazoned in royal magnificence, were soon to receive our new subjects in majestic splendor in the breathtakingly beautiful Alhambra.

CHAPTER XXXIX
Cristobol Colon and Ysabella

The fall of Granada created a sensation throughout Europe. Rome commemorated the event by a solemn procession led by the Pope and Cardinals to St. Peter's where High Mass was celebrated with the Pope proclaiming "From this day forward, Ferdinand and Ysabella shall be known as 'the Catholic Kings!'" Everywhere there was rejoicing and shouts of laughter. In England, King Henry VII ordered special services to be conducted in the St. Paul Cathedral.

Cristobol Colon was very much in evidence. His face appeared in every crowd. He was at Santa Fe for the dedication of the town's ceremonies. He joined Medina Celi's grand contingency for the surrender ceremonies at Granada. He was a success in quietly reminding me he was patiently waiting.

I needed to make a decision about him and soon. I pulled out the written report submitted some time back from the second Commission I had appointed. In their carefully written words they recommended that we terminate our negotiations with Cristobol Colon. I decided to provide the money for his travel expenses to Santa Fe and see him once more.

At the appointed time he arrived in my chambers. After the customary greetings I told him I was sorry that I must defer to the wisdom and advice of my

Commission. I wished him well and "God speed" in his quest for a new sponsor. Colon was stunned! Without a word he turned on his heel and rushed out of the room. Colon had many loyal friends in my Court. One of his most recent supporters was Luis de Santangel, a fiscal officer of the Crown of Aragon, who was fascinated with the prospect of discovering a new route to the Indies. He was in my Alcazar on other business, and saw Colon hastily leaving my quarters. He waved a greeting but Colon brushed by him without a sign of friendly recognition. De Santangel came to my quarters asking for an audience with me. He wanted to know what had happened.

I explained my decision not to underwrite the expedition. Concern registered on de Santangel's face. He asked if I would give him permission to underwrite the "loco" scheme. Then, looking directly into my eyes, he boldly said, "Your Highness, who has always shown a resolute spirit in matters of great consequence, should not lack it now for an enterprise of so little risk. What about the expansive glory for Spain you so dearly cherish? Gone! Dashed to the ground!"

I reflected on that for a moment. A "hot flush" of energy rushed through my body, and then, too, I reminded myself that de Santangel was an astute business man. He had become very wealthy in a short time. I knew that if his sharp business acumen was so keen for a new route to be discovered to the Indies, possibly I should rethink this "scheme." My thoughts raced -- "How could I finance such an undertaking?" We had just concluded ten long, very costly years of war. True, I had reclaimed the Crown jewels and I could pledge them once again. Money. I always needed money.

De Santangel's direct confrontation with "What

about the expansive glory for Spain...?" caused an almost automatic response and I stated, "I will assume the undertaking for my own Crown of Castile and if the funds in the treasury are inadequate, I am prepared to once again pawn the Crown jewels to finance the expedition."

I dispatched a messenger to catch up with Colon and bring him back to Santa Fe. Colon had reached the little village of Pino-Puente when my messenger caught up with him urging him to return for another audience with the Queen.

It was early in the afternoon when Pulgar showed Colon into my chambers. I had been busy pouring over papers and looked up as he entered. He started to bow, but I waved him to a chair inviting him to sit down. Suddenly I wanted to know this man. There was another chair placed close to Cristobol and I moved across the room and sat down opposite him, just as I would an old friend. I wanted him to be at ease, and commented about the pressing matters of clearing up all the after-effects of our war with Granada and planning for a bright future for my people. Then I asked him to tell me all about this proposed exploration. I wanted to have a clear picture of all the possibilities it presented. I listened carefully, watching his animated face light up as he spoke of that new route he was certain to discover. He went on about the glories that would be heaped upon Spain, and the untold riches that would be ours. Carefully he injected the possibility of Christianizing the new lands. We would send our priests and church laymen to build the churches and teach the people to love God and his Kingdom of Hosts.

Colon was an extraordinary man, of that I was certain. I asked him about his childhood and his education. He told me he was born in Genoa, Italy. His father was a weaver. He had been given some early schooling at Pavia where they were teaching mathematical sciences. He became so engrossed in the possibilities of using mathematics to guide ships, he boldly signed on as a water-boy at the age of 14. He continued to sail the Mediterranean, in and out of all the ports of Egypt, Greece, France and North Africa. Fourteen years ago, sailing along the far western end of the Mediterranean, a stormy sea capsized their small ship and Colon swam to the sandy shores of Portugal. It was here, listening to those Portuguese explorers who were developing the science of navigation, that this idea came to him. Within his mind, he knew that he, Cristobol Colon, would stun the world with his successful voyage.

Our conversation lasted for four hours. Cristobol had an unusual spiritual philosophy. He wasn't exactly Catholic, but his zeal for Christianizing the world was remarkable. We talked about the politics of other nations, European Courts and the ocean mariners. For one who had only the bare rudiments of an education, he surely had developed his mind with a keenness rarely demonstrated, and I now understood why the nobles were impressed by him. I was beginning to succumb to his spellbinding personality, too.

As the afternoon was drawing to a close, I said, "Cristobol, against the advice of every single, solitary knowledgeable advisor, I am going to underwrite your expedition. The Crown of Castile will honor your request for the posts of Governor, Viceroy and royalties." A broad smile broke over his face. He was jubilant! He started to walk from the room and then he stopped and turning around, asked, "And an Admiral?" I looked over at the stack of papers on my desk needing my attention and said, "Yes, and an Admiral, too."

Smiling to myself, I watched this stranger, now my friend, and thought, "Cristobol, you won on that point." How few people in my lifetime ever gained the upper hand in their negotiations with me. Tomorrow I would open discussions with the Valencia merchants to borrow the money for the expedition. I heaved a big sigh. That meant once again the Crown of Saint Fernando and my ruby necklace would not be "mine."

Earlier in the day, Ferdinand and some members of our Royal Council had left Santa Fe for the city of Granada to meet with Moors who held responsible offices and were working with us for a smooth transition of government records. The news that I had met with Cristobol Colon in his absence soon reached him and he mounted his swift horse and galloped back to Santa Fe. From my quarters I heard the pounding of hoofbeats and looked out to see my husband jump down from his horse and almost run toward the entrance of our quarters. He burst into the room, his face flushed with anger, and his brown eyes flashing. My first reaction was to "wonder what had happened in Granada to cause such anger?" Before I could ask, he shouted, "How could you -- how could you!" He was gesturing with his hands, pointing his finger at me, and I said, "How could I what? Tell me, what has happened in Granada that is so severe that you have allowed your temper to get out of control?"

Ferdinand's voice became even louder as he shouted, "Nothing went wrong in Granada. It is the secret meeting you held with that imposter from Italy that I am angry about. I heard the wildest rumor that you met in secret with Colon and agreed to finance his wild schemes. Tell me, how in Satan's Hell are you going to pay for it? Where is the money to come from? You, Ysabella de Trastamara, who have always been so frugal insisting that money not be wasted are as 'loco' as that red headed stranger!"

"Ferdinand," I said, keeping my voice level moderately low, "I make the decisions that concern Castile. You make the decisions that concern Aragon. I have never, at any time, ever made one single suggestion to you about how to handle Aragon's affairs. And I will thank you, now, not to interfere with mine. Castile, and Castile alone will underwrite every aspect of Colon's 'scheme' and if he discovers a new route to the Indies, it will be Castile -- not Castile and Aragon -- but Castile that will bask in the glory." I stood up and without flinching looked directly into Ferdinand's eyes and stated, "I, Ysabella de Trastamara -- alone -- will accept the responsibility to outfit three small ships, and I, Ysabella de Trastamara -- alone -- will claim the new sea route and the new territory for Castile. You and Aragon can go mind your own business and I will mind mine for Castile!"

Ferdinand was speechless. Finally he said, "But Aragon needs troops, ammunition, horses, lances, lombards, food, clothing, wagons, medicines to win our battle against France. Now that we have won Granada, we must win battles to secure our northern border. I need that money you are so foolishly spending on this 'scheme' for Aragon, I need..."

Quietly I interjected. "Ferdinand, now is not the time to create a military disturbance with France. We haven't recovered from the overwhelming costs of the Granada campaigns. There is absolutely no way that I can ask my people to underwrite your campaigns for

Aragon. No, absolutely no Aragon military..."

Before I could finish, Ferdinand turned on his heel and stomped out of the room. I heaved a sigh, sat down at my desk and began writing out lists for supplies we would need for Colon.

I sat and pondered over this unexpected task I had given myself. I determined that Ferdinand's outburst would be a momentary flare-up, for over the years I had weathered several of them. I knew that my treasury was very low and that I would have to use my powers of persuasion with the merchants to give me a considerable discount when I ordered the supplies.

The die had been cast. Ferdinand still insisted the idea was preposterous. On the appointed day, April 17, 1492, Cristobol Colon was shown into our chambers and as Pulgar handed me the document, I handed it first to Colon who glanced through it quickly, signed his name with a dramatic flourish, then to "My Lord, the King." After signing it, Ferdinand handed it to me and I signed my name, attached the royal seal, and bade Colon "God speed." Soon he would engage the fair winds of the Atlantic Ocean which would blow him all the way to the Americas.

CHAPTER XL
Colon Sets Sail for the New World
Expulsion of the Jews

Colon's project was now underway. De Santangel was bubbling with enthusiasm. He was at the little port of Huelva overseeing every detail of the outfitting of the vessels.

I sent requests to Sevilla as well as to other Andalusia ports requesting they complete my orders for supplies free of duty and charge the Crown the lowest prices possible. Cristobol needed only three vessels. I decided to withdraw two small caravel which Castile maintained on a twelve-month basis for public service. These two ships were outfitted with new sails, new ropes, a heavier anchor and more room created to hold supplies of food, water, bedding and other items for a long voyage. My friend, Fray Juan Perez, the respected guardian of La Rabida, was ecstatic. He rushed to inform the head of the Pinoza family expressing his belief that Colombo's voyage would succeed. The Pinozas were very wealthy, distinguished families in Palos with broad seafaring based business activities. They had a large fleet of ships and were eager to assign one of their larger ships to the Crown for Colon's venture. Fray Perez and the Pinozas soon had the third vessel equipped with all the supplies. I sent up a prayer of thanks to God for this lifted my financial burden considerably.

One problem had been resolved, and now another yet to ponder. It had been ten years since I had formally signed the papers for the Inquisition. I had prayed with all my heart that one God, one religion, one nation and one people we would become. Turmoil, deceit, distrust, anger and terrible suffering had been inflicted by the Catholics against the Jews. Strong and defiant, the Jews continued to be a closely knit group and things continually seemed to go from bad to worse in our relationship with them. When I had agreed to the Inquisition, the only people to be sternly dealt with were those who professed to be Catholics, but in reality were practicing a totally unrelated religion.

Our war with Granada had ended, and even though the Moors had been left with considerable freedom, I faced the possibility it would be years before they were absorbed into Spanish life and customs. From those ancient days when the Moors conquered the Peninsula, their strongest supporters were the Jews who became their allies and abettors. Would history repeat itself? I decided that I would expulge the Jews, not only protecting Granada from their devious influence but their persons as well. It would free them from Torquemada's over zealous activities, saving their lives and property.

It was a long and painful decision. As I signed the decree and handed it to del Pulgar, he read it through. Then he read it again. Looking up at me he said, "Your Highness, I have served you long, and I hope well. I have admired, respected and truly love you. But this action, this decree, I cannot condone. If your Highness will allow, I should like to tender my resignation from your service."

I was stunned! Pulgar gone from actively orchestrating my daily affairs? It never crossed my mind that he would ever leave. I knew his family background was Jewish but he was a sincere, devout Catholic. These were his people. I understood. I nodded my head for I was totally speechless. Fighting back the tears, I asked, "What will you be doing?" He quickly answered, "I think, your Highness, I will write. I have been in your service for many years and have kept volumes of notes. I will find a little house near the seashore and pore over these notes and write the history of your reign."

My spirits lifted. Who better than del Pulgar could write about those tumultuous, chaotic years where every day there was a new crisis commanding my immediate attention. Yes, that gave me comfort and lessened the pain. I asked, "Pulgar, have you decided upon the title of your book?" He was thoughtful for a minute, obviously he hadn't. Then he said, "Yes, I'll title it, 'The Catholic Kings.'"

Time rushed onward. In Rome they had elected Alexander VI as our new Pope. I had used my considerable influence hoping to elect our Grand Cardinal Mendoza but that was not to be.

In late July de Santangel advised me that all the vessels for Colon's expedition were completed and the last of the supplies were being placed on board. He and Colon were having a problem finding adventurous sailors and he wondered, "Could I help?" It hadn't crossed my mind that there would be few who would take such a gamble as Colon presented. I reasoned that, "Thinking men would question the wisdom of such and outlandish scheme." Our prisons were over-crowded so I sent out a call for "volunteers." We soon had enough sailors to man every station in those caravels.

The historic time was nearing for Colon to set sail from the port of Huelva. On August 3rd, amidst the cheers and shouts of joviality the noble lords of the houses of de Santangel, Medina Celi and Medina Sidonia rode through the streets to cheer their brave compadre on and wish him well. The priests had arrived with religious artifacts, ready to bless the ships. The royal flags of Castile were hoisted to the top mast of the Nina, the Pinta and the Santa Maria. Colon and the rest of his crew scrambled aboard. The nobles untied the strong ropes that had held them moored casting the ships out to sea, westward bound with great expectations.

Shortly after Colon had set sail, I received word that Don Beltran de la Cueva had died. Then the disturbing news that on August 27th, the brave and daring, forceful, charming Rodrigo Ponce de Leon, Marquis Duke of Cadiz had died. It seemed totally incomprehensible that this vibrant man's life had ended at the age of 49. It was Ponce de Leon who had struck the surprise attack at Alhama, continuing to participate in every campaign until Granada had surrendered. Ferdinand's life was saved three times during the conflict by his daring interventions. He spent his last days in the quiet and solitude of his beautiful mansion in Sevilla.

For nine days our entire Court mourned, for this bold hearted cavalier was loved and respected by everyone. Dressed in military splendor with his famous sword by his side, his body lay in state in his palace in Sevilla for several days. Finally, through the streets of the saddened city he was borne and placed to rest in the tomb of his ancestors in the great chapel of the Augustine Church. Moor banners captured during his battles with the Infidel during his young years were carried high to keep alive the memory of his dare-devil exploits; exploits which would live forever in the annals of history; exploits as undying as his great soul.

CHAPTER XLI
Cristobol Colon's Triumphant Return

In September we moved our Court to Aragon's lovely seaport city of Barcelona. It was now time to begin the negotiations with Maximilian for the marriage alliance between his children, Archduke Philip and Archduchess Margaret, and our own Juan and Juana. Austria's House of Hapsburg was a powerful family who wanted an alliance with Spain as much as Ferdinand and me. The uniting of our families should contain the over-zealous Charles VIII. Ferdinand was enthusiastic about the prospect of once again outwitting the French King. The thought of our combined power in a marriage alliance could make a strong impact in containing King Charles' interest in Italy. Envoys came and went while negotiations were carried out. In the meantime, Ferdinand was dealing with Aragon's other administrative concerns.

For the past several years, he had presided over the Court of Justice administering swift decisions in every case that came before it. Early in October, at the close of a morning court session, he was leaving the Palace of Justice walking down the marble steps. Suddenly Juan de Canamas, a lowly worker, lunged at him with a sharp sword attacking Ferdinand from behind and aiming directly at Ferdinand's head. His first sharp blow struck Ferdinand at the neck, and the second deep thrust slashed his shoulder. Ferdinand fell down shouting, "St. Mary preserve us! Treason, treason!"

Aides rushed forward to capture the assassin, others dashed out the door racing for doctors, and still others gently lifted their fallen King and placed him on a cot. The doctors arrived and stopped the profuse bleeding. Both wounds were very deep. Ferdinand's life was saved by the heavy gold chain he always wore around his neck for it had prevented the assassin's sword from inflicting a fatal wound. It was a long, painful recovery period, and for the next three months, I never left his side as I nursed him back to health. Our concern and prayers for his complete recovery was on everyone's mind. His strong will and disciplined, alert mind were healing balms that no medicines could match. It was nearing the Christmas holidays when he was well enough to resume his Friday morning activities in the Palace of Justice dealing fairly with his people.

Louis de Santangel, a member of our Council of Advisors, was ever ready to present new ideas for change. Early one February morning he arrived at my quarters quite unexpectedly, his eyes flashing with an expression on his face conveying he had very special news. He announced he had just met Elio Antonio Martinez de Jarava, a brilliant Latin scholar, who was creating a new language. My first reaction was the thought, "Who needs a new language?" I certainly knew I had not been entertaining any thought for that kind of change and I wondered where de Santangel conceived the idea that this would be of interest to me. Prudently, I did not state my thoughts. I respected de Santangel and decided that I would humor him and spend a few minutes with his new friend.

Jarava strode into my chamber with such an air of confidence about him, I was impressed. I immediately sensed that standing before me was not only a brilliant Latin scholar, but a gentleman who exuded charm and grace. In his hands was a book, and after the courtly introductions, he placed the volume in my hands simply stating the basis for the new language was Latin. He had established grammatical rules to be used in such a manner it would enable people everywhere to easily learn to speak our language.

I listened as he went on to explain his ideas and why he had developed them. From my own serious study of Latin, I understood exactly what he was doing. My mind raced backward remembering many of the difficulties I had faced communicating with my subjects in Murcia, Galacia, Asturias and Estremadura. Everyone had a slightly different language borne out of centuries old heritages. There were those early Castilians who inherited the Roman remains, later interspersing words from Arabic, Visogothic and French. A common language spoken throughout all the kingdoms loomed into my mind. Without hesitation and without further discussion, I immediately signed the proclamation directing Martinez de Jarava to prepare new text books and establish classes, first in the Universities and later our private and Catholic schools. I made a mental note to order more paper and ink in order for the books to be ready for study immediately.

In March, 1493, an excited aide rushed, unannounced, into our chambers. As he burst through the doors, the expression on his face and bouncy walk seemed to convey he had something of great importance to tell us. He had run so fast to our Alcazar he was gasping for breath. Standing before us, trying to steady his nerves by taking a few deep breaths and contain his excitement, he then proudly announced, "Colon has returned! He has discovered a new land!"

That "hot flush" of energy rushed through my body again. I looked at Ferdinand, his face registering incredulous disbelief. I was waiting for "My Lord, the King" to ask the first important questions, but quickly noted he was so surprised he was speechless.

I asked the aide, "Tell me, where is Colon? When did he arrive back? Did everyone who left with him arrive safe and well?" Oh, I had a hundred questions on my lips, but the doors of our chamber again opened and Pietro Martire, my First Secretary who replaced Hernando del Pulgar, was showing Luis de Santangel into the room. I motioned for the aide to be seated in a chair at the end of the room, and de Santangel, bowing low with a flourish, made the official announcement to us. Ferdinand had rebounded from his state of shock and we invited de Santangel to sit down and tell us everything he had learned.

De Santangel stated that all of the details he had heard were still rather sketchy, but a courier had arrived in Barcelona proclaiming only that Colon had returned from his voyage, sailing into the quiet harbor of Palos about noon on the 15th of March, 1493, proclaiming he had discovered a new route to the Indies! The excited de Santangel, who had a great gift with figures, proudly announced, "Colon sailed back into the harbor of Palos gone exactly seven months and eleven days."

His news was rather sketchy, for he hadn't taken time to get all the details because he was anxious to report on the success of the expedition to us. We spent an exciting hour talking and joking about the Admiral whose "loco" scheme would soon stun the world. Anxious as we were to get more details, we decided to wait until Colon arrived in Barcelona to hear from his own lips all about his voyage and his epic discovery of the eastern shores of India.

I swung into a flurry of activity sending dispatches everywhere, to every city, town and principality in my realm, and of course, to the Pope as well as all of the diplomats whomever and wherever they were. We made grand plans to welcome Colon and his brave sailors back to our land with parades, speeches and an elaborate banquet to be presided over by the Grand Cardinal Mendoza. It is not possible to put into words my own emotions of this historic event. Obviously, there was no way I could begin to comprehend the magnitude of Colon's discovery nor the unfolding of the world role Spain's historic destiny would become.

Colon was anxious to present himself at our Court in Barcelona and after spending a few days with Fray Juan Perez and the Pinoza family, he departed from Palos taking with him the colorful products he had brought from his foray into the New World countryside. Natives wearing their simple costumes and decorated with rudely fashioned gold collars and bracelets traveled along with him. His sailors carried exotic tasting fruits and unusual plants. There were several unusual looking four-footed animals, as well as the brightly feathered birds making up the colorful pageant as they made their way north, creating a stir in all of the towns and cities causing Colon's progress to be much slower than his scouts had anticipated.

From everywhere crowds of people appeared to gaze at this extra-ordinary spectacle and at this remarkably brave man who brought the exciting news, "He had discovered a 'New India.'" As he passed through

Sevilla, every housetop, window, and balcony was overcrowded with spectators straining to just catch a glimpse of him. His fame was quickly spreading throughout all of Castile.

It was the middle of April before Colon reached Barcelona. All the nobles and cavaliers of our Court dressed in their finest silk jackets and satin breeches, mounted their gold and silver saddled horses, and waving brightly colored banners, rode to the gate of the city to personally escort him into our royal midst.

Ferdinand, Infante Juan, and I seated ourselves under a superbly crafted red and gold silk canopy of state and waited for his historic arrival. As Admiral Cristobol Colon, Viceroy and Governor of the new lands approached our dias, we rose from our seats and raised our hands in a military salute to our Admiral and invited him to be seated before us. Ferdinand and I had decided to receive him with the honors we had always reserved for those of high rank, great fortune, or an accomplished military success. The act of seating a person of Colombo's social and dubious family background was an unprecedented event for our haughty and ceremonious Royal Court.

I looked into the face of this explorer and I knew this was Cristobol Colon's proudest hour. This was the moment he had savored. The moment that spurred him ever onward in his quest for proof of his inner convictions. He had succeeded in destroying the snobish intellectual's long-contested theory the earth was flat. He had flinched as they laughed when he presented his sound arguments that the earth was round. His pride had been wounded as he suffered through their sneers, skepticism and contempt for his scientifically researched ideas. Now he had won the prize!

Aware that his long trip from Palos to Barcelona was strenuous and tiring, I suggested that he get a good rest and tomorrow we would listen to his historic account of his voyage. I assured him that I wanted to hear every detail. I wanted to know everything about this new land, the natives, precious metals and plentiful minerals.

At the appointed hour Colon arrived at our Court displaying his grace and polished manners, sedate, dignified and enthusiastic about the brilliant future that would be Castile's as the result of his successful voyage. He described the white beaches, peaceful coves, rocky cliffs, mountainous terrains, trees, ferns and bright flowers. He spoke of the several islands that he sailed around, each one more beautiful than the other possessing rich soils to grow food in abundance. He expounded upon the exotic fruits and vegetables noting he had brought some specimens back with him. He expressed the strong belief in the assurances he had received from natives there were precious gold and silver mines in abundance in the interiors of those islands. Nodding his head toward me he confided the natives had no system of idolatry, making it quite simple to bring Christianity to their shores.

Colon's account of this land didn't seem to fit the description of those voyagers who had rounded the tip of Africa and sailed up the eastern coast to India and brought back the spices. The natives he brought back with him didn't fit the description of those I had heard about, but that did not dampen my excitement. My mind was filled with thoughts of gold and silver -- mountains of it! It was all right that he did not discover a new route to India. I was very pleased.

As Colon finished his fascinating account of his

adventure and exploration, Ferdinand and I, together with others attending this historic meeting, prostrated ourselves as a gesture of our gratitude. The solemn strains of the Te Deum began to quietly echo from the Royal Chapel in commemoration of this glorious occasion.

In my characteristic manner, I soon had all of my secretaries sending dispatches to every foreign office in Europe extolling the wonders of this "New India" Cristobol Colon had discovered for Castile. I made certain that each packet prepared was signed by both Ferdinand and me, sealed with wax and stamped with our royal insignia. I was now ready to bask in the glory of an adventure that would ignite the finest minds throughout the entire European continent.

Diplomats from every country in Europe began sailing into Barcelona's harbor, anxious to meet the *Catholic Kings* who had won the prize of Granada, the fabled Alhambra, and now an exotic land across a broad and expansive ocean to the far, far west. As their requests for an audience were received, Ferdinand and I proceeded to array our Royal Court with our ladies-in-waiting dressed in the most exquisite silks, satins and brocades. Jewels sparkled around their necks, heavy gold bracelets inlaid with precious gems encircled their wrists, their high-swept hair was kept in place with delicate jeweled combs. The nobles and cavaliers, pages and aides were suitably dressed in an opulence which would dazzle the visiting Europeans.

I recognized the importance of this diplomatic opportunity to present our Court to Europe and I chose elaborate dresses made from precious gold cloth. My thinning head of hair was always covered with lace mantillas which were now very fashionable at my

Court. Red was my favorite color. I would have a seamstress sew spangles of lozenges in crimson and black velvet on my mantillas adding a dramatic effect and to some of the lozenges I would attach a large pearl. Preparing for my children's weddings had brought every jewel merchant in Europe to our shores to display their brilliant precious gems. I couldn't resist adding more rubies, diamonds and pearls to the Crown jewels. I was especially fond of the pink toned balas rubies from Persia, some as large as a pigeon's egg. When those flamboyant diplomats swept into our Court they stared in amazement at the diamonds, rubies and pearls I wore. The gold dresses and bejeweled lace mantillas presented a spectacle for which they were not prepared.

Latin was the language all European diplomats and Ambassadors spoke and I watched their faces light up in wonderment as I responded to their questions in Latin. Ferdinand had always insisted he had no time to learn the difficult language and as the diplomats arrived for their audiences, he sat quietly on his Throne while I spoke in Latin extolling the probable wealth and vast resources of the new land, making an emphatic impression on my guests that the new land Colon had discovered was Castile's.

CHAPTER XLII
Ximenes Cisneros and Church Reformation

Colon's sensational discovery created a stir among the European communities. Those brilliant men of science congratulated each other, concluding they were living in a fantastic age. They had witnessed a great event.

Ferdinand and I urged Colon to prolong his stay in Barcelona, presenting him with such honorable distinctions as invitations to our Court and splendid gifts. As Ferdinand rode through the city, the Admiral would accompany him mounted on the beautiful spirited horse we had given him. As they made their appearance along the broad avenues and narrow streets, smiling crowds gathered to wave and shout greetings to Castile's latest, and now famous, hero. The courtiers of our Court rushed to be among the first to invite him as their very distinguished guest of honor to their elaborate parties and receptions.

Colon obviously enjoyed savoring his victory, but more than the social whirl of activities, his interests focused around the Crown's reaction to his discoveries, taking notice that both Ferdinand and I would clearly define the magnitude of his discovery, and in our determinations, compensate him with appropriate importance.

We decided to establish a Board of Indian Affairs and appointed Juan de Fonseca, Archdeacon of Sevilla, an ambitious prelate with a shrewd capacity for business, as the Administrator and added two subordinate assistants to serve with him.

Directly after Colon's historic return, Ferdinand and I applied to the Court of Rome with a request that Pope Alexander VI confirm our new discoveries and invest us with the same recognition -- or to the similar extent of jurisdiction -- the Holy See had conferred in the past on the Kings of Portugal. While Ferdinand and I were not in complete agreement with such an acknowledgement by the Pope, we decided if such a conferment were given to us, it would deter other nations from making an attempt to explore our new lands. In our application to the Pope we carefully pointed out that in no way would our new discoveries interfere with those rights formerly conceded to Portugal by the Holy See. We emphasized our major interest and future activities would be directed toward bringing Christianity to the natives. We recognized many competent persons were already making applications to the Court of Rome for a title to territories that we now considered were in our possession. We concluded our application noting we were unwilling to go ahead with any aspect of further explorations without the sanction of his Holy Office.

Pope Alexander responded to our application and on May 3, 1493, publishing a bull stating, "Because of the great services of the *Catholic Kings* in the cause of the church -- especially the subversion of the Moors -- and their willingness to develop a wider scope for the prosecution of our pious label, and of pure liberality, infallible knowledge, and plentitude of apostolic power, the Holy See now confers upon Ferdinand and Ysabella, reigning Monarchs of Castile and Aragon, the possession of all lands discovered, or hereafter to be discovered by Spain, in the western ocean." Another bull followed the next day clearly establishing the intention of the Pope's original grant bestowing upon Spain, "All land Spain may discover west and south of an imaginary line and to be drawn from pole to pole."

I read both communications through several times before deciding that I could cautiously move forward with my next plans. First, I wanted to begin the spiritual teachings to those Indians Colon had brought to Castile. My keen interest in their spiritual welfare was ceremoniously celebrated with the baptism of two of the Indians, with Ferdinand and our son standing beside them, permitted to take a Spanish name. One of the Indians remained with our Court to become part of our son's retinue. Others were sent to Sevilla where they would receive their religious instructions. I planned to have them later return to their native country to bring the teachings of Christianity to their people.

By the end of May, Colon asked permission to take his leave of our Court, for he was anxious to return to Andalucia to supervise preparations being made for his second historic voyage. After paying his respects and receiving our good wishes and prayers for a safe journey, he took his leave from our presence. The nobles and cavaliers of our Court again mounted their favorite horses, bridles and saddles glittering with gold and silver, raising their colorful banners high into the air, escorted Colon to the entrance gate of Barcelona.

Fray Hernando de Talavera was now the new Bishop of Granada and I invited him to help choose my next confessor. Talavera had been my spiritual advisor for many years and I was very proud to make this appointment to the newly created post.

France still had not returned Roussillon and Cerdagne to Aragon and now Charles VIII was spoiling to expand his kingdom into Italy. I had never wanted to become embroiled in a war with any of our European neighbors. After winning our triumphant victory in Granada, the marriage contracts now finalized with Maximilian and the discovery of a new land, Spain's position in world affairs had catapulted us into a highly visible and powerful position in the domination of world affairs. I convinced Ferdinand that we were in a favorable position to negotiate a successful Treaty with France. Ferdinand really enjoyed battle skirmishes, because when carefully planned, he knew he would win. All of his life he had dreamed of leading Aragon's military might against France and trouncing them on their battlefields. That took money and we faced an enormous mound of debts for repayment. I convinced him that we could successfully enter into negotiations with France and conclude it in our favor. I soon appointed Gonzalo de Cordoba to the task of delicately orchestrating the sticky negotiations.

I had kept my thoughts to myself about the future role of Spain's armies. The Granada conflict was over and there were many soldiers who had elected to remain in our military camps. How could we keep their morale high with all the inactivity? I was giving that some contemplative thought one day, when an idea popped into my mind that we should teach them to read and write. Their time could be devoted to scholastic learning instead of developing skills with dangerous swords.

For several years I had been hearing stories about a printing press, a Chinese invention brought to Europe. King Louis XI of France would never allow even one press into France. I had a totally different view. When I first heard about it, my thoughts raced back into time wondering what my father's reaction would have been. Somehow, I knew he would have embraced the magical, remarkable abilities of this new machine to rapidly produce printed books. I asked the Cortes to pass a "duty free" law for imported printing presses. During the ensuing years our intellectuals would be busy choosing the books to be published, printed and distributed throughout our universities.

I decided to invest money in books and hire qualified teachers for my soldiers to learn to read and write. Ferdinand voiced his loud objections. "Our soldiers wasting their time in the frivolous activity of reading and writing? Every nation in Europe will be laughing at us. It has never been done before!" Yes, indeed, it had never been done before, but "change for the betterment of my people" was what I wanted. Learning to read and write was a privilege my soldiers would have.

One morning Pietro placed a dispatch on my desk from Bishop Talavera. He was suggesting that I contact a Franciscan monk, Ximenes Cisneros, and seriously consider him as my next confessor. The Bishop noted in his letter that Cisneros "has a brilliance rarely matched by any of todays' religious leaders, coupled with a purity of motive, a steadfast faithfulness to his ideal of simplicity and piety faithfully demonstrated throughout his entire life." I remembered I had once heard his name mentioned when the Bishop of Siguenza appointed him chaplain of the cathedral in that city.

Several years later I had heard rumors that Cisneros had entered the Franciscan Order and remained at the Monastery de San Juan de los Reyes in Toledo until completing his novitiate. Later I had learned that he had retreated to the quiet and solitude of the Franciscan Monastery at Castanar. In 1482 I had elevated Mendoza to the Grand Cardinal and Primate of Spain and Mendoza appointed Cisneros to a post in Salceda where he still resided.

When Cisneros was shown into my chambers for our first meeting, I observed a tall, rather gaunt appearing sixty year old man standing before me. I thanked him for coming and told him I wished for him to be my confessor. A look of surprise crossed his face and then he raised his hand saying, "First, your Highness, please allow me to express my deep gratification and appreciation for the kindness or your consideration of me. But if I were to accept this great honor, might I place a few restrictions upon my role and freedoms?"

I nodded my head in assent, and Cisneros said, "I must not be required to live at Court or give political advice. I want the freedom to eat at any neighboring monastery or even, if I so choose, in the streets."

I knew that many monks in the Franciscan Order were strict vegetarians and thoroughly understood why he wanted his diet to remain "untainted." Those terms were acceptable. Then I invited him to sit down and be comfortable while we got to know one another.

I had sensed from the beginning this gaunt appearing man sitting before me was truly a unique individual. Now I was very curious to discover what set him apart from other Franciscan monks. Within a short time I had the mystery of the "puzzle of Ximenes Cisneros" pieced together. He was brilliant -- absolutely brilliant! He spoke with an eloquence. His fluent speech flowed, and his words, carefully chosen, had content and purpose. All of my life I had watched from afar the life-styles and habits of our holy men and I questioned their elaborate homes and abhorred their mistresses. It didn't seem correct that one who had professed to follow the "holy way of life" should flaunt the violation of the Church's holy laws. I decided to broach the subject of celibacy and the simplicity of a priest's life-style, as it related to our society, with Cisneros.

He responded with a thunderous denunciation of those practices and assured me he had been quietly chipping away at some reforms which were now underway at his church in Salceda. My head nodded in approval. He spoke with such assurance and brilliance, I was curious about his family background and education. He told me his family was very, very poor. The priests at Salamanca had given him his education and eventually they recommended him very highly to Rome where he completed his studies. While in Rome he made a profound impression upon the Pope and just before his return to Spain, a letter from the Pope referred to as a "Expectative" was presented to him.

Upon his return, Cisneros presented his letter to Alonso Carrillo, then the Bishop of Toledo. Apparently Carrillo had yearned for such recognition but had never been given this honor by the Pope. When Cisneros presented his letter, Carrillo's childish reaction was to promptly throw him in jail.

During Cisnero's six long, solitary years in prison he spent his time in daily meditation, study and prayer. These years of discipline made an impact upon Cisneros which changed the course and direction of his life.

As the door closed after Cisneros' departure, I paused to reflect upon our conversation. I was profoundly touched by this holy man. Why? I didn't know. My keen instincts, honed now with years of experience, had given me confidence "to know." Would that I had been able to read a crystal ball, for if I could, I would have looked into it to see a vision of this man's future and destiny -- a Cardinal, the Archbishop of Toledo, and after my death, the Regent of Spain!

CHAPTER XLIII
Marriage Alliances

At the close of the mourning period for Prince Alonso of Portugal, Ysabel returned to Castile. How my heart ached for my daughter, for she was so sad. She refused to take part in any of our Court activities choosing instead to devote her days to prayer, withdrawing from the world.

I wanted my daughter to have a normal life. The new heir to Portugal's Throne was Alonso's brother, Prince Manuel, who wanted Ysabel to be his bride, dispatching notes to her in a timely manner. Ysabel ignored them. Ferdinand and I had agreed that we would not force our daughter into a marriage against her will.

In 1495 the Portuguese Prince was crowned King Manuel of Portugal and he made a formal offer to us asking for her hand in marriage, but our daughter rejected his proposal.

Our negotiations with the House of Hapsburg were completed, and we signed the marriage alliance for our youngest daughter, Catalina, to become the bride of England's future king, Prince Arthur. In my secret thoughts I wished, "If only Ysabel could see the wisdom of marrying Manuel." The destinies of all my children looked very bright. Juan, soon to be married to the Archduchess Margaret of Austria, would be the next king of Spain; Juana, betrothed to the Archduke of Burgundy would become the Archduchess upon taking her marriage vows; and Catalina was to become the future Queen of England. How much I wished for my Ysabel to be the Queen of Portugal. There was still a marriage to plan for Maria. Yes, each of my children faced a bright future and I was happy.

Early one frosty morning in March, 1495, I heard the distinctive sounds of the hooves of horses below. The speed with which they raced into the courtyard seemed to carry an urgency that my ears hadn't been attuned to since the close of the Granada conflict. I looked out the window and noted Mendoza's pennons held aloft. Swiftly his men dismounted and their quick gestures conveyed to me they were telling my pages they had come on an urgent mission.

I heard the rapid pace of footsteps echoing throughout the stone-tiled halls and suddenly the doors swung open. Mendoza's First Secretary entered, first bowing, then standing tall and erect, his voice filled with emotion, he announced that the Grand Cardinal Mendoza, Archbishop of Toledo and Primate of Spain had died at his home in Guadalahara.

I had known his life was drawing to a close and as inevitable as death is, I still was not prepared for this great loss. Mendoza was the scion of the most distinguished family in the realm. Wealthy and powerful, he had lived in extra-ordinary splendor. This worldly Mendoza had been my loyal and trusted subject; a great man whose unmatched skills as a statesman would never be replaced by another. Our nation would mourn his passing. I would miss him.

A few days later Mendoza's First Secretary asked for a private audience with me, and it was granted.

Arriving at the appointed hour, he bowed and then presented to me a sheaf of papers. It was Mendoza's last Will and Testament, appointing "Her Royal Highness, Ysabella de Trastamara, Queen of Castile and Leon, as the executrix of his vast estate." I was too overcome with emotion to read it through, and graciously thanked Mendoza's secretary for his thoughtfulness in bringing it personally to me, rather than sending it by courier.

The prestigious appointment of the new Archbishop of Toledo weighed heavily on my mind. It was an Office which the church hierarchy fought for as diligently as they once fought for the Grand Mastership of the Orders of Santiago, Calatrava and Alcantara. These squabbles had been stopped when I moved for Ferdinand to be elected their new Grand Master when each of those offices had become vacant. This had eliminated the in-fighting which I always detested, and it also allowed the Crown to administer over these religious-military Orders giving us broad control over church affairs as well.

Ferdinand's illegitimate son, Alonso, born prior to our marriage in 1469, had been appointed by Ferdinand to the post of Bishop of Zaragosa when he was only six years old. Now at the age of twenty six, Ferdinand immediately suggested that Alonso should be appointed to this highly influential post.

I had been studying Cisneros carefully for the past three years. He had a will of steel, and the manner in which he overcame obstacles in his path was absolutely remarkable. He never wavered in his devotion to God; his conversations were peppered with a brilliance I had never encountered; and he continued his simple living habits. I was amazed at the energy with which he tackled everything for it did remind me of myself just a few years earlier. But most amazing was the fact Cisneros was eighteen years older than me.

Ferdinand continued to press me for a decision in favor of Alonso, but I had other plans brewing in my head. I was ready to tackle -- head on -- the church reforms that had been dear to my heart all my life. I was convinced that Cisneros had the brilliance, dedication and fortitude to mount a strong campaign to rid the church of the offensive practices of fathering children, keeping mistresses, spending money given to the church on vast lands, large homes, and thus becoming their personal wealth. It was true, Cisneros came from humble beginnings, and this high church Office had always been reserved for church clerics of noble birth. After thoughtful deliberations, I decided to enter into negotiations with Pope Alexander to obtain the appointment of Cisneros as the new Archbishop of Toledo.

I had been carefully studying Mendoza's Will. He had asked that his body be entombed in a chapel to be built within The Cathedral at Toledo. I met with The Chapter administering the affairs of The Cathedral, and each shook their heads saying, "The Cathedral is completed. We will make no changes nor further additions." I caught the finality in each of their voices and decided not to raise an argument. Quietly I moved around this magnificent building as they pointed out to me how totally complete The Cathedral now was. I nodded my head in agreement.

Two days later, a group of men with picks and axes met me at midnight at the doors of The Cathedral. We entered and I pointed to them the exact space where Mendoza's new chapel was to be built. Then I stood back and watched them chop a hole in the wall large enough for the Grand Cardinal's chapel. As the Queen, I had the last word.

Early in April the dispatch confirming Cisneros as the next Archbishop of Toledo arrived from the Pope. I thought a most appropriate time to present him with the good news would be directly after my confession. Everything moved along in a timely manner and I handed to Cisneros his letter. He took it into his hands, kissed it and then placed it upon his head. Then, opening it he started to read the contents. Quickly he folded it up and handed it back saying, "Your Highness, there has been some mistake, this letter is not for me."

I had to smile at his response. I handed it back to him suggesting, "Read it through, there is no mistake for that is your name and your new title." He opened it again reading aloud, "Alexander, Bishop and servant of the servants of God, to our venerable brother, Friar Cisneros, Archbishop of Toledo," and then he stopped. Without another word he handed it back to me and left.

I thought to myself, "Will wonders never cease!" Who would ever have dreamt that anyone would refuse to accept the highest religious office in the land. Cisneros did, and "No!" he would not accept the office as the next Archbishop of Toledo. I continued my campaign with steady persistence, never allowing my determination to waver. For six months we jockeyed back and forth and finally after another papal brief, he was consecrated as the new Archbishop of Toledo on October 11, 1495.

Cisneros quickly dismantled the extravagantly furnished arch-episcopal palace. The priceless tapestries were soon placed in a museum. The gold plates and candelabras were sold and profits given to charity. Down came the velvet curtains and out went the canopied beds. The household servants were reduced to ten friars to maintain the premises. Cisneros now had a comfortable home.

Pope Alexander was displeased with the new life-style of the Archbishop and soon dispatches arrived from Rome ordering Cisneros to refurbish the palace in a manner befitting an Archbishop. Cisneros had taken the vows of obedience and soon pieces of furniture began arriving and drapes were rehung at the windows. Appropriate paintings and sculpture were placed throughout and reluctantly, he donned the jeweled robes for Mass. When he attended the banquets, he still requested to be served the plain, simple Franciscan foods.

Cisneros' living adjustment now made, I was ready with my boundless energy -- almost matching his -- to begin the church reforms. For literally hundreds of years priests of the major Orders of the Church had gradually devised their own lax rules of ethics, deportment and life styles, deviating drastically from those Catholic edicts established by the great church leaders centuries ago. As a little girl I gaped in wonder at the opulent houses, fine carriages, and beautiful horses that our priests displayed. Sometimes I thought about their piousness. It seemed to me instead of money given by the people to the church to spread Christianity and feed the poor and hungry, it was used to buy large tracts of land, train armies, build fortresses and great houses in which to live, purchase gold candlesticks, import hand carved furniture with marble tabletops, paintings and priceless tapestries. Those extravagant life-styles were sanctioned by all clergymen. Priests displaying such abundant living styles were known as conventuals. A very small number of priests who practiced the strictest disciplines were known as the observantines.

Many priests of every Order had mistresses who bore their children. This was disgraceful! Pious nuns would find themselves pregnant, hiding behind the walls of a quiet monastery located far from the center of activity until the baby was born and placed in an orphanage. It was time for reform. Time to redefine deportment, ethics, and life-styles. We would focus upon such abuses as spiritual apathy, luxurious homes and sexual restraint. Discipline and virtue would be a welcome replacement.

I wrote to Pope Alexander asking for a bull which would give me full authority to proceed with the reforms I entrusted to Ximenes. Cisneros would deal with the priests and I would handle the delicate balancing of the nuns. I devoted every Wednesday afternoon sitting with them in the quiet of their monasteries sewing. Sometimes I made Ferdinand's shirts, but more often I embroidered religious scarves which were later given to churches throughout the kingdoms. At those Wednesday afternoon gatherings the nuns and I talked about the church. Sentence by carefully calculated sentence, I wove the conversation around the changing patterns for the emergence of discipline and piety within the church. It wasn't long before I observed they were moving out of their old, tired ideas and beginning to inject new habits into their daily care of the monasteries and religious ceremonies. It was working and I thanked God for His help.

Cisneros attacked the reforms deciding the Franciscan conventuals presented the worst excuse for priests that he could possibly imagine. They had sunk in vice and scandal enabling them to become very rich, lazy and untrustworthy. Dressed in his brown Franciscan habit, he tied bundles of books together and hoisted them on the back of his faithful mule. Down the dusty roads they trod, directing their lofty mission at the most opulent houses of the conventuals. After arriving at the monastery he would circle around the exterior and make a minute investigation of all its land and possessions. Then he would summon the entire Chapter, present his findings and asked them to renounce their vain ways and return to the Franciscan principles established by St. Francis of Assisi and those of St. Peter. If this approach failed, he soon moved to take a more drastic measure.

Those temperamentally unsuited for the Franciscan Order quietly departed with pensions he provided for them. Those who wished to continue in their service to God -- but refused to change -- were inexorably expelled, or even worse, excommunicated.

For literally centuries church officials had lived in great splendor never having to obey the laws of the church. These deposed priests soon began writing letters of protest to Rome loudly denouncing Cisneros. An alarmed Alexander decided to send the General of the Order, Gilberto Delfini, to investigate the complaints and return to Rome with a full report.

Delfini, confident in his position and anxious to make an impression upon Alexander, departed from Rome and upon his arrival in Spain failed to present himself before Cisneros. Evidently he was not anxious to become embroiled with Cisneros for he had learned that Cisneros' brilliant mind, so articulate and direct in his approach to any given situation, was no match for him.

Deciding that I, too, had been an instigator creating all the problems, he requested an audience with me which was promptly arranged for him. He arrived dressed in magnificent Vatican splendor and without so much as the customary bow or a greeting of any nature, he stood stiffly before me. Looking directly into my eyes he began his well rehearsed speech. For nearly ten minutes he proceeded to accuse Cisneros of incompetence, heresy, dishonesty, thievery, and disloyalty to the Pope. After lodging all the grievances against Cisneros, he stopped for just a second or two, and then blurted, "You are a stupid woman for appointing him Archbishop!"

"Father," I retorted, "have you taken leave of your senses? Do you realize to whom you are speaking?" He shifted his feet, pulled his shoulders back and replied, "I realize perfectly well to whom I am speaking. Ysabella of Castile, who is dust and ashes like me." Turning swiftly on his heel he unceremoniously rushed out. His report was promptly delivered to Rome. Pope Alexander was so displeased with Cisneros, he ordered the reforms to be stopped.

I had no intention of that happening. I had stood up to other Popes. Unruffled and with a sense of great purpose, I carefully selected three representatives to present my defense as well as Cisneros' to the Vatican. So skillfully did my ambassadors handle the delicate matter of the need for reforms and present the merits of the common cause, Pope Alexander promptly composed a new bull which not only sanctioned the continuance of our reforms, but he ended by appointing Cisneros his Apostolic Commissioner.

CHAPTER XLIV
Colon's Fateful Second Expedition

The unfathomable riches to be mined from Colon's new discovery captured everyone's imagination. There was an explosive flurry of activities in every direction. Eager Castilians began jockeying for positions to sail to the New World on Colon's next voyage. They would stake out their claims and untold riches would be theirs "just for the taking." It was a heady experience for all of us.

The entire Spanish Court shared in everyone's excitement and infectious enthusiasm. From border to border, my royal couriers raced over the dusty roads, across the newly erected bridges, to the cities far and wide delivering my dispatches promoting the spirit of discovery and colonization. Throughout the rest of my life, I never lost sight of a new land destined to bring expanded opportunities, recognition of our rank as a world power, and envious prestige to Castile.

From every kingdom of Castile, Leon and Aragon the brave, courageous, and stalwart adventurers arrived at the southern shores of Andalucia, dreaming of riches and just rewards. Sailing out of the harbor of Palos with Colon on his second voyage were overzealous cavaliers and hidalgos eager to become rich and powerful men in Hispaniola. The cavaliers were of noble birth, educated by private tutors; the hidalgos, sons of successful, wealthy merchants had attended the finest schools. Of leadership and work experience, they had none. They just clambered aboard those ships moored in the port city of Palos and when the anchors were pulled, the ropes untied, the ships given a shove away from the wharf, they were westward bound for the New World.

The long voyage had begun. The cavaliers and hidalgos decided they were no longer required to obey Spanish laws. Since Colon was a foreigner and of such low birth, it was improper and an indignity for their esteemed personages to respond to his commands. Demeaning was the word they would shout back at him as he attempted to establish a proper stance for cooperation. All during the long voyage they lounged on the decks, demanded the best food, told ribald stories and boasted of the riches they would have that would make them powerful subjects in the realm.

Three months later, Colon's caravel sailed into the harbor of Hispaniola with the cavaliers and hidalgos scrambling to be the first to touch the eastern shores of the fabled East Indies. They were met by the simple natives who still declared the white men had come from heaven, falling on their knees before them in thanksgiving to their Creator. These spoiled and lazy men lost no time in provoking such outrage with their cruelty and overbearing attitude toward the Indians, who, in turn, vigorously objected. The defiant Indians soon stymied the efforts of the Spaniard's colonization.

One area reflecting the Indian's outrage was their decision to neglect their fields. They were willing to starve themselves, and in so doing, they would starve their oppressors. The snobbish cavaliers and hidalgos absolutely refused to help with any labor in the fields to grow food, insisting that was too demeaning. The only dirt they intended to turn was to be that which was filled with gold.

In order to avoid famine, Colon resorted to reducing the daily allowance for food. He insisted, without distinction of rank, everyone must work. The high-minded, haughty hidalgos and cavaliers complained loudly at these indignities inflicted upon them with this demeaning drudgery. The priests, too, were outraged that their food was being rationed.

Ferdinand and I were so intent upon this discovery bringing untold wealth to us, I was sparing no expense. With every warm, friendly letter from Colon describing the beauty and novelty of the New World he was exploring, he attached endless lists for supplies to be sent. Every minute suggestion the Admiral made was acted upon promptly.

Several sea captains returned from their voyages to the colony with disturbing reports -- or maybe it was rumors -- I wasn't really certain. They stated the new colony was seething with discontent. I would listen to their conversations, read through the disquieting reports, and then review with my exchequer the total costs for this very expensive adventure. In silence I studied the reports of the meager returns being brought back to our shores by those able sea captains.

It was obvious to Ferdinand and me that it was taking much longer to colonize the new land than we had originally believed. We continued to support Colon throwing our full weight behind him, and in the process passed various ordinances in his favor, extensively enlarging his power and privilege base. Our letters to him contained our glowing acknowledgement of his loyalty and distinguished service to the Crown, reassuring him of our strengthened confidence in his integrity and prudent decisions.

We were bombarded with complaints of the colonists accusing Colon of maladministration and of the oppressive and unjust severities he imposed. All of those accusations were so vague that Ferdinand and I chose to make light of them and countered those reports by expressing we thought Colon's situation was difficult to resolve. Cautiously we decided we would send an agent to the colony to make inquiries -- a trusted agent who would report to us his findings. We would be careful in selecting an agent we thought would be dutiful and understand the difficult position Colon faced.

I had repaid the loan made by the Valencia merchants on the Crown jewels. When they were returned to me, I removed my ruby and pearl necklace and started to place it in the hollow of the carved wooden cross. Then I put the necklace back with the other jewels, knowing that never again would I need to use the jewels as collateral for emergency loans and no longer should I secure the safety of my necklace in its hiding place.

Our treasury was again over-burdened. The broadened areas of the Crown's activities continued to drain our hard won resources. We were embroiled in the Italian conflict for the Kingdom of Naples had nearly been overrun by the French. The elaborate wedding preparations for Juan and Juana were being made and I was sparing no expense. My endless lists with so many activities stretched longer and longer with no end in sight.

In the spring of 1496, Cristobol returned from the

colonies. Ferdinand and I were more than just a little anxious to receive a verbal report from our Admiral, Governor, Viceroy and dispatched a note to him saying, "Come to us when you can do it without inconvenience to yourself, for you have endured too many vexations already." We both signed the letter, sealing it with the Crown's official stamp and then handed it to my royal courier instructing him to personally deliver it to Colon in Sevilla.

The building blocks for Spain's firm foundation for the next century's historic role were being placed. Our marriage alliances with the House of Hapsburg and England would curtail France's expansive thirst for power and prestige commanding her armies to invade its neighboring borders. It was the beginning of the golden era of Spain's glorious future.

CHAPTER XLV
The Death of Ysabella's Mother

The church reforms were now systematically moving forward and other branches of government were running smoothly. My attention was focused upon the children's weddings. Juan's proxy wedding had been solemnized at Malines in November; and as 1495 approached, I was looking forward to Juana's proxy wedding which would take place in Valladolid in January.

My elaborate plans for my daughter's departure to Burgundy in a special fleet of ships were underway. The small armada would deliver Juana to her bridegroom in Antwerp and would return to our shores with Juan's bride, the Archduchess Margaret.

All winter long I worked upon the lists. First there was Juana's elaborate wardrobe. I wanted my daughter to be one of the most elegant, fashionable ladies in the European courts. No expense was spared in ordering the gold cloth, silks, satins, brocades, delicate laces and exquisite beading. I chose her jewels with thoughtful deliberation. Juana, still headstrong and defiant, failed to show for many important fittings, choosing instead to ride with her father, totally ignoring all of the plans being made for her brilliant future.

I had decided to build twenty ships to carry Juana, her household, immediate wedding party and guests who would choose to sail with her to attend the wedding.

To every kingdom I sent orders for all the special provisions. My expanded shopping lists continued to lengthen. How many sides of beef would be needed? I placed an order for eighty-five kilos of hung beef. How many salted herrings would be devoured? I decided upon one hundred fifty thousand. Then there were eggs -- ten thousand should be enough. Chicken was a favorite delicacy, so I placed special orders for one thousand fowl. There would be much revelry on board as they sailed northward; four hundred barrels of wine should keep them in high spirits.

Everyone was excited. The guest list lengthened so I expanded the fleet. Soon there were one hundred ships to be built, and then I found it necessary to increase it to one hundred twenty. Finally one hundred thirty seaworthy ships were bobbing in the harbor. By the end of July the wedding armada was ready to be placed under the able command of Ferdinand's cousin, Admiral Don Fadrique Enriques.

The marriage treaties for both Infanta Juana and Princess Margaret stipulated that neither should bring a dowry because the maintenance for each of their households would be borne by the host country. I had three reasons to be concerned about my plans being a success. Juana was young. Juana was bossy. Juana was temperamental. I carefully orchestrated everything with a well planned systematic course for her to follow. I knew her sharp tongue could get her into trouble at Court so I selected servants whose implacable loyalties to Juana and to Spain I knew I could trust. I chose her chaplains, chamberlains, steward and treasurer; and her ladies-in-waiting were from the most distinguished noble families of Castile and Aragon.

By midsummer all the equipment, supplies and crew had arrived at the northern port of Laredo. Everything was inspected and ready, and on August 5th, my five children and I arrived at the port city.

Hundreds of guests had already arrived, swarming like busy bees over the docks with baggage and servants. Instead of hundreds, there were thousands of people arriving to attend the wedding -- so many I lost count. Many of our distinguished families had brought as many as two hundred fifty people in their individual suites. My chronicler, Pietro Martire, insisted there were twenty thousand people boarding those ships. I just shook my head in wonderment and silently prayed for their safe arrival in Burgundy.

It was the middle of August before all was ready and every last person had scrambled aboard the top-heavy ships. Admiral Fadrique was ready to escort the first ship out of the harbor when a gusty whirlwind with a fierce gale blew in. The small ships tossed in the harbor's choppy waters for two days. On August 18th, the masts were raised, sails now billowing in the light breeze, anchors were pulled, ropes untied and amidst loud cheers and well wishes, the one hundred thirty ships cast out to sea soon to disappear over the horizon.

As I watched that flotilla sail northward, a terrible feeling of guilt came over me and my stomach churned. Somehow I sensed that all would not be well with Juana and her handsome new husband. I lingered in Laredo for a few days anxiously waiting for word of everyone's safe arrival in Antwerp. Instead, one of our merchant ships limped into the harbor bringing the ominous news there were terrible, terrible storms all along the western

French coast with many ships dashed against the rocky French shores.

Still anxious, and not having received any word from Fadrique, my children and I joined Ferdinand in Burgos. Finally in November we received word that Juana and Philip were married on October 20, 1496 in Loirre. I should have been relieved but anxious thoughts for my daughter's well being continued to surface.

We were still at Burgos when I received a dispatch from my faithful friend and servant, Governor Pedro Bobadilla, simply stating, "Your mother is dying. Come quickly."

My tiny, frail, sixty-four year old mother was sinking fast. Taking her hand in mine I tried to tell her that I loved her and that I was here beside her. Gasping for air and clutching her glass beads, she tried to utter for one last time, "Mine, mine, mine," but her soul took flight and her body went limp in my arms.

The final rites over, numb, bleary-eyed and weary, I returned to my quarters to write some letters. So engrossed in total concentration was I, that I didn't notice an aide had come in and placed some items on my desk. Finishing the letter to the Bishop of Granada, I glanced across the table, and there, gleaming as the rays of the late afternoon sun shone upon them, were my mother's glass necklace, broach and ring. For thirty four years they had represented to her the symbol of her royal birth, something none could take from her. I took the worthless pieces into my hands, and with the tears rolling down my cheeks I began to sob. I cried for the pain that Enrique had caused when he demanded her jewels. I sobbed for my father who had neglected his duty to provide for her. I wept for her lonely, empty, solitary life.

CHAPTER XLVI
Marriages and the Death of the Heir to the Crown

Europe was experiencing the worst of winters. The seas were too dangerous to sail and Admiral Fadrique decided to wait for favorable weather. It was a long, cold, damp and hungry winter in Burgundy for my people. The northern Europeans were rude and ignored their Spanish guests, pushing them off to the hostile port city of Antwerp. The rude gales churned the deadly waters for five long months and my people suffered in icy misery. Food was priced beyond their means to pay for it. Disease broke out. The Admiral fell ill. Many, too many to think about, died from exposure and famine.

The Spanish fleet set sail from Burgundy in March, 1497 to bring my people and the vivacious Austrian Princess home. The party docked at Santander and as soon as word was received of their arrival, Ferdinand and Juan mounted their steeds and galloped northward to greet her.

Margaret was everything I could have wished for in a daughter-in-law. She was beautiful, intelligent, witty, charming, well-mannered and her court etiquette was impeccable. My son was overjoyed for this truly was a "match made in heaven." They triumphantly progressed through the countryside arriving in Burgos at the Constable's splendid Casa del Cordon where I was staying. I was surrounded by my ninety ladies-in-waiting, all exquisitely dressed in white lace and cream-colored brocades. I had chosen to circle my throat with rows and rows of gleaming jewels. As my future daughter-in-law knelt before me, her beautiful long red hair fell around her shoulders like a heavenly cloud, and deep inside I knew my son's marriage was going to be perfect. Yes, absolutely perfect.

For five months I had been preparing for my new daughter-in-law. I ordered a new carriage. This was the first carriage in our family. Often my nobles had suggested that one be purchased for me, but when I noted the cost, I quickly opted to ride my faithful horse. My itemized list for Margaret was endless. There were clothes, gold plates, candelabras, furniture, Flemish tapestries, girdles, silver services, silk sheets, rare cabinets filled with Oriental damask, and bronze candlesticks. Oh, it was an endless list I made for my son and his Archduchess. To Juan I gave the cities of Salamanca, Zamora, Toro, Arevalo, Jaen and Ronda.

The city of Burgos took on a carnival-like atmosphere. From every balcony the flags were flying. Fresh bouquets of flowers were placed in windows or tied to posts. Musicians appeared on street corners singing new ballads composed in honor of the future king and his Archduchess.

On Sunday, April 3, 1497, the brilliant marriage ceremony conducted by Ximenes Cisneros, Archbishop of Toledo, was performed before all the grandees of Castile and Aragon and representatives of the House of Hapsburg.

Watching this holy ceremony binding my son in matrimony with this beautiful Austrian Archduchess was one of my happiest moments. Granada was ours.

A rich new land had been discovered. Spain was stable and prosperous and by my side was my devoted husband.

Ysabel was beginning to have second thoughts about her future and within weeks after Juan's wedding she decided to accept King Manuel's wedding proposal. All of my dreams were falling into place.

On September 20, 1497, in Valencia de Alcantara, my daughter became the Queen of Portugal. Life was good. God was omnipotent, and I was very, very happy.

Time was rushing onward. Gone were the days when I could spend my hours in the saddle or work into the wee hours of the morning. My doctors now urged me to rest often. There were running sores that would not heal breaking out on my legs, baffling the doctors. I was concerned, but I made the doctors promise not to speak to a single, solitary soul about them. After the gruelling preparations for Ysabel's royal wedding, totally exhausted, I was ordered to remain in bed for a complete rest.

Juan and Margaret were living in Salamanca sending us happy notes regularly. They were expecting a baby and were bubbling over with happiness. Suddenly Juan became ill with a high fever. The alarmed doctors sent couriers racing south to Valencia to notify us. Quickly Ferdinand mounted his horse and galloped over the countryside to be at our son's bedside. It was too late. When he reached Salamanca, our nineteen year old son was dying and on October 4th, 1497, he drew his last breath.

The news of Juan's death struck like a knife into my heart. I was dazed. I couldn't accept it. He was the heir to our thrones. I had to trust the wisdom of God who had taken him, but for the rest of my life I would mourn his passing. To comfort me, Ferdinand brought Juan's favorite greyhound dog who, too, missed his master. Juan's faithful dog became my constant companion, never leaving my side.

It was early in 1498 when we received the news that Margaret had given birth to a tiny, stillborn son. The new dream that had been formulating in my mind for my grandson to become the next king of Spain had quickly been snuffed out. My heart was breaking.

CHAPTER XLVII
Colon Returns to Castile in Chains

The preparations for Colombo's departure on his third voyage were making very slow progress, primarily hindered by the Administrator of the Board of Indian Affairs, Bishop Fonseca. For some reason, unknown to me, Fonseca had developed an apparent deep hostile attitude toward the Admiral. During the months following Fonseca's appointment to oversee the Indian affairs, I had received several reports describing him as a very irritable man with an almost unforgiving temper. Fonseca's powerful position gave him every opportunity to successfully oppose the preparations for Colon's next historic voyage.

The preparations for the ocean voyage went forward and now nearly completed, a search in earnest began for sailors to man the ships. The unfounded rumors of the terrible conditions in the colony had spread like wildfire everywhere. No one wanted to brave the choppy seas, endure long hardships, hunger and desperation. It was one more dilemma placed before me to resolve. After careful thought and discussions with Ferdinand, the Royal Council and other advisors, we again decided to unlock the gates of our prisons and commute the sentences of those who would volunteer to go to the new colony. From the port of St. Lucar, on May 30, 1498, Colon once again sailed out of our harbor loaded with supplies and dangerous convicts, never dreaming of the shocking state of affairs waiting for him upon his arrival in the islands of Hispaniola.

Colon sailed into the now comparatively familiar calm harbor of the main island, confident that all of the problems of the past were behind him and looking forward with enthusiasm to accomplish many things. Gold had been discovered on the main land and small shipments of the precious ore were being placed on board ships bound for Spain. Before leaving for his return to Spain, Colon had transferred the responsibility of governing to his brother, Bartholomew. The overbearing hidalgos and cavaliers, ignoring every sort of discipline and law abiding exhortations from Bartholomew, completely paralyzed the operations. The colony was in wretched ruin. Those colonists who had revolted against Bartholomew had the colony in total disarray. The mines which held such high hopes for Colon and the Monarchs were now idled. The poor, unfortunate natives had been subjected to inexcusable overwork, terror and inhuman oppression. The common cry of the cavaliers and hidalgos was, "Only the strongest survive!"

Colon plunged into this chaotic situation meeting the difficult task of restoring order. Within days after his arrival, the very crew that had sailed with him were encouraged to join the forces of the rebels and mutinied against him. Colon was forced to resort to negotiations, entreaty, force and to some extent finally succeeded by giving concessions -- concessions he thought patched up the differences. It was a deceptive settlement, for the rebels only wanted to wring the concessions out of Colon and then continue to essentially diminish what authority he had left.

Those long, tedious negotiations and concessions had gone on week after week, month after month, taking nearly a year to establish a segment of civility in this God-forsaken land. The cooperation Colon so desperately needed and had worked so hard to restore continued to be threatening as the dissention of those feuding, self-seeking cavaliers continued. Rumors continued to reach Spain that things were going from bad to worse in the colony. The most absurd accusations against Colon and Bartholomew were constantly placed on my desk. Some reports even went so far as to state Colon and Bartholomew were using every tactic imaginable to establish an independent government.

The supreme confidence I had placed so totally in Colon never allowed me to waver for one single, solitary moment or to suspect his loyalty. I was concerned and becoming very uneasy as day after day the barrage of reports arrived. I finally began to have increasing doubts. I thought possibly Colon's real problem was he did not have the talent and capability to govern. Still pondering this serious situation and making no real progress in resolving it, a communique arrived with one of the royal couriers informing me that several of the antagonistic, trouble-making rebels had arrived with a number of Indian slaves from Hispaniola. These rebels wasted no time in gaining the public's attention and loudly acclaimed to all who would listen to them that the great Admiral, Governor, Viceroy Cristobol Colon, had assigned these slaves to them. They proudly displayed the unfortunate Indians on their clumsily erected stages.

I read that communique through and through. Colon had so many times written, and also spoke often with Ferdinand and me, telling about these gentle islanders who would be so receptive to our Christian teachings. I decided I had better dispatch a letter to Colon immediately and confront him with this development, asking him if he had actually consigned these quiet men to a life of slavery. Suddenly reports were received that another ship had arrived and advertisements were appearing for the sale of many Indian slaves in the Andalucia markets. By now I was visibly alarmed. I commanded the sale of those Indians to be suspended immediately and then asked for an opinion of a council formed of theologians and doctors, asking them to make a determination as to the conscientious lawfulness of the sale of any human being.

I sent a dispatch to all those churches active in training priests who were to become the missionaries, instructing that they be taught to speak the language of the Indians. In every single personal letter, as well as nearly every ordinance devised, I urged -- over and over again -- our absolute obligation to those natives. "We must give them their religious instruction and we must be kind and gentle to them in every way."

Another alarming dispatch arrived proclaiming two more vessels had now arrived from the Indies with three hundred slaves on board waiting to be sold in the marketplace. I sent a small group of advisers directing them to find "By whose authority were these Indians damned to become slaves in Castile?" They meekly returned with the matter-of-fact statement, "The Admiral had granted these concessions to the mutineers." I was appalled, indignantly asking, "By what authority does Colon venture to thus dispose of my subjects?" Orders for all Indian slaves to be returned to their homeland immediately were issued. The few Indians assigned to the Crown were also given their freedom, released from their bondage and returned on the next available ship to the New World.

After much soul searching and round-the-clock discussions, I reluctantly agreed to send a Commissioner to investigate the affairs of the colony. I made the unfortunate appointment of Don Francisco de Bobadilla, a poor knight of Calatrava. The new Commissioner would need the firm backing of the Crown with full authority to restore the colony. I invested in him the supreme powers of both civil and criminal jurisprudence. He was instructed to bring to trial and pass sentence on everyone who had conspired against the authority of Colon and the Crown. He was further authorized to take possession of the fortresses, vessels, public stores, property of every description, and to settle matters with all the officers. By my royal command, without distinction of rank, he was to return the troublemakers to Spain. Upon their arrival they would be severely dealt with by me.

Immediately upon his arrival in Hispaniola, Bobadilla organized a pretentious parade to proclaim his absolute authority. Next he commanded Colon to appear before him. Without any hesitation Colon promptly arrived at Bobadilla's headquarters to make his report. Bobadilla looked at this tall, blue-eyed man standing so straight and confident before him, and ordered his aide to place Colon in chains and imprison him. His next act was to send incompetent people scurrying around to gather evidence against Colon. Piecing together the bits of gossip they had gathered, Bobadilla listed page after page of crimes Colon had committed. He then entrusted the report to the personal care of the next sea captain sailing for Spain. Colon was placed aboard that sea captain's ship with explicit orders from Bobadilla, "Colon was to be chained in irons throughout the entire voyage home."

Ferdinand and I were troubled about the far reaching authority I had given Bobadilla. The very last thing I could possibly have imagined would have been that he would take such immediate drastic measures against Colon. The nobles, along with every member of our Court, were outraged that such severe action had been taken against Colon. It was a national disaster! Such an indignity to be heaped upon a hero who had done so much for Spain and the civilized world.

The royal couriers raced from Cadiz to Granada bringing to me the official dispatch sent by Bobadilla. I ordered Colon to be immediately released from those irons and that he be given his complete freedom. Further, my envoys left with a personal letter from me, written in my own hand, to give to Colon. I instructed Colon to travel immediately to Granada, escorted by the colorful envoys I had sent.

Colon traveled in royal style revived by all the reassurances and kind disposition of his Monarchs. Being informed of his arrival, we immediately sent an aide to bring him to us. When Colon entered the room, I hardly recognized him. His red hair was now streaked with grey, offset by his sunken blue eyes which gave the illusion of blank spaces where his eyes should be. His drawn face and tragic thin body was a shock to me. He walked with a painful limp. It was obvious with every step he forced himself to take, he was in excruciating pain. He stood before us straight and tall, without the once envied graceful movements, visibly shaken and unable to utter a single word.

Before me stood this heroic man whose incredible journey changed the world as we thought it was. Ferdinand remained silent, but I spoke out to express my sorrow and absolute indignation that one of my own trusted servants had forced him to endure such pain, suffering, agony and humiliation. The words poured from the very depths of my heart. As I looked at this wasted, broken man standing before me I realized that I--alone--must take the full responsibility for Bobadilla's actions. Tears filled my eyes and flowed down my cheeks. My concern for all the pain and suffering he had endured was too much for the fragile emotions, which he had held in check for so many months, finally spilled over. He dropped to his knees, his body shaking with uncontrollable sobs. For the first time since I had been crowned the Queen, I was mortified and ashamed of a terrible act imposed by my subjects upon an individual.

CHAPTER XLVIII
Death of Daughter Ysabel

A ll of Europe now watched the shifting tides of the Spanish Monarchy. Far away in Netherlands, Philip, the Handsome, our son-in-law, declared himself heir to the Crown. Word reached us that the royal Courts of Europe were preoccupied with the titillating gossip about our daughter's sharp tongue and her passionately jealous outbursts caused by Philip's wandering eyes and notorious love affairs. Juana never wrote to me. I knew nothing of her life at the Flemish Court. One by one her carefully chosen advisers returned home in disgust, and only then was I able to piece together the disturbing situation. I was very uneasy. Philip, the future sovereign of Spain? Ferdinand and I echoed an emphatic, "No. Absolutely not."

I was not anxious to become embroiled in arguing with Philip's father, Maximilian. I had a strong feeling that it was Maximilian who encouraged, and yes, even perhaps ordered, Philip to make such a bold announcement.

We immediately summoned our daughter, Ysabel, now pregnant, and her new husband King Manuel to Spain. They arrived in Toledo in March of 1498 and on Sunday, April 29th, before the grandees, prelates and other important officials, the Cortes dutifully recognized Ysabel and Manuel as heirs to the Castile crown. Then we traveled to Zaragosa where they were acknowledged as the successors to the Crown of Aragon.

It was a difficult time for my delicate daughter, and it was unfortunate it had been necessary to bring her home now. She was having a very difficult pregnancy and we decided she should remain with us until after the birth of her baby.

Late in the afternoon on August 22nd, 1498, she went into a long, painful and difficult labor. I was by her side giving her comfort and good cheer, and on August 23rd, she gave birth to a tiny baby boy. What a rush of joy and excitement I felt as the doctor wrapped the tiny baby in a blanket and placed him in my outstretched arms. Cradling him, I moved to a window to study his face. Did he look like me, Ferdinand, his father, or his mother? I couldn't decide. His tiny wrinkled pink face and reddish brown hair favored the Trastamara side, of that I was certain. As he squirmed in my arms and began to fuss, I rocked him gently to and fro and started to sing a little lullaby. Suddenly Ysabel screamed as if racked by pain. I heard the doctor exclaim, "Oh, no!" As I turned around he was closing her eyelids and gently, ever so gently, he drew the coverlet over her still, lifeless body.

Ysabel was dead! With my little "king" still in my arms, I stumbled down the corridors searching for Ferdinand. He was in a meeting at the end of the hall and when he saw the tiny baby in my arms, his eyes sparkled and he bounded toward me to get a glimpse of his first grandchild. My face registered the news, for as he drew nearer he knew Ysabel was gone. Without a word he gathered our grandchild and me into his arms and I cried as if my heart was breaking. First mother, then Juan and his tiny son, and now Ysabel.

Fall was one of my favorite seasons and I especially liked to be in Burgos at this time of the year. The Monastery La Cartuja de Miraflores was now completed and the tombs of my father, mother and brother had been transported from Valladolid to Burgos, my mother and father's placed before the altar. Ferdinand wanted no part of the dedication ceremony I planned. He was so angry with me because I ordered the tombs to be placed directly in front of the altar. He was certain his Aragon nobles would not approve. This had never been done before. On the appointed day, Ferdinand and I arrived at the Monastery and attended the ceremonies, just as I had planned them. I gazed at those tombs and marveled at the beauty which the sculptor had wrought with his tiny hammers and chisels. They were a national treasure! I was pleased, yes, very pleased.

All was not well with the brilliant alliance Ferdinand and I had so carefully managed when we established the Spanish-Hapsburg dynasty. The Flemish Council of Burgundy approached the union very cautiously. For decades the Low Countries had been embroiled in wars and rivalries, weakening themselves from within and unable to defend their country. Over the years the Flemish Council had carefully orchestrated a delicate peaceful co-existence with France.

Philip was only three years old when his mother, Mary of Burgundy, died leaving him the Low Countries as his inheritance. The Council took total charge of his life and the overseeing of his formal education. As the young Archduke matured into a young man, he was weak, indecisive, and vacillating, unable to make decisions. The Flemish Council capitalized upon his weakness and manipulated him at every turn with their crafty policies, thus retaining the power in their hands.

All that my daughter cared about was Philip, for she was passionately in love with her handsome, blonde, charming Prince. Philip was her whole life and whatever it was that he wanted, she acquiesced. Not long after their wedding those servants so carefully chosen to surround her became dissatisfied and decided to leave. With the exception of her treasurer, Martin de Moxica, all of her Spanish household returned home in disillusionment. As soon as they had departed, Philip promptly placed the Flemish Prince of Chimey in charge of her entire household. Cristobol Barroso was her newly appointed chamberlain. To Mme. de Halwin went the post of overseeing her mail, dictating her every move, and deciding what Court functions she would attend. Juana's ladies-in-waiting were curtly dismissed and soon replaced with untrustworthy native spies.

It was from those returning to Spain I learned that Burgundy was not honoring the Marriage Treaty making no provisions at all to pay Juana's household. Those who returned applied to Castile's treasury for their back pay. I was gravely concerned about this flagrant violation of our Agreement and asked our Spanish Emissary in Burgundy to lodge a mild complaint. When this produced no results I requested the Bishop of Catania to make a representation to Philip personally. It was a useless exercise in futility. For the first time in my adult life my hands were completely tied. I had no power to change any aspect of my daughter's predicament. There was no way for me to intervene and come to the aid of my child. Using my considerable influence I was adamant in insisting that the Flemish allow Castile to provide Juana with proper funds for her household.

The Flemish finally permitted me to send 2,000 Flemish escudos which were delivered to Moxica, who, by this time, had joined with the Flemish. As soon as the money was delivered to him, payment vouchers were prepared for Flemish retainers; then Mme. Halwin forced Juana to sign them. Juana's immediate servants received nothing. Juana had no money at all.

Again, I sent an emissary to discuss the matter with Philip. Still vacillating he side-stepped the matter insisting that Ferdinand and I were applying too much pressure upon him to comply with the Marriage Treaty. Then, too, the Flemish and Hapsburg elements were constantly badgering him to continue to keep peace with France. From every side there were pressures. What could he do?

In July I sent my agent, Tomas de Matienzo, Sub-Prior to Segovia's Convent of Santa Cruz to Brussels. Over a period of several months he had meeting after meeting with Juana. In ciphered letters to me he relayed Juana's responses. He had asked her, "Why did she not inquire about anyone from her country?" Juana replied, "I no longer know anyone from Spain."

On Assumption Day two priests arrived to hear her confession and she ignored them completely. Matienzo asked her, "Why?" Juana didn't answer. Matienzo reminded her, "Your mother would not approve." This elicited the sarcastic response, "I kiss my mother's hand for telling me how to run my life." "Why do you not write home?" "I will do so soon." "Why not today?" "Because I have nothing at the moment to say." Endlessly on and on it went until finally Juana grew tired of the intolerable interviews and decided to remain mute, refusing to converse at all.

Matienzo continued to send his ciphered letters

to me, constantly complaining about the food, people, climate, his illnesses, habits, and customs of an uncivilized country, and he always needed money. He remained in Burgundy until after Juana gave birth to her first child, Elinor, and then deciding nothing more could be accomplished, I recalled him to Spain.

My two youngest daughters surrounded me with their love and attention. They were both so intelligent and wise, and I prayed their futures would be filled with happiness. King Manuel waited until the proper mourning period for Ysabel was over, and then he asked for Maria's hand in marriage. Linked to Portugal Spain was destined to be, for Maria wisely accepted and I was once again preparing for another royal wedding.

Shortly after Maria's ceremonies were behind us, Ferdinand and I accompanied our youngest, Catalina, to the northern port in Spain where she boarded a vessel and sailed off to England to become the young bride of their future king, Prince Arthur. How much I loved this perfect child. I wanted her life to be happy and fulfilled.

In May I left for Granada with Ferdinand and our little grandson, Miguel. I traveled more leisurely now. Ferdinand jokingly said, "with proper dignity." Those wild rides during the early years of my reign might not have conveyed all the "pomp and dignity" my High Office commanded, but it did bring solutions to my people's problems. I no longer traveled on a horse, but was carried on a special platform where I could either sit or recline. I would gladly have traded this "dignity" my mode of travel now dictated for the hectic and dangerous wild rides of my younger years.

Surrounded by my loved ones in the peace and beauty of the Alhambra, I hoped to regain my health. I prayed the beauty of the gardens and the quiet, peaceful surroundings would restore my tired body. The open sores on my legs were not healed, instead new ones festered and opened. It was so painful to walk because the sores affected every muscle in my legs. My weight was increasing at an alarming rate. Seamstresses were busy measuring and fitting and before a new dress was even completed I had gained several pounds and more inches. They had to start all over again. This was disturbing. What should I do? I didn't want my subjects to see their over-weight Queen and wonder if I was dying so I sent for some Franciscan monk habits. I put one on and it fell in nice folds around my body, disguising my waist and swollen legs. Because of the open running sores eating into the flesh, my bloated hips, huge thighs and enlarged legs, I waddled like a duck when I took my steps.

I inspected myself in a mirror wearing my new monk habit, put on my now familiar cap covering my very thin hair, and placing my favorite hand carved wooden beads with the three crosses around my neck, my royal attire was complete. If God so willed it, for the rest of my life this monk habit would be my royal wardrobe. My subjects concluded I was increasingly turning my inward thoughts and prayers toward God.

Colon was making his fourth settlement trip to the New World. So far, our ships had not returned home laden with precious jewels, gold and spices. Somehow I thought if we gave it time, a lot of time, the new land's wealth would gain for Spain a regal place in world history.

Without any hesitation, both Ferdinand and I decided upon the complete restoration of the Admiral's honor, and he had a right to the "ten percent royalties" which the Crown had awarded to him. As far as his titles, I wanted to reserve my judgment and wait.

We selected Don Nicolas de Ovando of the Military Order of Alcantara, and Commodore of Larea to establish order in Hispaniola. I immediately gathered an armada of Spanish galleons which would carry a very large contingency of troops, supplies, food and other necessities. Ovando would arrive with such an ominous force representing the Crown there would be an immediate and complete restoration of civil liberties.

In late 1499 we received the unsettling dispatch that Philip had appeared before Guy de Rochefott, the Lord Chancellor of France in the cities of Flanders, Artois and Charolis, swearing himself the vassal of Louis XII, King of France, and promising to carry himself toward Louis as his 'sovereign lord' until his death.

Time rushed onward. Juana gave birth to her second child, Carlos, and during that summer in Granada, on July 20th, 1500, God called our little two year old Miguel home.

Juana would inherit the Crowns.

CHAPTER XLIX
Juana 'La Loca'

The political climate in Brussels dramatically changed when word began to circulate that Juana and Philip were the heirs to the Spanish throne. Clearly the awesome power which Philip could eventually wield would directly affect every European nation. He was presently the Sovereign of the Low Countries, and upon the death of his father he would inherit Austria. There was no doubt he would inherit the entire lands and properties belonging to the House of Hapsburg, and when crowned as the King of the Spanish empire, he would be Europe's most powerful Monarch. Suddenly all of Europe turned their eyes towards Flanders. Anxious to further diplomatic relations and develop firm friendships, a steady stream of diplomats arrived from Germany, Austria, France, England, Spain, Denmark and the Pope.

At the age of three, Philip had been separated from his father and taken to live at the Court in Flanders, as a result, ties which bind a father and son together were very weak. This left the control of the weak minded and vacillating Philip vigorously contested between Flanders and Spain.

After the death of our little Miguel we dispatched our emissary to Flanders, directing him to have an audience with Philip and Juana, and to deliver to them our hand written invitation to visit us, and upon their arrival they were to be duly sworn by the Cortes as the next Monarchs.

I was deeply concerned about Juana. Still never writing, I had no knowledge of her activities or how she was handling the Flemish people. I sent my first chaplain, Juan de Fonseca, the Bishop of Cordoba, to befriend her. Fonseca found Juana isolated and in an agitated state of nervous depression. In a letter I received from him he wrote, "No living souls aid her with a single word."

It had been two years since Matienzo had been recalled to Spain and Juana appeared eager for company. She looked upon Fonseca as an educated family friend and an important man of culture. Fonseca decided he might be able to reach her if he became a "story teller" weaving stories of Court intrigues to capture her attention. As he deftly told stories about internal rivalries, jealousies, envy and Court intrigues, Juana sat in rapt attention listening to every word, playing it over in her mind. Grasping the significance of Court intrigues she exclaimed, "That's why my Spanish servants disappeared!" Then she began to remember a lot of things that had strangely happened which took the control of her life out of her hands. Fonseca was pleased. He thought he was making considerable progress. Soon Juana would be able to discern when others were manipulating her. I felt a little easier as I read these ciphered reports.

The Flemish Council, so successful in the manipulation and control of Philip, chafed at the idea of him traveling to Spain for they knew Philip's undisciplined mind could easily be swayed by others. For that major reason they found many ways to delay

Philip and Juana's departure. Carefully calculating the effectiveness of their conversations, they assured Philip, "Yes, you must go to Spain and be sworn as their next King. You must only go for a very brief stay and your own Flemish advisers and friends must travel with you." The first segment of their plans completed, they next opened and successfully concluded negotiations for a marriage alliance with France. Louis XII was anxious to betroth his tiny baby daughter, Claude, to Philip and Juana's second child, Carlos, thus cementing a powerful alliance between the two countries.

When word reached our Court that our little grandson's marriage had already been arranged, Ferdinand and I were stunned. All of those carefully thought out plans when our own Marriage Treaty with Maximilian was completed were unravelling. An alliance between France and the Low Countries was the very last thing we could have considered happening only a few short years ago.

We sent our new Ambassador, Fuensaida, to Brussels instructing him to use his considerable influence to aide Juana and Philip in quickly making their travel plans for their homecoming festivities. Conveniently for the Flemish conspirators, Juana became pregnant again and her doctor would not permit her to travel and on June 15, 1501, our little granddaughter, Ysabel, was born. Fuensaida's dispatches to us were filled with obvious frustrations. He tried to apply pressure to get a commitment for a definite time of their departure. He would write to us, "Some say they will leave at the end of October, and others say at the end of November. I believe nothing for nobody tells the truth. But in truth, they have no more desire to go to Spain than to hell."

Finally we received word they were leaving Flanders, but the meddlesome Flemish Council secretly arranged for them to travel overland through France. Louis XII had invited Philip and Juana to leisurely travel through the French countryside to Spain and along the way, they were to be feted as only royal persons should. Early in November, 1501, Philip and Juana left Brussels with an enormous retinue and an endless train of baggage-cars with furniture, silver, tapestries, and even kitchenware.

King Louis sent a heavy detachment of lancers to escort them through France in a slow procession, stopping at all of the villages for a kingly reception. A solid friendship between Philip and Louis sprang up and with this accomplished, Louis allowed them to travel south but no longer escorted by the French envoys. The severest weather conditions prevailed with blinding snowstorms and drenching rains. The rivers of southern France overflowed their banks and wagons mired down in a quagmire of mud. Finally they crossed the Pyrenees with only half of their belongings.

On March 14th, our nobles met them in Burgos and escorted them to the Alcazar in Tordesillas. Then it was on to Medina del Campo and Segovia, hoping to reach Madrid by Holy Week. Leaving Madrid they expected to arrive at Toledo soon; however, Philip became ill with measles forcing them to stop at Olivos. As soon as word was received of this unfortunate delay, Ferdinand left immediately for Olivos to meet his son-in-law.

Juana chanced to look out the window of the upper gallery when she saw her father ride into the courtyard. Overjoyed, she ran through the gallery, bounded down the stairs, and swept out the huge door and into her father's outstretched arms. Our now radiant daughter clung to her father's arm as she lead him to Philip's bedside. Philip made a feeble gesture to sit up and reached out to grasp Ferdinand's hand to kiss it. Ferdinand withdrew his hand and signaled instead for a chair to be placed by the bedside. Juana wound her arms around her father's neck and beaming with obvious happiness, she translated the conversation between Philip and her father.

On May 7th they arrived in Toledo riding through the cheering streets, first to The Cathedral where Ximenes Cisneros, Archbishop of Toledo, stood at the portal with his tall jeweled cross. After the short service they proceeded up the hill to the great Alcazar where I was waiting for them.

I studied my flighty, nervous daughter and my spoiled, conceited and overbearing son-in-law. Juana had not matured at all. It was all too obvious. She lived only for Philip, passionately in love with him, jealous of his every move, and too possessive. What kind of a Queen would she be? How would she handle Spain's brilliant future? I was troubled and Ferdinand was alarmed. Far into the night we reviewed our options, deciding our only hope would be "time" -- time for the children to see the wisdom of remaining in Spain to learn the Hispanic ways of governing. Time . . . it was my only hope for my country's future.

Philip was ranting and raving for he wanted to go riding, hunting and jousting. Elaborate plans were being made; however, before the festivities had gotten underway, we received a dispatch from England informing us that our precious Catalina's husband, Prince Arthur, was dead. Our Court immediately went into nine days of mourning. On May 12th, the full Requiem was presented at San Juan de Los Reyes with a *"representative"* of Arthur on a bier of black velvet, its starkness relieved by a white damask covered cross. Philip displayed obvious boredom and bad manners as he yawned through the entire service.

Just as the mourning period ended, Ferdinand's uncle died in Aragon and the Court again went into mourning. Philip was thoroughly disenchanted and quite vocal in expressing how much he detested everything Spanish, making very pointed comments about our custom of mourning for the departed -- especially for people we had never even met. Any slight suggestion or effort to give him training in statecraft or diplomacy was met with a curt rejection. He was conceited, undisciplined and quite frankly, a very rude, angry young man.

On May 22nd, at the great Cathedral in Toledo, the Castilian Cortes swore in a radiantly beautiful Juana and sulking Philip as the next Monarchs. Ferdinand had quietly ordered that the Archduke of Burgundy, Prince of Austria's arms not be carried in the procession. Philip was furious vowing to himself that when he was presented to the Cortes in Aragon, he would demand his banners and shields be displayed.

Ferdinand left in July for Zaragosa to handle the arrangements for the next ceremonies. Philip continued to complain; his servants got into brawls with the Spaniards; and because of the differences in food and climate, many of his people were ill. Days of waiting to be summoned to Zaragosa stretched into endless weeks. Three months had gone by and still no summons to Zaragosa.

Meanwhile Ferdinand leisurely made his way through the countryside to Zaragosa, sauntering along the dusty roads craftily drafting plans for his snobbish son-in-law who had displayed an obvious admiration for Louis XII. He vowed he would not so readily hand his Crown over to this spoiled royal "egg-head."

The summons to Zaragosa was finally presented to Philip in October. Hurriedly he and Juana departed with a great flourish as their banners were struck and they mounted their prancing ponies leading the grand procession out of the courtyard and down the dusty roads. I watched from my window as they gathered in the courtyard below. Juana, in her excitement -- or haste -- had forgotten to bid me goodbye. I thought to myself it was just as well for I was not feeling well and to put up with any sort of her pretenses would have made my day more difficult.

Arriving in Zaragosa, an anxious Philip immediately placed his demands before Ferdinand, insisting that he properly be accorded his Sovereign rights with his banners and shield displayed. Wily Ferdinand, stroking Philip's big ego, nodded his head in agreement.

Juana and Philip stood in rapt attention before the Cortes of Aragon, ready to be pronounced heirs to the Throne. First the Cortes recognized Juana as heir to the Throne. Then turning to Philip, in grave, dignified tones they announced, "Philip, Archduke of Burgundy, Prince of Austria and of the House of Hapsburg shall henceforth be recognized as the future queen's consort, and only during your marriage. Further, if Queen Ysabella should die and King Ferdinand remarry, and if a male child is born, then that child becomes the Crown Prince of Aragon and heir to the Throne."

Philip was stunned. The smile on his face suddenly became a frown. He could find no words to utter for an acknowledgement. Through his mind raced the thought, "So that was why Ferdinand took so long. He was holding private meetings with the Cortes to present this 'bastard' plan." Silently he vowed he would get even with his father-in-law. Yes, indeed, he would repay him in kind. Juana had not grasped any part of the Cortes pronouncement. She was aware only that her charming Prince suddenly became disenchanted.

Philip was friendly, cool and politely distant with Ferdinand, for they had remained in Zaragosa to attend to additional business being debated by the Cortes, and Philip was invited to accompany Ferdinand to the sessions.

I was not well and had decided to be taken to Madrid. My couriers delivered the dispatch to Ferdinand keeping him informed of the move. Ferdinand pounced upon an idea and quickly paid a call to Philip announcing that I was very, very ill and he must rush to Madrid to be by my side. The Cortes still had important business to conclude so he would deputize Philip, and Philip would then officially preside over the meetings. Suddenly Philip bristled with importance. He sat up straight in his chair, pulled his shoulders back as if to say, "Well, now, this is the role for the Archduke of Burgundy." Ferdinand made a swift exit, and with great expectations the arrogant Philip prepared for his next encounter.

The first order of business of the Cortes was to raise funds for war against France. Philip looked around at the serious faces of those men and realized he had been tricked. He had pledged his undying loyalty to Louis and now he must become directly involved in raising funds to wage a war against him. He was beside himself. Suddenly he bolted from the room, mounted his horse and raced towards Madrid. It was an angry son-in-law who demanded an immediate audience with us.

Ferdinand and I were astounded with his pretentious announcement that he must leave immediately for Flanders. He insisted he had received a dispatch from the Flemish Council urging him to return to Flanders immediately. There were heated exchanges between the three of us. Knowing there was nothing for him to do in Flanders, we presented every solid argument we could think of to convince him to remain in Spain. "Juana was pregnant and could not travel." His reply to that was just a shrug of his shoulders, staring defiantly into our faces. Next, "He had not had enough time to become acquainted with Spain." Philip countered that his government had given him only one year to be away. That year was up and they have demanded that he return.

We petitioned the Castile and Aragon Cortes to issue a royal command that he "refrain from offending the Sovereigns by a quick, untimely departure." Philip ignored the command and continued to insist his presence was needed to resolve troubles at home.

Realizing we had exhausted every argument, there was nothing left to do but announce that "We will not permit Juana, five months pregnant, to leave Spain until after the birth of her child." Without even blinking an eye, Philip coldly and calmly stated, "Fine, I can leave without her."

Juana was beside herself. She threw one of her famous temper tantrums, begging, pleading and crying. Philip merely looked at the pitiful, pregnant, disheveled woman before him as if she were a total stranger. Picking up his riding gloves and fastening his sword around his waist, he motioned for his aides to saddle his horse. Watching from her window, Juana screamed and wailed as her husband rode away.

While we waited for the birth of Juana's child, I tried to reach out to her but she remained distant and non-communicative to me; however, she was outspoken to others and the servants. She complained bitterly and placed the entire blame for Philip's sudden departure directly upon me. In fact, her treatment of me was almost unbearable causing the tongues to wag and create such a stir throughout the Court and beyond. I would never have tolerated it but I feared too much agitation could affect her high-strung emotions. I prayed daily that she had not inherited my mother's incurable insanity. I desperately wanted to help her and prayed she would understand the gravity of the role she was destined to have for Spain.

After the birth of her baby son on March 10, 1503, Juana grew even more difficult, spending her days longing for Philip. Possessive and jealous of his every move and gesture, her agitation increased as she thought of the mistresses he must now have. Word reached us from various sources Philip had traveled through France and arrived at Savoy, leaving somewhat later for Innsbruck, Switzerland, and presently we understood he was in Bavaria. Juana was constantly planning her departure issuing orders every day for her things to be packed.

All through the spring and summer Juana and I discussed her return to Brussels. I had a thousand reasons for her to remain. Juana had a thousand and one reasons to leave. Every gruelling session with her left me emotionally drained and after each encounter my strength failed and I had to spend days in bed. Finally, firmly convinced I could not reach her, I departed for Segovia instructing that Juana be taken to La Mota, a large brick Alcazar given to Ferdinand and me by the Duke of Alba situated just outside Medina del Campo.

La Mota is an isolated, bleak and lonely Alcazar. Admittedly, I placed her there not to imprison her, but to allow her time to think and resolve her passionate longings for a husband who cared nothing about her. To the best of my knowledge, Philip had not sent a single note to his wife since he had departed months ago. There was no word from him rejoicing for the son which she had borne for him.

Something finally prompted Philip to sit down and write to Juana. In his letter he stated bluntly, "It will be better for you to leave Spain now, or you may never, ever get away." All Juana could think of was that her husband had sent for her. He must love her, and she was leaving to join him. Frantically she issued orders for her baggage to be packed. She sent out inquiries for mules, wagons, and supplies. There was a torrent of energy unleashed for she now had firmly made up her mind -- she was leaving.

Word of the flurry of activities at La Mota reached my ears and I promptly dispatched Bishop Fonseca to intervene. It was late in November and the blustery cold, strong winds blew throughout the isolated valley where La Mota was built. Fonseca arrived at La Mota just as Juana was mounting her mule ready to ride out of the courtyard. Juana observed Fonseca making his authoritative entrance and knew instantly why he was there. Haughtily she pulled her mule up to him, and glaring in his face she spit out that she was leaving. Fonseca countered with a command that the Queen had ordered her to stay. Juana pulled on the reins urging her stubborn mule to move. Quickly Fonseca ordered the drawbridge raised and Juana knew she was trapped. She lashed out at the Bishop with a fury, screaming at the top of her lungs and threatening him with bodily harm. The Bishop beckoned a servant to unlock a gate at the back and he slipped out. Juana's anger was not vented for she still had more to say to him. Scrambling up the steep, rocky steps to the top of the battlements, she looked out to see the Bishop and his horse moving off in the distance. Her screams and tormented cries echoed throughout the valley. After Fonseca disappeared into the distance, she stumbled down the steps and crouched at the iron bars of the gate. Her frantic emotions spent, now in a dazed, catatonic state, she gripped the bars with hands that froze in an iron grip. Tears that had been flowing from her eyes were now replaced with a glazed, glassy stare. The frightened servants dared not go near her.

All through the night she clutched the gate with her iron grip. Late the next afternoon she released her grip, moved a few feet to the guardhouse and sitting down on a little stool began her five-day vigil. "Here they stopped me. Here I will stay."

An excited courier brought this disturbing news to me in Segovia. I dispatched Cisneros and the Admiral to La Mota. Finding Juana still crouched in the guard-house they tried to speak with her. She glared at both of them, heard everything they said, and turned away. They failed in this mission they told me, and they were very sorry but there was nothing more they could do. I knew then that I had no choice. I must go to Juana. This shocking melodrama had to end!

My tall, burly litter carriers hoisted me aboard their strong shoulders and in an even gait they swiftly carried me over the dusty roads for my final encounter. Word had been sent ahead to notify Juana that I would be arriving and for her to have my rooms prepared. Juana turned a deaf ear to this command. When I learned of this, I decided to remain in Medina del Campo to rest and gather my strength.

Juana was still defiantly sitting in the guard-house when I arrived. With the tenderness only a mother who loves her child could understand, I tried to urge her to go inside the Alcazar. Her only words, spoken with rigid determination and totally unrelenting, "Here they stopped me. Here I will stay."

Realizing that any further efforts would be fruitless, I ordered my beefy litter carriers to boldly pick her up and carry her into the Alcazar. My heart was breaking, my strength was ebbing, my hand was shaking, but I had to write Ferdinand to let him know -- "I put her in."

That night I prayed that the entire episode would be blotted out of everyone's memory, that this ordeal which Juana had just passed through was now over and behind her. It was too late. The damage was done, and for the rest of her life her people would know her as Juana "La Loca."

CHAPTER L
The Death of Ysabella

The horrible ordeal had ended, sapping my strength to such a degree it was impossible to return to Segovia. Juana needed us and as soon as Ferdinand had finished with some of his business he joined us at La Mota. Juana loved her father dearly and it was so helpful to have him near. The doctors and clergy agreed that we must allow Juana to return to Flanders, and we ordered a small fleet to take her home. Baby Ferdinand would remain in Castile. Philip had returned to Brussels and Juana was dreaming of the days when she would be with him again. As doting grandparents, we taught her little son to walk and talk.

All was readied for Juana, and in March we accompanied her to Laredo. The small boats sailed out of the harbor and I never saw her again.

My doctors ordered me to rest but the realm's business continued to occupy my mind. My life would be ending soon -- that I knew -- and many things needed to be accomplished. There was no time to waste. As always, there was my constant concern for the people. From my personal income I supported hospitals and convents and I was anxious for reports from them. I met with university officials to discuss curricula for added studies in botany and archeology, and I worked earnestly for fixed salaries to be paid to our professors.

My weight was a growing concern and by now it was almost impossible for me to walk. In the morning, dressed in my Franciscan robe, my hefty litter bearers would gently lift me from my bed to the couch. My eyesight was failing and an aide would read to me choosing the activities at home and abroad he knew interested me.

The news from Brussels was disturbing. From the gossip mills of the European Courts came the devastating news that when Juana returned she discovered Philip had a mistress with long, blonde curls. One day Juana came across the lady reading what Juana was certain was a love-note from Philip and she demanded it. The defiant lady tore the note up and swallowed the pieces. An enraged Juana spied a pair of scissors and with panther-like movements she grabbed the scissors with one hand and the blonde curls with the other. The rival screamed and pulled away, but Juana's strength never failed her. Hair that was not clipped with scissors was pulled out by the handful, leaving a bleeding scalp and only a few wisps of hair.

Catalina in far off London wrote regularly. Her deceased husband's brother, Prince Henry, had proposed and she accepted. No wedding date had been set, but I wrote wishing her happiness, good health and a long life.

Time rushed onward. More discoveries in the Americas were reported by our returning sea captains. Our Grand Captain leading our Italian armies finally routed Louis XII at Carellano and Gaeta forcing the French army to surrender. Ferdinand was proclaimed the King of Naples. At long last the Peace Treaty with France was signed at La Mejorada.

Ferdinand never left my side. Sitting in silence

we drew strength from each other. Sometimes I would catch a tear falling down his cheek. I knew he was saddened for together we had been a mighty team. But God was calling, and homeward bound I was soon to be. Now I must make the effort to write my Will. The Cortes had met in July of 1503, nearly a year ago, requesting that I draw my Will naming my heir to provide for the proper transition of governmental affairs. That must wait for there still seemed to be time.

In July Ferdinand came down with a very high fever, and I caught it, too. Ferdinand's physical stamina was strong and soon he was up and about. I wasn't so fortunate for the fever continued to linger. Throughout the rest of the summer I lay on my bed weakened by the fever, listening to the reports of events around the country and continuing to handle official business.

Word was received that all of Europe knew that the ebb and flow of my life forces had nearly run its course. Public prayer and processions were held for me throughout the continent. Friends and envoys from Italy, France, Germany, Denmark, Greece, England and Sweden arrived, knowing it would be their last audience with me. My secretary and chronicler, Pietro Martire, continued to comment that never in history had foreign diplomats and Ambassadors traveled so far for their final "good byes." Another first he would proudly state. An Italian visitor, Prospero Colona, requested an audience stating, "I have come all the way to Spain in order to meet a woman who rules the world from her sickbed." I had to smile when Pietro brought his request forward. "Yes, of course, I will see him," was my prompt response.

My body was weakening, my breathing slowing down. The fever had never left me and I was constantly thirsty -- my throat was so dry. Somehow I must find the strength for my Will. I heard Pietro just this morning say it was "October 7th." I knew it was time to draw upon my remaining strength and decide about the important things left to be finalized.

Pietro placed the quill and paper by my side and as I grasped the quill in my hands, the words seemed to flow and take shape filling the pages.

First, my burial. I asked that "My body be taken to the Franciscan Monastery of Santa Ysabella in the Alhambra at Granada, and be laid to rest in a low and humble sepulcher, without memorial, other than just a plain inscription upon it. The funeral must be very simple, very plain, and the money saved be distributed among the poor."

Funds from my personal estate were to "go to several charities and marriage portions for poor maidens; and ransoms to be paid for our Christians still held in prisons by barbarians."

"My debts, if there are any, must all be paid within a year after my death."

I thought about certain lands and appointments that had been made among my royal household, and as I gave it considerate thought, I decided it had gotten out of hand. I asked that "the grants made with land and annuities be revoked."

I urged my successors "that they be vigilant in maintaining the integrity of the royal domain and above all, never to divest our nation of our title to the important fortress of Gibraltar."

Then . . . "I bequeath the Crown to my daughter, as 'queen proprietor,' and the Archduke Philip, as her husband. After mature deliberation and with the advice of many of the prelates and nobles of the kingdoms, should Juana be declared mentally incompetent, then I appoint King Ferdinand, my husband, to be the sole regent of Castile until our grandson, Charles, is able to take command."

To my "beloved husband, Ferdinand, I beseech the King, my Lord, that he will accept all my jewels, or such as he shall select, so that seeing them, he may be reminded of the singular love I always bore him while living, and that I am now waiting for him in a better world, by which remembrance may he be encouraged to live the more justly and holy in this." And now it is finished.

I looked at Pietro and asked for the date, and he replied, "October 12, 1504." What a remarkable coincidence. It was just twelve years ago, on this very day, that Cristobol Colon discovered our new lands. A thought flashed through my mind, and I wondered if the date would be remembered throughout all of history.

I looked down at the paper in my hand, and writing the date, I then signed my Will, "Ysabel de Trastamara."

My body was so heavy and weak I couldn't move and my thirst was unbearable. Still, I lingered. My mind dwelt upon some unfinished pieces of business. Too weak to write, I dictated a codicil to my Will. First, I was concerned with government affairs. There were still several public measures which I had deferred because of my illness that bothered me. I requested the "Cortes to appoint a commission to make a new digest of the statutes and pragmatics, the contradictory tenor of which still occasioned much embarrassment in Castilian jurisprudence."

Then there were the natives of the new world. I "knew" Castile's knights and hidalgos were introducing slavery. I urged them to "quicken the good work of converting and civilizing the poor Indians, to treat them with the greatest gentleness, and redress any wrongs they may have suffered in their persons and property."

There were the revenues from the three religious Orders of Santiago, Calatrava and Alcantara. "Were they legal?"

As Pietro placed the paper before me, I signed it, "November 23, 1504. I am the Queen."

My time was very near and I was ready to go. Everyone was coming to pay their last respects, fighting back their tears and trying to be brave. They spoke in hushed tones, walked quietly for they wanted not to disturb me.

Beatriz was constantly by my side, as she had been all of my life. I wanted her to oversee a few last important points and I said, "Beatriz, my dearest friend, how I have treasured your friendship. Promise me, just promise me a few things?" Fighting back her tears, she nodded. "Promise that you will instruct the priest not to place the holy oil on my feet at my Last Rite. My legs are so swollen and covered with terrible running sores. I couldn't bear to have anyone see them." A tear or two rolled down her cheeks, and she nodded. "My burial clothes, please dress me simply in the Franciscan robe." Beatriz was still overcome with her emotion and I said, "Those are my wishes my friend, my dearest of friends. How God has blessed my life by placing you in my midst."

Reaching for my rosary I thought, "My soul is ready to take flight and I must prepare to meet God." Through my mind flashed the burning fires of the Inquisition and the slaves held in chains. With all my might I had tried -- I was a failure! I had worked all my life for the unity of Spain. I had advocated gentle treatment of the heretics and still the fires of the Inquisition burned more fiercely every day. I had freed thousands of slaves but far away in the new lands another and much worse form of slavery was beginning. I had borne a son to be King of Castile and Aragon and he had died. What a record of failure! I needed desperately to prepare the speech I would make before God, the Father. There would be no need to say, "Father, I have failed." He would know that. Then I will say, "Of Thy infinite mercy, forgive me. I tried and I failed."

My breath -- my breath was gone. My body went limp and my soul took flight.

The doctor pronounced, "Her Majesty is dead."

My ever faithful chronicler, quill and paper in hand, looked up at the clock, then wrote, "Noon, November 26, 1504. The Queen is dead."

A few days later Pietro prepared his letter for Talavara, the Bishop of Granada, and as he sat down to write, words forming in his mind, he wrote, "My hand falls powerless by my side for the very sorrow. The world has lost its noblest ornament; a loss to be deplored not only by Spain, which she has so long carried forward in the career of glory, but by every nation in Christiandom, for she was the mirror of every virtue, the shield of the innocent, and the avenging sword to the wicked. I know none of her sex, in ancient or modern times, who in my judgment is at all worthy to be named with this incomparable woman."

EPILOG

I n strict conformity with their beloved Queen's request, preparations were immediately underway to transport her body to its final resting place. On the morning of November 27th, an escort of cavaliers and ecclesiastics began their mournful march to Granada. Shortly after departing from Medina del Campo the chilly high winds blew in a driving rainstorm which continued throughout the long, morbid journey. Their progress was slow, impeded by nearly impassable roads. Bridges were swept into the swollen rivers and swift streams. Horses and mules lost their footings in the churning waters and as their riders urged them forward, the undercurrent of the rushing waters pulled them under and they perished. The entire country was under water. The sun refused to shine.

On a gloomy morning on December 28th, the weary and saddened procession arrived in Granada. After the simple solemn rites were said, the sun broke through the clouds and the remains of Ysabella were laid to rest in peace in the Franciscan Monastery of the Alhambra.

For the next twelve years, the future of Castile was in doubt as nobles and Kings became embroiled in plots seeking power, prestige and fortune as they grasped for control of the Crown.

When the funeral procession arrived in Toledo,

Ferdinand halted the cortege long enough to have a platform raised in the great square under the shadow of one of the most impressive Alcazars throughout all of Castile. Following the trumpet call and proclamation of the Court heralds, Ferdinand told the people he was resigning the Crown of Castile, and as was provided for him in his late wife's Will, he was now assuming the title as Governor of Castile. Then the accession of Juana and Philip to the Castilian Throne was proclaimed.

On January 11, 1505, the Cortes met at Toro to pledge their oath of allegiance to Juana, Queen and Lady Proprietor, and to Philip, her husband. Then, as directed in Ysabella's Will, after much discussion they determined Juana incapable of governing and moved to acknowledge Ferdinand as the lawful Governor of the realm, sanctioning Ferdinand's authority as the Regent and empowering him to nominate a Regent in the event of Juana's death.

Two prominent discontented nobles, the Marquis de Villena and the Duke de Najara, each having expansive land holdings Ysabella had reclaimed for the Crown, quickly sent an invitation to Philip to travel to Castile to take immediate control of the government. They were craftily planning the restoration of their former vast fortunes.

Cristobol Colon, returning from his fourth and last voyage to the Americas dropped his anchor in the harbor of St. Lucar on November 7th, 1504. Crippled by gout and concerned with other health problems, overcome with sadness with the death of the Queen, his benefactor, he remained in Sevilla hoping to regain his health. In May of 1505 he felt stronger and traveled north to the capital city of Valladolid where Ferdinand now held his Court.

Ferdinand received his distinguished Admiral with gracious words and gestures assuring Colon he truly understood the important services Colon had performed for Castile and promised faithfully the precise terms of the agreement signed by him and Ysabella were to be honored.

In vain did Colon wait for money. He borrowed heavily to live, and when Ferdinand was confronted, he deftly side-stepped the subject. Ovando was beginning to send large sums of gold and other valuable commodities to Spain, and as Ferdinand began to add up the percentages which were rightfully Colon's, he decided there would be no restorations paid to Colon. Not one maravedies. The dreams which had filled his every waking moment now dashed, Colon's health failed and on May 20, 1506, he expired.

By far the most ambitious and cunning of the Castilian nobles was Don Juan Manuel, Castile's Ambassador to the Court of Maximilian, and descendent of one of the most illustrious houses of Castile. This restless, ambitious nobleman craftily laid bold plans to become Philip's most powerful advisor. He would rule Castile while Philip played out his role as the King -- in name only. He began to sow the seeds of discontent among the Castilian nobles, as well as convincing Louis XII the time was ripe for his armies to invade Castile from the north. Philip was persuaded to send a letter to Ferdinand asking him to resign as the Governor and return to Aragon.

Manuel's seeds of discontent disrupted the fragile strings of government Ferdinand so cautiously held. Soon there were only two major nobles left to support him -- the Duke de Alva and the Count de Tendillas. The rest had crossed the imaginary line of battle and when

Philip and Juana returned to Castile, they would pledge their allegiance to them.

Concerned that Louis XII was intent upon sending his armies south, Ferdinand sent an envoy to the French King's Court with a proposal of marriage to his sister Germaine. Meanwhile, Emperor Maximilian and his son, Archduke Philip, were attempting to secure the Kingdom of Naples in Italy to them.

Ferdinand had lost the support of the nobles, and as the reports continued to arrive from Naples, all was not well there. Making plans for his second marriage, he asked for the Crown jewels of Castile to be brought to him. He stared at the gleaming treasure for a moment as if to block out the memories of the past, then he removed the ruby and pearl necklace he had given his bride thirty five years earlier. Next he selected the largest of the balas rubies, string after string of precious pearls, diamond clips and pins. His wedding gift to Germaine complete, he traveled to the small town of Duenas in Castile where, on March 18, 1506, they were married. Anxious to avert the storms of civil war that were still brewing and concerned with the turn of events in Naples, he formally resigned as the Governor and Regent of Castile and departed with his new bride for Italy.

Philip's life, too, came to an end shortly after his arrival in Castile. He fell ill with a fever and died on September 25, 1506.

A prelate of seven members was formed with Ximenes appointed at the head, assisted by the Duke de Infantado, the Grand Constable and Admiral of Castile, the Duke de Najara, a principal leader of the opposition, two Flemish nobles and an additional two members selected by the Cortes. Uncooperative Queen Juana refused to sign any of their writs which Ximenes presented for her signature.

Juana's deplorable mental condition continued to deteriorate. During her husband's illness she never left his side. After his death she now remained in a state of stupid insensibility, sitting alone in a darkened room, her head resting in her cupped hand, lips closed, as mute and immovable as a statue. When a summons by the Cortes would arrive, along with other pressing business requiring her royal signature, she merely waved it aside murmuring, "My father will attend to all of this when he returns. He is much more conversant with business than me. I have no other duties than to pray for the soul of my departed husband."

Juana's moody despondency continued at times exhibiting the wildest streaks of insanity. Toward the end of December, she decided to remove her husband from his resting place at the Monastery of La Cartuja Miraflores in Burgos and take the body to Granada. All of the arguments against it made to her by counselors and monks at the Monastery were fruitless. Their opposition served only to arouse frenetic, wild responses. Reluctantly, they removed Philip's casket from its resting place. After removing it from the vault, Juana demanded it be opened. She then reached out and touched the moldering corpse of her husband.

She instructed that the casket be placed upon a hearse drawn by four horses. In the dark of night on December 20th, she departed. The long journey was an interminable nightmare for those assigned to accompany her for she insisted they travel only at night. When they arrived at a small town or village the casket was placed in a church or monastery and the next day a funeral service would be held.

Ferdinand's enemies were writing desperate letters to Emperor Maximilian urging his immediate presence in Castile. Ximenes and the Grand Constable, the Duke de Alva, received full powers from the Cortes to act in Ferdinand's name until he returned.

Ferdinand and Germaine arrived in Valencia on July 20, 1507, met by the Dukes de Albuquerque and Medina Celi, Count de Cifuente and other prominent nobles. At Tortoles he was reunited with his beloved Juana. Ushered into his chambers by Ximenes, Ferdinand stared at the wild, haggard woman with an emaciated figure dressed in squalid clothes standing before him. He soon convinced her to travel to Tordesillas where Philip's remains were laid in a sepulcure in the Monastery of Santa Clara, adjoining the Alcazar, and until her death forty seven years later she kept her eternal vigil.

Ferdinand took immediate control of the government, striking unrelenting blows at the few dissenting nobles. Once again the nobles of Castile were ruled by a "foreigner," by a King many disliked, distrusted and disdained.

During the final years of his life, a fever from which he never totally recovered seemed to consume his body. From time to time he received letters from his daughter Maria announcing the birth of another child. Soon Maria and King Manuel had eight lively children. Ferdinand was very saddened and concerned with the historical events unfolding in England. Catalina, married to Henry VIII, was being divorced by the King to marry Ann Boleyn.

Impatient and ill at ease Ferdinand would change his residence as he moved from kingdom to kingdom hoping he would regain his strength. Finally on the evening of January 22nd, he signed his last Will giving the Crowns of Castile and Aragon to his oldest grandson, Carlos. Early the next morning on January 23, 1516, he breathed his last.

The reins of government were again placed in the capable hands of the ailing Archbishop of Toledo, Ximenes Cisneros, elected as the sole Regent of the land. On September 15, 1517, Carlos arrived on the northern shores of Castile and traveled to the Franciscan Monastery of Aljilera near Aranda to the bedside of the dying Regent. In tranquil peace, still in perfect possession of his mind and powers, the eighty one year old religious warrior expired on November 8, 1517. His work was finished.

* * * * * * * *

"Isabel of Castile" -- "Isabel La Catholica" -- "Isabella, The Queen of Queens" -- her name weaves the magic spell of romance, legend and story! Never in history has a woman been raised on such a pedestal of worship, for she rose to every crisis of her nation's history with brilliance and heroism. She, alone, turned the tide of misfortunes for her people and wrested their salvation. This crusader for the rights of all changed the course of civilization and the aspect of the entire world. Books have been written and ballads about her have been sung in every language around the world. She rose supreme in every relation in life, as a loving daughter, a perfect wife and a devoted mother. In many a critical moment of her reign, her untiring energy and dauntless courage conquered every danger, while her striking political wisdom inspired and confounded friend and foe alike. Absolutely forgetful of herself, she thought only of others, was magnanimous in forgiveness of all personal injuries and full of passionate earnestness in her devotion to God. In dealing with the dark shadow of the Inquisition, we need to be reminded that the virtues of Isabel were her own, while her faults were those of her time.

Thus ended a thirty year reign in which the young Queen assumed the mantle as a leader to her people, subduing the noblemen, the church, gaining control over the municipalities and creating a prosperous nation. She restored the faith of her people in the Monarchy. Her great dream, that Granada would once again be Spain's was realized. She left a legacy of noble examples, a foundation for unprecedented wealth and power -- for under her noble stewardship the several kingdoms into which the country had been broken up for ages were brought under a common rule; the ancient empire of the Spanish Arabs subverted; the kingdom of Naples secured; the historical union of her daughter to The House of Hapsburg providing the future King to play a vibrant role for leadership in Europe; and all the wealth of the New World -- all gained by using her intuition, instinct and fairness for justice without waging a war against her European neighbors. It was an incredible reign. It was a feat that no woman before her time, and none since, has achieved.

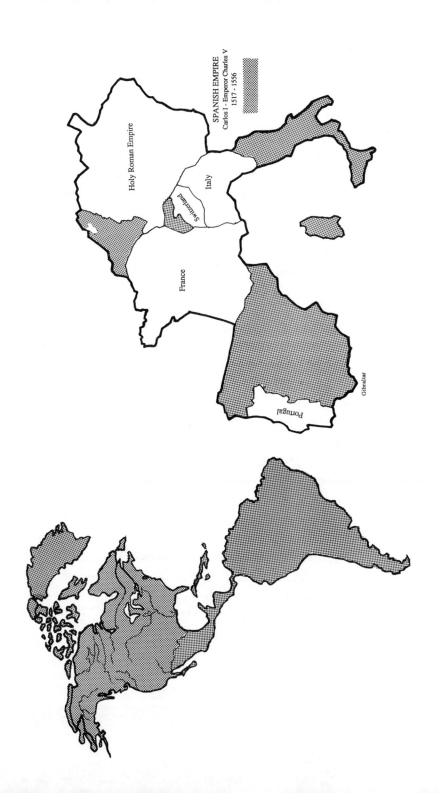

SPANISH EMPIRE
Carlos I - Emperor Charles V
1517 - 1556

Holy Roman Empire

Switzerland

Italy

France

Portugal

Gibraltar

REFERENCES

REFERENCE A
MAJOR HISTORIANS ON THE
REIGN OF YSABELLA

William H. Prescott: The most comprehensive English research data documenting the life of Queen Ysabella was compiled during the middle of the Nineteenth Century by the American historian, William H. Prescott. His first four volumes established the undisputed historical facts relating to King Enrique IV's reign of twenty years followed by thirty years under Ysabella and Ferdinand's rule.

Prescott was the first English speaking historian the Spanish government permitted to access the historical records, Chronicles and official documents.

For an index of his major work, "Ferdinand and Ysabella," see Reference B.

Enriquez del Castillo: Born in Segovia, he was an important member of the King's "Privy Council" as well as Chaplain and historiographer during the King's reign. He had an excellent opportunity to write his historical observations. Publication: **"CHRONICLE"**

Alonso de Palencia: Born in 1423, at age of 17 became a page to Alfonso de Carthangene, Bishop of Burgos. His eyewitness of scenes recorded the erratic and tumultuous reign of Enrique IV.

Alfonso, Ysabella's brother, appointed him as the Royal Historiographer during his short reign and after Alfonso's death, he attached himself to Ysabella, and was employed by the Archbishop of Toledo. On the accession of Ysabella to the Throne he was confirmed in the capacity as National Chronicler. Publications: **"CHRONICLE OF ENRIQUE IV" and "DECADES"**

Hernando del Pulgar: Secretary to Enrique IV and upon the King's death, became First Secretary to Ysabella, occupying that position until his resignation in 1492 to devote the rest of his life to writing about Ysabella's historical reign. Publication: **"THE CATHOLIC KINGS"**

Pietro Martire: Native of Arona, Italy, born in 1455, traveling to Spain in 1487 at the invitation of Castilian Ambassador, Count de Tendilla. Received with much distinction by Ysabella. In 1492 Martire became Ysabella's First Secretary after the resignation of Hernando del Pulgar. Wrote an account of the discovery of the New World, a book highly commended by subsequent historians and researchers. Publication: **"DE REBUS OCEANICIS ET NOVO ORBE"**

Gonzalo Fernandez de Obiedo Y Valdes: Born in Madrid in 1478, he was introduced to Ysabella's Court to become a page to Ysabella's only son, Juan III. In 1515 he traveled to the New World and remained there until his death. He occupied several important posts, one of which was the appointment as historiographer. Publication: **"HISTORIGRAPHER OF THE INDIES."**

Antonio de Librija: Born in Andalusia in 1444, he was a brilliant student at the University of Salamanca and later studied at the University of Bologna in Italy. His published writings are often quoted by major historians. Publication: **"LATIN CHRONICLE"**

Andres Bernaldez: 1488-1523. Curator of Los Palacios, a native of Fuent in Leon. He was Chaplain to Deza, the Archbishop of Sevilla and curator of Los Palacios, an Andalusian town not far from Sevilla. Bernaldez had ample opportunities to obtain accurate information relative to the Granada conflicts for he was living in the theater of action. Publication: **"CHRONICLE"**

Don Juan Antonio Llorente: Llorente was Secretary to the Tribunal of the Inquisition in Madrid (1790-1792) where he observed the proceedings of the Holy Office of the Inquisitions which was always shrouded in mystery. His official station afforded him an excellent opportunity to acquaint himself with the inner-working of the Inquisition activities. Upon its suppression at the close of 1808, he devoted his services to a careful investigation of the registrars of the Tribunals—both in the capitals and provinces. To his credit, his compilation of facts is the only authentic history of the Inquisition. Publication: **"HISTORY OF THE MODERN IN-QUISITION"**

Oviedo & Valdez: Commissioned by the Spanish government to research and write an in-depth account of the historical discoveries of Chistobol Colon. Their set of books provides an encyclopedic account of the Spanish conquest from 1492 to the late 1530's. Publication: **"HISTORIA GENERAL Y NATURAL DE LAS INDIAS"**

REFERENCE B
An Index of
"History of Ferdinand and Ysabella"
by William H. Prescott

WILLIAM H. PRESCOTT
AMS PRESS, INC., New York, NY
Volumes I, II, III, and IV

Volume I

Historical background of major reigns of both the ancient and Renaissance Kings of Castile and Leon

P. 13 History of the military Order of Santiago.

P. 19 (Notes) Description of robes of Order of Santiago and additional historical background.

P. 20 (Notes) Enrique IV's marriage to Blanche of Navarre.

P. 25-27 Origination of Cortes 1170.

P. 29-30 Origination of Santa Hermandad.

P. 40 (Notes) Ponce de Leon supports 13-year old son (Marquis of Cadiz) into battle against Moors.

P. 41-42 Introduction of hidalgos as the "rico hombres." (Notes) Description of their lifestyles.

P. 42 (Notes) Description of Castilian knights and their lifestyles.

P. 45 (Notes) "Fuero Viego" - Visogoth law reformation and Alfonso X's law reformation - "Siete Partidas" - Seven Divisions.

P. 49 Powerful position and wealth of Archbishop of Toledo.

P. 55 Narrative about Enrique III's demand for return to the Crown of land stolen by the nobles during prior reigns.

P. 110 Death of Enrique III, beginning reign of Juan II, Ysabella de Trastamara's father.

P. 111-112 Background history of Alvaro de Luna.

P. 113-119 Background history of reign of Juan II.

P. 129-132 Death of Juan II's wife, Maria of Aragon, and his second marriage to Ysabel of Portugal. Fate of Alvaro de Luna.

P. 133-134 Birth of daughter, Ysabella, and death of King Juan II.

MARRIAGE OF FERDINAND AND YSABELLA

PORTUGUESE CONFLICTS

REFORMS OF YSABELLA

VOLUME III

MARRIAGE ALLIANCES; DEATHS AND SUCCESSION TO CROWN OF CASTILE; CHURCH REFORMS

REFERENCE C
OTHER SOURCES

"TALES OF THE ALHAMBRA"
WASHINGTON IRVING

P. 61-66 Historical reign of Muhamed Ibn-I-Ahmar (1195-1271).

"CHRISTOPHER COLUMBUS"
ERNIE BRADFORD

P. 27-26 Early years of Colon's life and dream to discover new route to Indies.

"ADMIRAL OF THE OCEAN SEA"
SAMUEL ELIOT MORISON

P. 79-108 Colon's arrival in Castile and Queen's consent.

OTHER NOTEWORTHY
HISTORICAL PUBLICATIONS

Insights into the early childhood years of Isabella, studies in Madrid, marriage to Ferdinand, coronation and reign are well documented by other noted historians:

CASTLES AND THE CROWN: Townsend Miller
THE QUEEN OF QUEENS: Christopher Hare
ISABELLA OF SPAIN: William Thomas Walsh
ISABELLA OF CASTILE: Ierne Arthur Plunket
ISABELLA THE CATHOLIC: M. Le Baron de Nervo
THE CATHOLIC KINGS: Butler-Clarke